TO
Lisa ?

A very nice lady
who is as bright &
positive as people come.
Take kindred to heart
as you read it.
God Bless You
Mark Allen Young

HINDERED

The Fall and Impending Rise of Black America.

MARK ALLEN YOUNG

Bloomington, IN  Milton Keynes, UK

authorHOUSE®

AuthorHouse™
1663 Liberty Drive, Suite 200
Bloomington, IN 47403
www.authorhouse.com
Phone: 1-800-839-8640

AuthorHouse™ UK Ltd.
500 Avebury Boulevard
Central Milton Keynes, MK9 2BE
www.authorhouse.co.uk
Phone: 08001974150

First published by AuthorHouse 5/24/2007

ISBN: 978-1-4343-0091-1 (sc)
ISBN: 978-1-4343-0092-8 (hc)

Printed in the United States of America
Bloomington, Indiana

This book is printed on acid-free paper.

HINDERED IS DEDICATED
TO MY BELOVED SON

EMERY MARIO YOUNG.

INTRODUCTION

INITIALLY, MY MOTIVATION FOR WRITING "HINDERED" stemmed from anger. I was angry of young Black people across America due to prolific and senseless killings, a negative social image, Black on Black violence, drug dealing and fear peddling in Black neighborhoods, and a general ignorance to the impact that the youth are having on the Black race. I was blaming the Black 14-30 year old demographic for most of the problems the Black race is encountering. I felt as though they should know better, that they should care more, and as the most visible and energetic members of the Black constituency, they should have a much more positive influence within not only Black communities, but the world in general. The problems of gun violence, drugs, alcoholism, image, sexism, egotism, misogyny, materialism, narcissism and image could be corrected, eradicated, become a thing of the past, if Black youth only wanted it to be as such. That is how I felt in the beginning. As days expired, I began to realize that it is not for them alone to carry such burdens, but in fact, these burdens should be shared by all of Black America.

I now know that Black youth are just that, youth. I now know that the problems belonging to Black America (to be referred to as BA henceforth) cannot be solved by Black youth alone. I now know that it is almost impossible for Black youth to recognize and understand the big picture of American and world society, and how it all intertwines with and relates to BA. As my thinking evolved and my sentiments began to reshape, I dug deeper into the research galaxy. I would soon come across additional facts and figures that would expand my knowledge as to the extent of the problems of BA, ultimately resulting in a staggering conclusion as to the prospects of survival for BA right here in America.

I realized that the problems of BA are as tall, wide, deep and thick as any geographic phenomenon on Earth. The problems of BA are multifaceted, and are crippling and killing Blacks of all economic classes, ages, and gender. These problems are chronicled within hundreds of statistical facts and manifest themselves as dozens of diseases, conditions and shortcomings that together create a synergy of suffering that collectively and fundamentally puts the pieces in place to finish off BA in chess-like fashion: Checkmate! BA is living a dizzying, deadly and dysfunctional existence that effectively guarantees its extinction in America over the next three to five decades.

As a result of BA's present problems, a call to alarm has been necessitated, and everyone with a stake in the survival of BA must be enlisted to right the ship. And assuredly so, we all, including you, and me, have a stake in the future of BA within the context of all of America. And although initially my sentiments were somewhat off the mark, they would gradually morph themselves into a strong motivational force that called for me to wake up and make a decision to do something to help BA.

'HINDERED" IS AN empirical look at the plight of BA. The problems affecting BA actually affect all who live in America, whether or not you live in the inner city, are Black, White, or are of another race, and irregardless of gender. Although these problems are addressed in laser-like fashion specifically to BA, these same problems actually apply to our Latino brothers and sisters as well, as they run a close second to BA in many of the metrics to be identified. However, being a Black American myself, I am compelled to primarily focus on BA. In any case, let it be stated that much love and concern goes out to Latino America with the hope that one day we will all work together to accomplish a mutual goal of a fruitful and peaceful coexistence in both America and on Earth.

Before reading on any further, allow me to take a moment to make a very important request of you. "Hindered" contains a significant portion of statistical facts and figures. Some of these facts and figures you may very well be aware of, some you may not be. In the early stages of your reading, do not be taken by the statistical information presented. What "Hindered" attempts to do is to bring all of the important numbers and conditions together in a way that possibly has not been done before in a single printed context. The total number of these facts and conditions number in excess of seventy, and the intent is to give you, the reader, a strong awareness of the totality of all of these statistical powerhouses and their collective assault on BA. And so, my request of you is to not get bogged down in all of the statistics, particularly in the beginning, but rather try to picture how these diseases, conditions and shortcomings are at the heart of the baffling and crippling mortal existence that BA is mired in, even in your very own communities, and especially in your very own communities.

At one time, the successes of the Civil Rights Era seemed like the end of a vicious and painful chapter of life for Blacks in America, and the beginning of a joyous and opportunistic new one. It now appears that the celebrations of past successes were premature, and that not only is there much work unfinished, but BA has actually taken steps backwards. Whereas life goes on for most, this is not the case for BA. The reality is that BA has to find a way to stay alive. There are answers to the problems, but action is required of everyone to bring those answers to fruition. Time is of the essence, and BA can no longer waste time. My fears are real, and so are the facts. BA has a very tough and long road ahead

CONTENTS

PART I

NUMBERS

LOVE

GIVING BLOOD MANY YEARS AGO, WHEN I worked as a transfusion volunteer at Stanford Hospital, I got to know a little girl named Liza who was suffering from a disease and needed blood from her five-year-old brother, who had miraculously survived the same disease and had developed the antibodies needed to combat the illness. The doctor explained the situation to her little brother, and asked the boy if he would be willing to give his blood to his sister. I saw him hesitate for only a moment before taking a deep breath and saying, "Yes, I'll do it if it will save Liza."

AS THE TRANSFUSION progressed, he lay in bed next to his sister, as we all did, seeing the color returning to her cheeks. Then his face grew pale and his smile faded. He looked up at the doctor and asked with a trembling voice, "Will I start to die right away?"

BEING YOUNG, THE boy had misunderstood the doctor; he thought he was going to give her all his blood.

FROM LEE RYAN PALMER

(www.spiritual-endeavors.org/stories/four.htm)

3

A History of Help

IN 1816, IN LARGE PART BECAUSE of slaves taking refuge with Seminole Indians, there were Seminole wars. Tennessee militia colonel and former U.S. President Andrew Jackson made war on slave/Indian encampments and communities, and even went so far as to claim all of Florida by the United States. In 1862 President Abraham Lincoln signed a bill ending slavery in the District of Columbia. Nine months later President Lincoln issued his Emancipation Proclamation, setting all slaves free. Fast forward to more modern times, where in the 60's America experienced the Civil Rights Era. This era, led by Dr. Martin Luther King and other great leaders and heroes who fought for Black equality, would attempt to bring to an end the ongoing and explicit killing, brutalizing and mistreatment of the Black race in America.

On April 3, 1961, Dr. King told the world that he had been to the Mountain Top, looked over and saw a future where BA would get to the Promised Land. But what has happened since then? It seems that BA has lost its way. The Promised Land that Dr. King spoke of seems to be inaccessible to BA, as if being denied entry by some sort of invisible force field. 'Which Way Is Up?', a movie comedy starring the great comic Richard Pryor, was supposed to be just a movie that made people laugh, and not a slogan by which BA would live by. However, that seems to be the case as the Promised Land that Dr. King spoke of has yet to be found.

And now BA finds itself in the road-building business. To reach its destination, BA must build roads that are devoid of the numerous potholes and detours encountered in its travels of today. As BA undergoes its travels, it will see that the journey will not be made just by car, plane, or train, but by piggyback as well. Those that are stronger will have to carry those who are weaker. Those who are rich will have to subsidize those who are poor. It is quite necessary to help one another if BA is to make it to The Promised Land. That is the only way BA will find its way to survival, to improvement, and to success. Every scripture, every affirmation and every prayer ever invoked for the deliverance of a people will have to be called upon to bring about the survival and the safety of BA, as times have gotten just that bad, and the outlook for BA, right now, offers very little promise.

DR. KING, MALCOLM X, Muhammad Ali, and all of the Civil Rights heroes and individuals who fought oppression and racism in the Civil Rights era indeed carried BA on the strengths of their backs and the fields of their visions. And yet, presently there are millions of Black folk who do not have a clue as to the real meaning and purpose of the fight those brave leaders of the past fought. And fight they did, as valiantly and with as great a collective courage and skill as any people throughout history. However, BA cannot exhale entirely yet, because the battle is still not over.

Today, BA has even further to go than yesterday. Today, BA is still fighting, and still losing, as not much seems to be going right. There are millions of Black folk who have not for one minute put themselves in the shoes of the Black people of the past that were lynched, beaten, maimed, attacked by dogs, denied the right to vote and even denied the right to go to school. I have often time-traveled myself back to those days of the Civil Rights era, wondering what decisions would I make when threatened. Would I have been brave enough, smart enough or resilient enough to survive those brutal and inhumane times? How long would I have lived? What would have been the condition of my psyche while enduring the inhumane conditions of that era? Would I have been allowed to go to school? Would I have been magically blessed with a curiosity to learn and soak up knowledge and reading skills every chance I got?

Those are questions I ask myself even now. And yet today, hate and confusion radiates outward and inward within BA so much that although BA stands on the brink of extinction, it is still pre-occupied with materialism, wealth, class-ism, jealousy and an apathy that should cause all to cringe. Never mind that most Black ancestors had very little in terms of clothing and educational opportunity, yet stuck together to survive and fight for its rights. Today it is about me, me, me. Few Blacks, relatively speaking, are achieving much success in the present era. Meanwhile, as the losses mount everyday, the branches of Black genealogical trees whither away.

THE DOWNWARD DESCENT slowly gains micro-momentum everyday on a national basis. Citizens of Black communities are sort of like firework shows, where every once in a while a rocket flies high, straight, and explodes into a beautiful, radiant kaleidoscope of bright colors and sparkling lights. Sometimes there are the sparklers that glow brightly for a decent length of time. The sparklers build families, work towards careers and uplift communities. However, most of the time there are the firecrackers, which get one chance to pop, and end up dead, imprisoned, diseased, or uneducated, or the duds, who roam the world aimlessly with no goals, plans or understanding of the simple respects, niceties, or responsibilities in life that can take a person a long way. Sometimes they get caught up playing the fool seeking urban legend status, other times they end up being your neighbor. You see them introducing themselves to the world on national talk shows such as Maury Povich, Jerry Springer and Rikki Lake. At that point it's too late, as every Black person on the face of the Earth is once again embarrassed to no end.

The collaboration of African American slaves and Native Americans in the early 1800's should not go unnoticed. It is an enlightening revelation to know that BA was not alone, that there was help from Native American brothers and sisters. The same is still true today. BA is not alone. It was not alone in the 1800's. BA was not alone during the Civil Rights era, and BA is not alone today. There are many individuals of all colors who want to save BA, and strengthen its great nation, America. A chain is only as strong as its weakest link. What are required are real and meaningful strategies and moves initiated and maintained by BA. In direct to the point fashion, BA must show that it wants to save itself. It is time for substance, and not just rhetoric that rhymes. And it is a time for a plan that will work. That is how BA will find the answers to all its problems. That is how BA will survive. That is how BA will make it to the Promised Land.

The Quality of Life Statistics

THERE ARE MANY REASONS AS TO why BA is faring so badly. The well-being of any entity, be it a school, small business, shopping mall, government agency, large conglomerate, a municipality, a non-profit, or a person, has a way to be measured, evaluated, or diagnosed. Each problem within BA has its own root cause, and plays its own role in the intricate web of misfortune, dysfunction and death inducing behaviors that combine to choke the life out of BA.

The indicators used in assessing the state of existence for BA are referred to as the 'Quality of Life Statistics' and are categorized under two separate headings: The 'Mortality Metrics', and the 'Afflictions'. There are 74 separate areas in all, comprised of 17 Mortality Metrics and 57 Afflictions. Together they reveal the immensely sad story of how Black people are both living and dying, and also dictate the choices that must be made going forward to ensure the survival of the Black race in America.

The Quality of Life Statistics for BA give a clear indication as to where BA is going – namely, both to the grave and into the history books as extinct. The Mortality Metrics and Afflictions are calculated against the population change from the year 1999 to the year 2000. As will be seen, Black people everywhere, both new members of the population and those of forthcoming years, face an uphill battle against tremendous adversities. The following list comprises the seventeen causes of population decrease in BA. Although immigration is a metric that swells the number of Blacks in America, "Hindered" focuses on native Black Americans and their diminishment in America, starting from the year 2000, and projecting out. The following 18 items, minus African and Caribbean immigration, comprise the Mortality Metrics, which reveal the top causes of death of Black people in America.

- **The Population change from 1999 to 2000:**[1]

  (1999 pop. - 34,862,000; 2000 pop. – 35,470,000) gross pop. gain of 608,000

1) **Number of people within increase that are immigrants:**[2]
   (From Africa and from the Caribbean = 126,000.) 608,000 – 126,000 = 482,000

2) **Cardiovascular Diseases of the Heart**[3] 105,571
   (arrhythmia, arteriosclerosis, etc.)   482,000 – 105,571 = 376,429

3) **Cancer**[4] 63,500
   (lung, breast, colon, pancreas, prostate)   376,429 – 63,500 = 312,929

4) **Coronary Heart Disease**[3] 51,265
   (heart attacks,)   312,929 – 51,265 = 261,664

5) **Stroke**[3] 19,221   261,664 – 19,221 = 242,443

6) **Accidents**[5] 12,277   242,443 – 12,277   = 230,166

7) **Diabetes**[5] 12,021   230,166 – 12,021   = 218,145

8) **High Blood Pressure**[3] 10,582   218,145 – 10,582   = 207,563

9) **Infant Mortality**[6] 8,771   207,563 – 8,771   = 198,792

10) **HIV/AIDS**[7] 8,723   198,792 – 8,723   = 190,069

11) **Homicide**[5] 7,867   190,069 – 7,867   = 182,202

12) **Chronic Lower Respiratory Diseases**[5] 7,607   182,202 – 7,607   = 174,595

13) **Nephritis & Nephrosis**[5] 6,911   174,842 – 6,911   = 167,684

14) **Influenza/Pneumonia**[5] 6,069   167,684 – 6,069   = 161,615

15) **Liver Disease & Cirrhosis**[5] 2,737   161,615 – 2,737   = 158,878

16) **Alzheimer's Disease**[5] 2,728   158,878 – 2,728   = 156,150

17) **Suicide**[5] 1,962   156,150 – 1,962   = 154,188

18) **Asthma**[8] 1,000   154,188 – 1,000   = 153,188

ON THE SURFACE it appears that from the year 1999 to 2000 BA has added 608,000 people to the Black American nation. However, when both the 126,000 immigrants and the 328,000 deaths are subtracted from the initial 608,000, BA is left with an adjusted number of only 153,000 (rounded down from 153,188) people. These 153,000 new members to Black America will face many life-threatening challenges and conditions, which will continue to take a total on Black lives, and greatly diminish their chances of having healthy and productive existences.

The net population growth of 153,000 from the year 1999 to the year 2000, when calculated against the population of 35,470,000 Blacks in the year 2000, resulted in a population growth rate of .0043% for the transition year 1999 to 2000.

In the year 1999, there were 112,483 Blacks living with HIV/AIDS. In the year 2000, there were 121,903 Blacks living with HIV/AIDS. The increase of 9,420 Blacks living with HIV/AIDS from the year 1999 to the year 2000, when calculated against the 121, 903 Blacks living with HIV/AIDS in the year 2000, resulted in a growth rate of Blacks living with HIV/AIDS of 7.7% for the transition year 1999 to 2000.

In the year 1999, there were 851,902 Blacks imprisoned across America. In the year 2000, there were 871,867 Blacks imprisoned across America. The increase of 19,965

BLACKS IMPRISONED ACROSS AMERICA FROM THE year 1999 to the year 2000, when calculated against the 871,867 Blacks imprisoned across America (pg. 50) in the year 2000, resulted in a growth rate of Blacks imprisoned across America of 2.34%. The Black HIV/AIDS growth rate of 7.7% and the prison population growth rate of 2.3%, both tower over the census population growth rate of .0043%.

BLACK PEOPLE FARE much worse than all other ethnic groups in every single Mortality Metric, with the exception of Teen Pregnancy and School Dropouts. With most of the Quality of Life Statistics, Blacks fare 20 to 50% worse off than other ethnic groups, and some even surpass the 50% threshold.

First there is cardiovascular disease (CVD), which is the number one killer in America for all people and accounts for almost four out of ten deaths for all African Americans. Next is Asthma, where an estimated 3.4 million Black Americans are afflicted. How about the fact that African Americans account for half of all new HIV/AIDS cases? Blacks also run twice the risk versus all others in terms of first-ever stroke, and Blacks have a 50% higher death rate due to diabetes. Overall, in the year 2000, the death rate to population ratio was .092% for Black people, and this percentage is derived by dividing the total number of deaths in the year 2000 (328,000), into the total population of the year 2000 (35,470,000). Almost one person died for every ten people who live in BA, a shocking statistic, and unbeknownst to most people in America.

The media coverage of the Mortality Metrics and the Afflictions is piecemeal at best, which helps explain the mass non-action status of BA. At what seems like a pace of one health report per week by way of conventional media, the cumulative effect of all the Mortality Metrics and Afflictions goes somewhat unnoticed, allowing them to gain momentum and reach their highest level of toxicity. The sense of urgency that is required to move millions of people into action to save themselves is not there, and thus, the extinction process moves forward.

HIV/AIDS – The Super Fuel

THE USA TODAY, IN ITS JUNE 14, 2005 issue reports in its Health section that there is an estimated 1.039 to 1.185 million people nationwide that are infected with HIV. It also says that Blacks represent almost half of the infected. Additionally, it says that there are about 25% of those who are infected with HIV whom do not know it. This information comes from the CDC.

On November 9, 2004, CNN reported that a man had been arrested for intentionally exposing 17 women to HIV/AIDS. This phenomenon is not new, although it rarely makes headlines. This is the wild card that exists within the HIV/AIDS situation, and it must be recognized. The 'angry' infectious carriers that intentionally spread the virus are indeed a serious problem in Black communities, as this occurs more often than most people might think. Is this a new sort of dysfunctional cycle that needs to be aggressively treated? As angry infected people infect others, is there a good chance that those infected may intentionally infect others as well? What are the percentages of this happening? What research is being conducted to find out? This may be as important a component as there is in the fight against HIV/AIDS and if not yet, should be included in the educational process concerning HIV/AIDS. If it will save lives, then it is worth the time and effort to discover what types of people are practicing this behavior, who the typical victims are, and how often this is happening.

Additionally, not all intentional HIV/AIDS spreaders are 'angry' individuals. There are many people who simply refuse to give up their sex lives for all the right reasons. These people lack the proper 'balance of conscience' and choose to sentence their sex partners to death for the price of an orgasm.

OF LATE, THERE has been much talk about guys who live on the 'Down Low', or DL. These are bisexual guys who are spreading the virus because while they routinely sleep with men, they also continue to sleep with women. Whether referred to as 'Down Low, or being bisexual, there are people who are paying a huge price for the promiscuity of these people. It is not simply a matter of sexual orientation choice. It is a matter of life and death, and those who have become infected with HIV/AIDS as a result of the secret, dual bisexual lives of individuals on the 'DL' can attest to that.

The result has been that in the last couple of years, Black women have accounted for the majority of new HIV/AIDS cases in America. Not only does this trend have all of the customary negative implications expected with this deadly virus, but it also diminishes the ability of the Black race to reproduce. This reduces future children, parents, grandparents, grandchildren, and so on. This exponential effect on BA should not and cannot be ignored any longer by members of Black communities. The HIV/AIDS epidemic is wreaking havoc to BA in a way that could only have been imagined in our worst nightmares.

More Quality of Life Facts

- Among African American children, ages 1-14, cancer ranks third among the leading causes of death surpassed only by accidents and homicides.[4]

- African Americans have the highest death rate from colon and rectum cancer of any racial or ethnic group in the U.S.[4]

- Lung cancer is the leading cause of death in African Americans.[4]

- Prostate cancer is the second leading cause of cancer death among African American men.[4]

- In 1997, African American high school students were somewhat less likely to eat fruits and vegetables and more likely to eat high-fat foods compared to White students.[4] High fiber diets play a considerable role in preventing heart disease and cancer.

- According to the Center for Disease Control (CDC) Youth Risk Behavior Survey, cigarette smoking increased in 1999 among African American high school students to approximately 34% among males and 23% among females.[4]

- Minorities with cancer often suffer more pain due to under-medication. Nearly 62% of patients at institutions serving predominantly African American patients were not prescribed adequate analgesics.[4]

****

- Data from the 1998 Behavioral Risk Factor Surveillance System show that more than one-third of African American adults (33.9%) reported no leisure-time physical activity with African American women more likely than men to be physically inactive (39.9% versus 25.9% respectively.[4]

- In 2000, Cardiovascular Disease (CVD) accounted for 33.5 % of deaths among African American men and 40.6% among African American women. The overall death rate in 2000 from CVD was 343.1. The death rate was 509.6 for Black males; 397.1 for Black females.[3]

- Coronary Heart Disease (CHD) accounted for approximately 16% of deaths among African Americans. The overall death rate in 2000 from CHD was 186.9. The death rate was 262.4 for Black males; 187.5 for Black females.[3]

- Compared with Caucasians, young African Americans have a

two to three-fold greater risk of ischemic stroke (caused by a clogged blood vessel).[3]

- The prevalence of High Blood Pressure (HBP) in African Americans in the United States is among the highest in the world. The overall death rate in 2000 from HBP was 16.2. The death rate was 46.3 for Black males; 40.8 for Black females.[3]

- Among African Americans, 45% of men and 46% of women have high total blood cholesterol levels.[3]

- 77% of African American men and 61% of African American women are overweight. 50% of African American women and 28% of African American men are obese.[3]

- Physical inactivity is more prevalent among African Americans than Caucasians. African Americans are one of the least active groups in terms of overall physical activity. 44% of men and 55% of women are sedentary, with no leisure-time physical activity.[3]

- Among African Americans age 20 and older, 2.5% of men and 3.2% of women have had a stroke.[3] The 2000 overall death rate for stroke was 60.8%. The death rate was 87.1 for Black males; 78.1 for Black females.

- Among African Americans age 20 and older, 37% of men and 37% of women have high blood pressure.[3]

****

- **Alcohol**

- African Americans comprise 21% of the 257,000 Americans injured in drinking-related motor vehicle crashes each year. Although they drive less, the average African American teenager is twice as likely to die in a motor vehicle collision. African American children ages 5 through 12 are at three times the risk of dying in an automobile collision than are White children of the same age. [10]

- On average, one African American is injured every 10 minutes in alcohol related crashes. [11]

- Alcohol is the most widely used drug by African American youth. [11]

- Alcohol contributes to the three leading causes of death among African American 12-20 year olds; homicide, unintentional injuries (including car crashes), and suicide. [11] It is probably safe to assume that alcohol plays a major role in sex activities.

- 40% of African American teens ages 12-17 and 35.1% of African Americans ages 18-20 are among the most frequent magazine readers, versus 19.2% and 19.7% of non-African Americans in these age groups. [11]

- African American youth saw 77% more alcohol advertising in national magazines than did non-African American youth in 2002. [11]

- For beer, distilled spirits, and low-alcohol refreshers in 2002, alcohol advertising in magazines reached more of the African American underage audience with more ads than it reached African American young adults ages 21-34. The alcohol industry routinely refers to 21-34 year olds as its target audience. [11]

- Of the advertising that overexposed African American youth, alcohol advertisers concentrated in 13 magazines accounting for 80% of the exposure of African American youth to alcohol advertising in 2002, including Sports Illustrated, Vibe, Cosmopolitan, ESPN the magazine, Jet, and Entertainment Weekly. [11]

- African Americans account for more than a third (38%) of

the 816,149 AIDS cases reported since the beginning of the epidemic and about half (49%) of the 43,158 cases report in 2001 alone. [12]

- African Americans will account for more than half (54%) of the 40,000 new HIV infections estimated to occur in the U.S. each year. [12]

- As of the end of 2001, there were 151,530 African Americans estimated to be living with AIDS, or 42% of the total of all people living with HIV/AIDS in America. [12]

- The AIDS case rate for African American men in 2001 was 8 times that of white men (109.2 per 100,000 compared to 13.7). Among women, the AIDS case rate for African American women was almost 20 times the rate for white women (47.8 per 100,000 compared to 2.4).[12]

- HIV was the leading cause of death for African Americans ages 25-44 in 2000, compared to the 4th leading cause of death for Latinos and 5th for whites in this age group.[12]

- Although African American teens (ages 13-19) represent only 15% of U.S. teenagers, they accounted for almost two thirds (61%) of new AIDS cases reported among teens in 2001. A similar impact can be seen among African American children under the age of 13.[12]

- Black children represent almost two-thirds (62 percent) of all reported pediatric AIDS cases.[13]

- Black senior citizens represent more than 50 percent of HIV cases among persons over age 55.[13]

- One in 50 Black men is HIV-positive. One in 160 Black women is HIV-positive.[13]

- More than a third of African Americans (35%) say HIV/AIDS is the most urgent health problem facing the nation compared to 13% of whites. However, concern among African Americans, as well as the public overall, has been decreasing over time.[13]

ON A RECENT trip to Dallas, Texas, a friend and I were having a conversation about life in Dallas. Over the course of our conversation, he floored me with the revelation that his son attends a school where over half of the Black kids there have HIV. It has not been ascertained whether or not this information is accurate, yet I had an immediate feeling that this revelation could very well be true. And if it is, the same could be true for other high schools, and middle schools as well, in Black communities across America.

FOR BA TO have any chance at a perpetual future, the children of BA have to be protected. There is no future if there are no children. If Black children die, all of BA dies. This scenario in itself should be enough to spur every Black citizen in America and beyond to action. I wonder aloud, will this be the case?

New Shameful Data and Outlooks

ON AUGUST 24, 2006, ABC Primetime broadcast a special entitled, "Out Of Control: Aids in Black America. This television special disclosed startling new facts:

- 40% of men in prison have sex with other men. Many of these inmates say that upon release, they will resume having sex with women, although a great deal of the have not been tested for HIV/AIDS. Additionally, prisons do not want to incur the necessary costs to identify and treat HIV/AIDS infected inmates.

- Dirty needles account for one-third of all HIV/AIDS cases in America, yet the federal government will not sponsor a clean needle program.

- Prominent leaders such as T.D. Jakes and others made statements such as "Paul provided no scriptures as to how to deal with AIDS", and "Blacks cannot focus on just one problem".

IT IS SHAMEFUL that these so-called leaders are either not smart enough, caring enough, or generous enough to mount an all-out attack on AIDS. There are strategies that all of BA can utilize immediately that will be very effective in the slowing down of this disease. Instead of lying down, BA needs to get up and take remedial action with a sense of urgency.

IT WOULD BE nice if the government could make all of the problems of BA go away. It would be wonderful if the manufacturers of the weapons of mass destruction already here in America, namely the cocaine that comes out of South America and the heroine that comes out of Asia and Latin America, were to be made gone. The privatized prison corporations would be scrambling for inmates, and that's for sure. The point is, BA need not to worry what others do or do not do, but to concentrate on what BA can do.

If BA ever gets to where it needs to be and gets back to solid ground, it had surely not ever lose its footing again. Statistically, Black people are the most ill people in America, and also the entire world. The fact that only 13% of whites and 35% of Blacks believe that the threat of AIDS is the number one health concern in America says a lot in itself, specifically that the 'concern' meter may need to be calibrated.

MANY PEOPLE BELIEVE that the best way to fight HIV/AIDS is to follow the ABC method: Abstinence, Being faithful, and Condoms. In my opinion, that condom thing can be thrown out of the window, as they are not the answer. For the purposes of conducting a quick survey, answer this one question: Would you kiss someone you knew had HIV/AIDS? Probably not, and thus the condom debate may now be laid to rest It is the entire sexual engagement that is the problem, not one facet of it.

Pass along one message, and one message only to the youth of BA: Abstinence, man, Abstinence. Abstinence, testing and monogamy are the tools of the trade. This is a message that needs to be understood now, not in a year or two. HIV/AIDS is taking names, killing people and is not a respecter of persons.

The Motherland

SUB-SAHARA AFRICA CONSISTS OF 46 COUNTRIES. They are physically located below Algeria, Libya, and Egypt. Included amongst the countries that make up Sub-Sahara Africa are Angola, Ethiopia, Ghana, Kenya, Mauritius, Senegal, Somalia, South Africa, Sudan, Uganda, and Zimbabwe. The boundaries of the Sahara are the Atlantic Ocean on the west, the Atlas Mountains and the Mediterranean Sea on the north, the Red Sea and Egypt on the East, and the Sudan and the Valley of the Niger River on the south. The beautiful continent of Africa is truly of Biblical proportions. It is also the most ravaged and turbulent continent of all.

The population of Africa is 804,000,000. It is the third most populous region in the world. Within the region, 50% of the people are less than 15 years old. It simultaneously owns the world's highest birthrate, world's shortest life expectancy, world's highest population growth rate, and the world's lowest economic growth rate. Some of the AIDS-ravaged countries have a lie expectancy of less than forty years. Large amounts of farmland are becoming extinct while 70% of the workers are farmers. Only 37% of the people have clean water to drink, while at the same time, Christianity is the most widespread religion.

UNFORTUNATELY, RAIN FORESTS are being destroyed. This is a very tragic occurrence, because not only do the rain forests provide clean air and deter the greenhouse effect but many of the plants and animals found in rain forests are found nowhere else on Earth. Most importantly, cures for certain diseases come from species of the rain forests.

Because too many trees have been cut down it is warmer than it should be, and this has placed many animals and plants at risk. Elephants and rhinos are endangered because of poachers. Famine continues to rise in large part because desert expansion continues due to the over-planting and destruction of trees. The accompanying droughts have turned farmland to wasteland. Crops are burned and stolen due to civil wars and this results in starvation and bloodshed, which in turn creates millions of refugees. At the same time, the U.S. interests are Angola oil and preventing the spread of communism.[14]

AFRICA IS HURTING and Africans are dying by the millions. African land is ravaged non-stop. However, Tarzan is still swinging. South Africa, which is predominantly White occupied, has almost the largest portion of the world's gold and diamonds, and is one of the richest nations in the region.

Death in The Motherland

IN THE YEAR 2002, THERE WERE 2.4 million people that died from AIDS in Sub-Sahara Africa. Only 37,000 died in North Africa. That same year there were 3.5 million adults and children that were newly infected, and 29.4 million people living with AIDS with ten million of those young people (aged 15-24) and another three million being children (under 15 years of age). Malaria still claims about as many African lives as AIDS. Preventable childhood diseases kill millions of others. There are even more serious medical conditions that claims millions of lives in Africa, including: cardiovascular diseases, poor nutrition, syphilis, famine, acute lower respiratory infections, diarrheal diseases, peri-natal conditions, measles, tuberculosis, cerebral-vascular diseases, ischaemic heart disease, and maternal conditions.[15]

Crisis in Africa

AFRICA IS AN EXTREMELY HETEROGENEOUS CONTINENT, and human rights violations come in many forms as well. From genocide, slavery, mass disappearances and torture, to denial of freedom of speech or of the press, there is little that will not be found in Africa. Destructive conflicts have turned Africa into a continent unable to turn its strength of diversity into opportunities for development. Africa is a continent in turmoil. Though rich in resources, the population is ravaged by repression, social violence, armed conflict, poverty, hunger, and forced displacement.[16]

IN THE LAST four years over four million have died due to the wars and arms in Africa, with over three million in the Democratic Republic of the Congo alone. Four million dead in four years; that's more people who have died per month than in the whole of the Iraq war. Four million dead in four years amounts to more Africans dying than at the highest rate during slavery. That's almost twice the number of deaths during the Middle passage during slavery over a 200 years period. Four million dead in four years; Imagine the heartache, pain, suffering, despair and injuries. Four million dead in four years and yet Africa does not produce many weapons. Four million dead, yet incredibly, not one person has been prosecuted for supplying the weapons of their destruction and death of the four million in the last four years.

His-story will focus on the recent Iraq war. But Human-story will remember the four million dead in Africa in the last four years, and how none of the weapon suppliers, war criminals, resource looters, and corruptors got away with facilitating the biggest, most expedient elimination of human life in the history of the world. In the end, it will make for great discussion, and that will be the end of it.[17]

Nearly half of the lives lost in Congo are children, with most victims killed by disease and famine in the still largely cut-off east. "In fact, Congo is the deadliest war the world has seen since the end of the Second World War and these staggering figures have gone largely ignored by the media and world leaders," said Dr. Richard Brennan, director of the International Rescue Committee's Health Unit.[18]

THE MEDIA DOES not cover this story nowhere near the level that it should. At this time, the present media focus is on America's war in Iraq. Gun merchants that have found a home in Africa, and apparently will be in Africa for the long haul, until there is no one left to be killed. These wars are about money, as arms dealers make a 'killing' financially as the weapons of destruction they sell results in the loss of millions of African lives.

The media also says very little of the ineffective drugs that are being used in the fight against malaria, which presently kills as many people as AIDS. In order to get the real skinny concerning Africa, one has to look away from traditional television and newspaper reporting and into books and the internet. But these sources are nowhere near as fast and far-reaching as their traditional rivals. In the meantime, millions more will continue to die, while relatively few will talk about it, and even less will know about.

The American Presence in Africa

AMERICA DOES HAVE A PRESENCE IN Africa. It seems that the red, white and blue is on the lookout out for the black, as in oil, and the green, as in money. There are probable gold and diamond interests as well. A trio of American companies, Shell, Bechtel, and Fluor, serve as examples of the American presence in Africa. However, it is my hope that the present attitudes and interests of Corporate America in Africa are not shared by the everyday citizens that make up the American people. It is hoped that their agenda is different from any agenda that the masses of Americans would have. Their agendas often times serve as a disgrace to most Americans. It is important that people around the world understand that the American Government and certain American corporations have very separate and different sentiments and intentions than many American citizens have, and I hope this statement is representative of the majority of Americans.

Shell

DURING THE 1990'S A POWERFUL PEOPLE'S movement emerged in the Niger Delta, Nigeria's main oil producing area, to hold the company accountable for massive environmental damage caused over decades by its operations there. This area was home to some of the sweetest crude oil in the world. Shell's operations on Ogoniland devastated the people's farming and fishing areas, which were central to their survival.

The movement was met with violent retaliation from the Nigerian military, supported and paid for in part by Shell Oil Corporation. Thousands were abused and hundreds were summarily executed. Shell admitted to having made direct payments to Nigerian security forces and importing arms. In fact, the company continues to have its own police force known by people in the region as the "Shell Police." Nothing is done to ensure that the population benefited from the company's presence, despite having the world's sixth largest oil producing capacity. To this day, Shell has failed to successfully clean up the damage left behind from production operations abandoned in 1993.[19]

Bechtel

As one of the largest construction and engineering companies in the world, Bechtel is the top contender for hundreds of millions (and potentially billions) in reconstruction contracts for post-war Iraq, despite conflicts of interest due to close connections to the Bush administration.

However, there are ongoing concerns about Bechtel's role in the Democratic Republic of Congo that has not received adequate attention. Bechtel was interested in winning business in the mineral-rich Congo and established an early and friendly relationship with the rebel leader Larent Kabila in 1997, before he took control of the whole country.

Coincidentally, one year after Bechtel initially expressed interest in the Congo by offering to draw up a master development plan and inventory of the country's mineral resources free of charge, coltan was discovered in the eastern region. This mineral is used in cell phones, computers and high tech devices. Since the discovery of the mineral, hundreds of millions of dollars have been made on the illicit sale of coltan to the U.S., Europe and Asia. [19]

Fluor

Fluor Corporation is one of the largest engineering and construction companies in the world, and is one of Bechtel's competitors for reconstruction contracts in Iraq. In the 1980's Fluor was accused of helping to further apartheid in South Africa through business dealings with the white government, where the company helped build what was at the time the world's largest plant producing commercial oil from coal.

Fluor also helped build oil refineries in apartheid South Africa, where it is the subject of "a multibillion dollar lawsuit claiming that it exploited and brutalized black workers. " Part of the claim includes accusations that "Fluor hired security guards dressed in Ku Klux Klan robes to attack unarmed workers protesting against poor pay and conditions.[19]

How to Really Help Africa

HUNDREDS AND HUNDREDS OF MILLIONS OF dollars have been raised to assist in alleviating the famine situation in Africa, and unfortunately, has not been enough to solve the problem. At the same time, hundreds and hundreds of millions of dollars, if not more, in the form of war profits, oil, and gems, has been extracted out of Africa.

There is a much smaller number that explains what is happening in Africa – the number four. There are four letters that it takes to spell the one word that explains the entire situation in Africa, and that word is evil. It is ultimate evil to allow millions of children, women, and men to die in the first place. To occupy Iraq while looking the other way at what is happening in Africa is inexcusable. The much greater losses are in Africa, and it seems as though things will not significantly change in the foreseeable future.

STUDY AFTER STUDY has shown that many factors affect how countries climb out of poverty. They include democratic government, low levels of taxation and corruption, and clear legal protection for the ownership of property and capital. But not aid! Virtually no evidence exists that aid does much of anything – other than make donors feel good. Aid to Africa will simply be wasted – swallowed whole by corrupt bureaucrats and African warlords. Once Africa is firmly under the control of the White man, progress will be swift and relentless.[20]

According to the U.N. and World Water Council, it is estimated that the $151 billion that has been spent on the Iraq War the first couple of years could have been put to the following uses:

- 678,000 new fire trucks
- Healthcare coverage for 82 million children or 27 million adults
- 20 million head start slots
- Could supply all impoverished people worldwide with food, childhood immunizations, HIV/AIDS medicine and clean water and sanitation for two years.[21]

TO DATE, THE money spent on the Iraq war has almost tripled the $151 billion mentioned above. The number of people, both Iraqi civilians and American soldiers, whom have lost their lives, is astonishing, and has surpassed the death total of 911. The number of American soldiers maimed and de-limbed brings tears to the eyes. And yet, it pales in comparison to what Black people all around the world are enduring.

The Good News

THE FACT THAT Black people are in serious peril around the world is not a secret. Here in America, the shame is that BA is not nearly doing enough, collectively, to change its destiny. It seems as though BA has thrown in the towel. Is there a method to this madness? Should not all of BA want to live? If so, to a person, what is being done about it?

The good news is that America needs us, just like we need America. BA needs to become a stronger American contingent, and this is in the best interests of America as well. People come to America the world over for one reason: opportunity. And BA needs to have the same mindset, which is one of recognizing opportunity and working hard to succeed. Individually, all of BA needs to have a better understanding of what is going on, and then take effective action. Up to this point, it is the lack of effective action that has made this entire ordeal so perplexing.

PART II

AFFLICTIONS

SERVICE

AN OLD MAN WAS WALKING ALONG the beach, when he came upon a part of the sand where thousands of starfish had washed ashore. A little further down the beach he saw a young woman, who was picking up the starfish one at a time and tossing them back into the ocean. "Oh you silly little girl," he exclaimed. "You can't possibly save all of these starfish. There's too many." The woman smiled and said, "I know. But I can save this one," and she tossed another one into the ocean, "and this one", toss, "and this one…"

Starfish……..
(www.inspirationpeak.com/shortstories.html)

PART II CONTAINS TWENTY AFFLICTIONS THAT BA has become all too familiar with. The majority of these Afflictions and their subsequent indulgence are a result of freewill, and the consequences of these choices are subtle, immense and far-reaching, resulting in a sort of slow-bleed of BA. These Afflictions go relatively unchecked as the impending harm associated with these Afflictions are interwoven into everyday behaviors and activities like the thread count of five-star hotel linens. They are so near as to not be seen for what they really are, and as such, are too close for comfort. Years of courtships with these Afflictions result in the disintegration of men, women and families.

Black youth are the fallen prey to this set of damnations. Possibly the biggest single obstacle facing Black America today is how to find a way to get Black youth on the right path to making the good choices. It is an epic battle, and what the Black youth of today need is the proper skill set to properly evaluate their every daily thought, decision and activity in order to give themselves a chance at real success in life. Is it possible for Black youth to clearly understand that BA is living in perilous times, and that they are the very heart of BA, as their decisions play a direct role in the future of every Black citizen in America. That same question can be posed to Black adults is it relates to their understanding of the same concept.

Black youth are definitely the key to the future of BA. They just don't quite realize it to the extent needed. Some might say that many of them act as though they don't care either. Black youth have to be shown that life has become 'realer' than they would want to admit. Whether it is abstaining from sex, to being courteous, to ridding Black communities of drugs, to respecting women, or to understanding that they have a better chance of getting in the NBA than they do of becoming a superstar rap artist, they must understand that Black youth not only have to make better decisions, they must make the right decision. Black youth must understand that they are needed to perpetuate BA in way that is proud, productive, and intelligent.

THE AFFLICTIONS ARE the other half of the Quality of Life Statistics, and they deal with the social phenomenon of life in Black Ame. As we take a look at these twenty Afflictions, it is my hope that all will be able to see how the simple, everyday activities and decisions effect the lives of a collective BA, understand how these activities and decisions work against BA, and realize that better decision-making and more self-restraint would by themselves elevate BA to not only a much higher standard of living, but also save lives.

The Black Family

ON THE PANEL of Tavis Smiley's Black Think Tank program entitled "The Black Family" was Dr. David Satcher - former president of Meharry Medical College and a former U.S. Surgeon General; Mr. Cornel West of Princeton University; Na'im Akbar - Psychology Professor at Florida State University; Judge Greg Mathis of television fame; Ms. Martha

COLLINS - EDUCATIONAL trailblazer of recent years; Dr. Orlando Patterson, - Sociology Professor from Harvard University; and Mr. Jordan Harris – President of "Youth Action".

Dr. Orlando Patterson provided some piercing statistics concerning the state of The Black Family. Some of the statistics he provided indicated that Black people:

- Have the lowest marriage rate
- Have the highest divorce rate
- Have the same results as above in regards to co-habitation
- Have the smallest number of network resources
- Basically, Blacks are "lonely" people[22]

THESE FACTS PROVIDE some insight into the state of the Black family. These statistics help to understand the state of Black men and women, and can play an important role in the correction of the family problems that exist today. For starters, Black youth have to be effectively taught that loving, outstanding families do not happen by chance, and that there is a system, an art to building tight-knit, close, loving families. Understanding how the Afflictions tear Black families apart is a lesson in that process.

It takes years to learn and understand that one's very own family is the single most precious possession a human being could ever have. It also takes a special understanding that the best chance at having a successful family is usually the first chance. If one is lucky, there might be a second chance, but it can often entail even more work than the first time. Wonderful and loving families are not found in grab bags, but built through hard work, dedication, and love. Having good relationships outside of the immediate family is similar. Young people need to know to know that life is not about a series of non-ending 'feel good' indulgences and one night stands, but rather long lasting, work-entailed relationships that add more and more meaning to their lives as time goes on. This is true with relationships in regards to:

- Parents
- Self
- Spouse or Significant Other
- Children
- Friends (usually a small number of true friends)
- Work
- Education

BUILDING HEALTHY AND long-term relationships is the foundation for meaningful and fruitful lives. Healthy, loving relationships contribute not only to successful individual existences, but also to just about any goal or endeavor undertaken. Having one's own family often serves as the pre-eminent motivation for achievement and success. To not have one's own family, or meaningful relationships with people we love, means to afford one the task of making sense of life on the most personal level. And this is especially true in Black communities and the extensive lack of the traditional nuclear family. An understanding of the nature of relationships could go a long way toward putting an end to the assembly-line creation of illegitimate children, broken families, and shallow, temporal associations.

Black youth are having problems shaping positive and meaningful value systems, and this stems directly from the lack of strong family units and healthy relationships in their lives. Ill value systems create ill-fated behaviors. The loser in all of this is BA. The family unit is undoubtedly the key to the success of any race or group of people. One-marriage families are fast becoming obsolete, as the myriad of critical problems in Black communities makes it much more difficult to both start and maintain families.

Too Much Television

ALTHOUGH TELEVISION VIEWING may seem to be a peculiar place to start when analyzing the Afflictions, it may well be the best place to start. You see, this is where BA first begins to fall apart. The effects of virtually all of the Mortality Metrics and Afflictions could be minimized to considerable degrees if only television viewing were decreased to a minimum. Children are not only what they eat and drink, but also what they see and hear. Black children exceedingly indulge in television viewing and video gaming, instead of the preferred alternatives of reading, physical exercise, studying, intelligent conversation, and family time. It starts from birth with the children watching Cartoon Network, Nickelodeon or The Disney Channel all day long. The reality is that the children would be much better off in a quiet room listening to 'quiet' sounds instead of watching the boob tube. And though this may be hard to believe, I must tell you that the same theory is true for adults also.

I firmly believe that television is one of BA's biggest societal problems. However, convincing others of the same is a problem in itself. Most people probably believe that television is not harmful, and this would be nice, if it were true. But it is not true. Like most indulgencies, if taken in moderation, television viewing would be okay for children. As the years go on, parental supervision and control can ensure a positive experience in regards to television viewing. But that is not what is happening. Children are allowed to view the incredible filth and junk on television with parental blessing, and statistics show that this is especially true for Black children. Television has become big brother, big sister, and momma and daddy. Ultimately, the television set has become the shaper of the value systems of Black children, and that is where things have gone too far.

IT SEEMS THAT most people do not quite realize just how much their children indulge in some sort of television viewing. First there is everyday television viewing, with all of its reality shows, music videos, and other bull-crap. This comes by way of cable television, satellite television, and the super-duper whammy of all television, digital cable television. What on earth can a person do with hundreds of channels except watch television and die? Then, there is the traditional movie going experience at the cinema. Next there are video rentals. This often leads to burning, or copying movies for personal possession. If they can't burn movies, then they just buy movies. This often leads to the re-watching of these same movies over and over again, in the event the children get 'bored'. And finally there is internet surfing, which is a form of 'tube' watching, and presently myspace.com is the boss of all websites in that command time spent on the internet. To finalize the deal, there is the king of it all, video gaming.

Now it is time to do the math. Add up the hours your children spend on the various forms of television viewing, including the internet. Many will find that over the course of days, weeks, months, and even years, there is not much time left for anything remotely resembling cognitive endeavors. Black youth are just barely reading one book per year outside of anything being required of them in school. Yes, reading has become quite the dinosaur. Imagine the heights Black children could achieve if they were to read books just one fourth of the time spent on the various forms of television viewing? They would be Carvers and Einsteins! Instead of watching television and underachieving for their entire lives, there are so many more productive ways to utilize their hours. The day is fast approaching when society will knock them backwards, leaving them to wonder what went wrong, and this is something that their present value systems is not teaching them.

Do not be fooled by the children's report cards, as many are simply tolerated and then promoted with few real challenges and accomplishments. Sometimes they are passed because they have nice personalities, and in any event, the challenge just does not exist to reach peak performance. This, too, happens as a result of the value systems of Black youth, and not nearly as much a result of indifference of teachers in the public school systems. Here is a simple test for you to give your children. Ask them to tell you three things about each core subject, which of course are Math, Science, Language Arts and Geography. The three things have to be formulas, principles, concepts, rules or properties, and not one-word answers or incomplete thoughts. You will be surprised at how many students cannot pass this simple test. And yet, it is a serious sign that they are not at one with their school lessons, and may be tell you that changes are of the order.

AND REMEMBER, THERE is an entire contingent of American students from private schools, and even more important, students of a foreign origin that are working hard to become movers and shakers in American society. They will be the surgeons, CPAs, supervisors, counselors, psychiatrists, administrators, and leaders of America, just as they are now, with or without Black students. Just what are you going to do about that?

Your Mission, If You Accept It

YOUR VERY FIRST mission, if you accept it, is to: GET RID OF ALL EXCESS CABLE CHANNELS IN YOUR HOMES! This is a tough mission for some, an easy mission for others. But remember, this will work wonders in helping your child to improve academically. Children are planted in front of television sets as soon as those little neck muscles are strong enough to hold up those cute, oversized heads of theirs. The next thing you know, the children are haunted by the words of the infamous boxer Mike Tyson, who once said in his very own unique voice after one of his fights, "It was over before it started". When we provide our toddlers with channels such as Cartoon Network and The Disney Channel, we have the intention of freeing up our personal time while providing them harmless entertainment, when in fact we have just introduced them to their number one failure option. Additionally, now the television becomes their primary information source, and also their best friend.

Remember that the internet is a big time waster and detriment in itself. It is quite often abused and misused. As a result, invest in filters to help you in the parenting of your children's internet surfing. Internet filters can be a tremendous help. A number of parents already control television viewing in their homes, and yet more parents are needed to do the same. The learning abilities of children would be peaked if they were to hear piano music, or were read to, or were to view educational channels such as Discovery, The Learning Channel, or as stated earlier, a quiet room, as there are so many more favorable and sensible options other than television viewing.

Something to Think About

As you brood over the following statistics, determine for yourself the role television viewing is commanding in the lives of Black children:

Nielsen Media Research conducted a study and concluded the following results:

- Primetime Television Viewing – Black teens ages 12-17 watched on average 1 hour and 50 minutes more television than all other ethnic groups. Black children ages 2-11 watch 1 hour and 26 minutes more television than all other kids.

- Daytime Television Viewing – Black teens watch 1 hour and 20 minutes more television than other groups, while black children ages 2-11 watch on average 1 hour more television than other groups.

- Late Night Television Viewing – Black teens ages 12-17 watch 1 hour and 30 minutes more television than all other groups, while black children ages 2-11 watch 1 hour more television than all other groups.[24]

- Yet another study revealed that 40% of Black 9-year-olds, 35% of 13-year-olds, and 24% of 17-year-olds watch six hours or more of television per day, compared to 14%, 8%, and 5% of White kids, and 22%, 19%, and 9% of Hispanic kids that watch six hours or more of television per day, in each respective age category.[25]

Growing up as a child in the sixties and seventies, we had to wait until Saturday to watch cartoons. Throughout the week, we would find various activities participate in to stamp out boredom. It was no problem concocting some sort of creative, educational or physical activity. Today, the activities of choice are usually a television show or a video game. The excessive indulgence in television viewing and video gaming destroys the minds of our youth like carbon monoxide poisoning, with both being silent and deadly.

THE ULTIMATE GOAL is to have your children watch absolutely no television at all on all school days, allowing television viewing on the weekends only. If this is not practical for you, then limit them to only one hour of television and no video gaming on school days, Monday through Friday. If you take the one-hour route, then limit their weekend television to something like four hours. Bring back creativity, education and reading in your homes. Grab a book and read along with them. Discuss the changes over with your children, give them a transition period, and make it happen. If you stick to this plan for thirty days, I guarantee that you will see a difference in their attitudes, personalities and study habits. However, keep in mind that these new time management skills cannot be taught if they are at a friend's house or somewhere else.

The minds of the children must be protected and nurtured with mental activities and quiet time. It takes more than just food and clothing to mold a successful child, and there are a lot more important things for kids to do in life than watch television for hours on top of more hours. In fact, practically everything else in life is more important than watching television.

It all comes down to this: The job of a parent is to provide children with the things that they need, not want they want. And when the children get some of the things they want, these things should be of a positive nature, and not a self-destructive one. Getting rid of video game systems and excess television viewing will prove to be one of the wisest decisions that you can make as a parent. And if you do it from the get-go, when they are infants, it will be much easier to build and maintain solid value systems within both your children's minds and your homes, as well as winning students in schools.

Video Gaming

YOUNG PEOPLE WILL play video games all day long, oftentimes without saying but a few words for hours at a time. You might hear an occasional expletive: "$#@%!" or "damn", or "nice move", but not much else. If this is how our youth spend their discretionary hours day after day, then how in the world will they compete in the real world? What about critical thinking skills, vocabulary or team building skills? In time, as they find themselves needing a job, we will hear the same " $#@%!", but only in reference to the job they needed, could not obtain.

Your next mission, if you want to protect your children and their futures, is to: GET RID OF ANY AND ALL VIDEO GAME SYSTEMS IN YOUR HOME! Sell the game systems to video game stores or simply throw them away. A better name for them would be 'video drug systems' or 'mind control systems' as kids will not bathe, do chores, brush their teeth, or anything else they are supposed to do if it interferes with their gaming time. Break the death-grips they employ on their joysticks and do them a favor take control. If there is not a video game system in your home, then – DO NOT BUY A VIDEO GAME SYSTEM! This is the sleeper step in contributing to the success of BA.

ON THE SUPPLY side of this equation, gaming continues to reach all-time highs as Corporate America caters to unintelligible demand. Full fledged criminal mentality games such as 'Grand Theft Auto' and 'True Crime: New York City' allow Black youth to further become enamored with the full array of vices - sex, crime, guns and violence – everything that growing boys and girls do not need. Corporate America should not be assisted in the destruction of the minds of Black children by buying their video games, allowing the children to rent them, or indulge in them in any way. Their deplorable and senseless games do not need to find their way into Black homes.

The biggest victims are the very young children, as it always trickles down to them. Nothing is worse than knowing that a small child of elementary age owns a video game system, as the younger they are, the more dysfunctional they will become just by playing video games. Young kids soak up video gaming like a sponge soaks up water. They love it, and corporate America knows it. Young children are at the mercy of the negative sensory overload they endure as they partake of the negative experience that video game.

There are ways to offset the video gaming experience. One of the best ways to do this is to enroll your children in activities such as sports teams or hobby clubs. However, enrollment is not enough, parents must make the time and arrangements to transport the children to their activities of choice. As this is done, the payoff will be forever lasting.

The time spent in front of these electronic boxes is alarming. The time has come to fight back against the onslaught of corporate advertising and senseless consumer spending. There should no longer exist the practice of spending good money on bad electronics. Think about what is good for the children, and only what is good for them. The time has come to take back the minds of the children!

Black Female Sexual Exploitation

YOUNG BLACK TEENS are contracting the majority of new HIV/AIDS cases. To explore why young, Black female teens are falling prey to this trap, a look at some of the phenomena that feed into these situations, in particular 'Black Female Sexual Exploitation', is necessary.

The sexual objectification of Black women continues today through negative sexual representations of Black femininity. Nowhere are these representations echoed more coherently than in popular hip-hop musical videos. In practically all of these videos, women generally wear bikinis, and this is particularly problematic because in most situations the women are not in a beach or pool setting. The women are obviously outfitted in bikinis merely to 'show off' their bodies and there is no real purpose or explanation a to why they are not wearing regular clothing.

Often there are dozens of scantily clad women in either bikinis or other revealing outfits, and the women generally outnumber the men by large ratios such as seven or eight to one, however, the men are usually fully clothed. This is of particular importance because it shows the opposite nature in which Black men and women are constructed and positioned. Their clothes represent their refusal to be reduced to mere body parts, although their female counterparts fall victim to this categorization. The women are 'put on display' for Whites, Blacks, and other audiences, which is reminiscent of the ways in which Black women were put on display historically.

THE REPRODUCTION OF certain stereotypes about Black womanhood in popular music videos are dangerous on two levels: first, these images are perpetuated in the Black community, affecting the self-esteem of Black adolescent youth, skewing the perception of what a Black woman should look and act like for Black females and males alike, and second, non-Blacks are privy to these images as well and continue to perceive

Black women as sexual objects that remain inferior to women of other races (who are not represented in the media in the same ways as their Black counterparts, especially in music videos).[26]

BET

BLACK ENTERTAINMENT TELEVISION, or BET, is the programming leader for the Black television viewing audience. It has music videos, gospel music, music videos, reality shows, music videos, sports programming, music videos and other programming, including music videos. Whereas Black people applaud BET and its programming efforts, the reality is that BET is more like the programming sewer leader in the industry. So much so, that it deserves a new name, which I will provide, free of charge, to its present parent company, Viacom. How about Black Bull$#!! Entertainment Television. Try Black Embarrassment Telemundo. You'll like this one: Bitch & Eggs TV. Next there is Black Excretion Television, and finally, Booty/Breast Excess Telethon. All would work just fine.

BA can be thankful to BET for being the largest, most continuous conduit of Black stereotypes and negative images in the free world. Never mind that it is not 'Black-owned', as its business platform was the same before BET's ownership changed hands. It was a pathetic television station then, and it is a pathetic television station now. The programming menu of BET is mentally toxic, being extremely high on sex and female exploitation and low on value. And like video games, it has trickled down to the young children. Just how many bikinis, breasts, and booties do the BA youth need to see? Apparently, as many as BET can squeeze in each hour, as long as it keeps Black kids glued to the tube and away from their books. Five will get you ten that under no circumstances whatsoever do the executives and managers at BET allow their children to view the crap they broadcast in the name of BET?

To SAY THAT parents need to pay attention to what their children watch is not the total answer, as parents cannot know everything. The quandary with BET is that Black people have a tendency to support entertainment-related endeavors that are endorsed with Black entertainment stars, such as compact discs, clothing lines, showcase programs, videos, and BET. Black youth are the collateral damage as they fall victim to the programming onslaught of BET, as it sells sex like drug dealers sell drugs. BET wants to addict Black kids to music by way of sex, and one of the consequences is that Black youth in fact get addicted to sex by way of music and its accompanying videos. Black parents endorse it by bringing BET into their homes. If Black youth were to see murders, marijuana use, or crack dealing every five minutes by Hip Hop artists in videos, rest assured that there would be even more homicides, marijuana smoking and crack dealing and drug use in Black communities than there is now. The same is true of sex. No other people serve up their children as an audience to the types of degrading, non-stop sexist programming that BET provides as Black people, and that is a shame.

The great irony is that the number one purveyor of sexual images to Black children is the recipient of numerous awards for its role in the fight against HIV/AIDS. This is public relations both at its best, and at its worst. That BET poses as a crusader in the fight against HIV/Aids is sort of like the fox watching the henhouse – "Get out of there, hens!" Go figure. Black children are negatively and sexually programmed hour after hour by a cable television channel that does not genuinely concern itself with the fact that Black people are dying like no other people in the world due to HIV/AIDS. The consequences of youth sex are HIV/AIDS, other sexually disease transmission, and teen pregnancy – but apparently, BET did not get the memo. But the reality is this: BET only exists because Black people support it.

THERE ARE OTHER problems associated with the 'most trusted' channel in BA. It can be problematic when supporting an entity without knowing of the facts and inner-workings of this entity. Here are some facts on BET and its advertising arm of its programming.

- Alcohol advertisers placed ads on 86 programs on BET in 2002, but 65% of advertising spending and two-thirds of the ads were on just six programs. Youth in general were more likely to see all six of these programs than adults, and four of the six drew disproportionate numbers of African American youth relative to African American adults.[11]

- 30% of African American teens are among the most frequent

television viewers versus 21% of non-African American teens.[11]

- Alcohol advertisers spent $11.7 million in 2002 to place ads on all 15 of the programs most popular with African American youth, including Bernie Mac, The Simpsons, King of the Hill, My Wife and Kids, and The Wonderful World of Disney.[11]

WHAT BA REALLY needs is for BET to be gone. BET's never-ending stream of sexual content continuously steps over a line that seems to extend further and further out. BET should be a channel that provides wholesome entertainment to families. Instead, BET promotes promiscuity, pimping, and orgies. Young Black girls learn to be groupies and freaks by watching the programming on BET. How many parents know that young Black girls of ages as young as 12, 13, and 14 years of age are performing lap dances at their parties? It does not take much imagination for young children to remove the bikinis, soap bubbles, and bed sheets that hide body parts in the music videos they watch. It does not take much for young children to envision the implied sexual acts of music videos. This is why television control is so important. There is a concept on the table that should be supported by all concerned – A La Carte!

A La Carte

IN THE NEAR future we will be blessed with a television-programming concept called 'a la carte'. A la carte is where cable TV consumers can pick the channels they receive instead of being forced to buy packages that have unwanted channels. Customers could avoid having violent or sex-laden shows, and this should save money also.
SENATOR JOHN MCCAIN (R-Ariz), introduced legislation on 6/7/2006 that would reward cable operators that offer the sale of cable channels on an a la carte basis. The FCC chairman Kevin Martin has called on Congress to pass the bill.

"The Parents Television Council is applauding Sen. John McCain for introducing the bill that brings consumers one step closer to having real cable choices and lower cable prices," PTC president Brent Bozell said in a prepared statement. "The forced subsidy of graphic and explicit content on basic cable must end," he said, adding that the current industry "solution" of family tiers "does nothing to give families choices and control over the content that comes into their homes."

The Concerned Women for America also endorsed McCain's bill, claiming that it would save consumers money and help parents to exile indecent programming without first having to pay for it.[23]

OF COURSE, THE cable television industry is fighting a la carte tooth and nail. Cable operators get paid by the number of subscribers they have, and although they claim to offer their customers diversity and choice, this is not true because customers are not being allowed to choose the channels they want. The result is that customers are stuck with crappy channels such as you-know-who, whereas American families actually deserve better. And remember, when threatened with higher prices, do not worry. Black children are already paying a greater price than could ever be measured in dollars and cents.

Radio Sell-Out

BLACK RADIO STATIONS present another set of problems to Black youth. Under the guise of music, children are being psychologically anesthetized to the realities of what is taking place in Black communities. The lyrics contained within today's music that is broadcast over the radio waves glamorizes problems associated with guns, drugs, sex, alcohol, and violence. These lyrics promote the behaviors associated with these vices as something necessary, vogue, and proper. Worse yet, it is apparently done with little or no opposition from Black adults. The number one tool used by today's Hip Hop artist to sell their music is sex, and it can be seen explicitly in their videos. It's a formula that seems to work for both the Hip Hop artists and the radio stations, as business owners continue to buy the advertising slots of these Hip Hop formats, even though these formats often are as far away as the other side of the world in terms of reaching their target audience.

BA seems to have taken the position that precious Black pre-teens do not really pay attention to the lyrics in today's music. It's either that or BA does not care. The lyrics in today's music are like the gateway to sexual imagery for young children. Black radio stations are probably the worst case of media poison because number one, there are so many of them, and number two, they are thought to be more child-friendly than television. Well, that is how it used to be. There is at least one Black radio station in each of the top two hundred or so cities in America. As in the case of BET, many Black radio stations are not owned by blacks, but by White entrepreneurs. Those that are Black owned would be well served to re-think their position and immediately change the urban format to one that is entirely family-oriented and geared toward resuscitating life back into Black communities. They would find that their advertising revenue would still be there.

THE FOLLOWING ARE some of the lyrics from some of the most popular songs of recent years. Keep in mind that these songs play as much as ten to twenty times a day, the artists that produce these lyrics are icons amongst young children, and has transformed what used to be a safe and entertaining medium into one of filth and disgust:

1) "It's getting hot in here, so take off all your clothes." (woman replies) "I am getting so hot, I'm gonna take my clothes off".
2) "You're a big fine woman, won't you back that ass up."
3) "Let me see you make your pussy fart, Good Lawd."
4) "Lick it right, lick it good, lick it like you know you should."
5) "I don't know what you heard about me. But you can't get a quarter out of me. 'Cause I'm a motherfucking P-I-M-P."

THE FOLLOWING ILLUSTRATES another negative effect that occurs as a result of targeted advertising on Black radio stations:

- African American teens ages 12-17 listen to more than 18 hours of radio per week on average, compared to 13.5 hours for all teens.[11]

- African American youth heard 12% more beer advertising and 56% more advertising for distilled spirits on the radio in 2002 than non-African American youth.[11]

- Rap music videos analyzed for a study published in 1997 contained the highest percentage of depictions of alcohol use of any music genre appearing on MTV, BET, CMT, and VH-1.[11]

- African American culture already abounds with alcohol products. A content analysis of 1,000 on the most popular songs from 1996 to 1997 found that references to alcohol were more frequent in Rap (47% of songs had alcohol references) than other genres such as Country Western (13%), Top 40 (12%), Alternative Rock (10%), and Heavy Metal (4%); also, 48% of these Rap songs had product placement or mentions of specific alcoholic brands names.[11]

WHEN THE MUSIC pioneers paved the way for today's artists, I would like to think that their intentions were to uplift the human spirit through song, and not serve as a means to glamorize the problems of Black communities as our children sing along. Yea, the ghetto is the ghetto. But it used to be that the ghetto was something people wanted to escape from. Now it's a place that is glamorized in lyrical fashion in many Black songs and serves as the main theme in Black movies.

It would be a good thing take to take a stand and boycott Black radio stations and BET. To demand cleaner lyrics in songs and to eliminate sexually explicit videos on television is a proper thing to do. The fate of and radio stations and television channels is controlled through the dollars of its customers. No matter who the owner, no matter who the artist, if the music or the show is negative, does not educate in a positive way, does not inspire Black children to succeed, and does not build up Black communities, then the business entities should not be supported. It is that simple.

Blacks survived slavery, and Blacks survived the wickedness of the Civil Rights Era. Blacks can also survive without BET, video games; and the present Black radio station formats. All are doing more harm than good.

Teen Sex

IN HER BOOK "Epidemic: How Teen Sex is Killing Our Kids"[9], Dr. Meg Meeker talks about how sexually transmitted diseases among teens has become a full-blown epidemic, a national emergency that's killing our kids, all kids. She states that in 1960, only two STD's existed. Today, more that 30 viruses exist. One in five kids over the age of 11 has genital herpes – a 500% increase since 1976. Dr. Meeker says that after their first sexual encounter, new studies show that teen-age girls have a 46% chance of contracting human papilloma virus, a virus that results in cervical cancer 93% of the time! Some facts from Dr. Meeker's book:

- Nearly 50% of African-American teenagers have genital herpes.
- Everyday, 8,000 teens will become infected with a new Sexually Transmitted Disease (STD)
- Nearly one out of for sexually active teens is living with an STD at this moment.
- One in five children over age 12 tests positive for herpes type 2.
- Adult diseases such as cervical cancer, pelvic inflammatory disease (PID), genital herpes, and HIV, have become diseases of children.
- Half of all students in ninth through twelfth grade have had sexual intercourse.
- For thousands of teens, one of the major causes of depression is sex.
- One out of every three girls had has sex by age 16, two out of three has had sex by age 18.
- The younger teenaged girl is when she has sex for the first time, the more likely she is to have had unwanted sex or non-voluntary sex. Close to four in ten girls who had their first intercourse at 13 or 14 report it was either non-voluntary or unwanted.
- One piece of good news is that teenagers who have strong emotional attachments to their parents are much less likely to become sexually active at an early age.

FLASHBACK TO THE seventies, when the primary concern focused on about five STD's – gonorrhea, syphilis, yeast infections, the clap, and crabs. Looking back, it was not bad, relatively speaking, compared to what is presently out there. Today, there are at least twenty-five STD's that today's children have to be concerned about. And as young Blacks are suffering and dying disproportionately from the STD epidemic, remember just what is at stake. Many young Black girls will not be able to grow up with the chance to get married, become healthy mothers and have the types of families they deserve, the types of families that give children a chance for a successful future. Many will also die prematurely.

Teen Pregnancy

- The United States has the highest rate of teen pregnancy and births in the western industrialized world. Teen pregnancy costs the United States at least $7 billion annually.

- The rates of both Hispanics and Blacks remain higher than for other groups, with Hispanic teens now having the highest teenage birth rate. Most teenagers giving birth today are unmarried.

- The younger a teenage girl is when she has sex for the first time, the more likely she is to have had unwanted or non-voluntary sex. Close to four in ten girls who had first intercourse at 13 or 14 report it was either non-voluntary or unwanted.

- Teen mothers are less likely to complete high school (only one-third receive a high school diploma) and only 1.5% has a college degree by age 30.
- Teen mothers are more likely to end up on welfare (nearly 80% of unmarried teen mothers end up on welfare), which makes it the biggest reason for getting on welfare, and one of the biggest obstacles to success for both Blacks and Hispanics.

- The children of teen mothers have lower birth rates, are more likely to perform poorly in school, and are at greater risk of abuse and neglect.

- The sons of teen mothers are 13 percent more likely to end up in prison while teen daughters are 22 percent more likely to become teen mothers themselves.

- The primary reason that teenage girls who have never had intercourse give for abstaining from sex is that having sex would be against their religious or moral values. Other reasons cited include desire to avoid pregnancy, fear of contracting a sexually transmitted disease, and not having the appropriate partner. Three of four girls and over half of boys report that girls who do have sex do so because their boyfriends want them to.

- Teenagers who have strong emotional attachments to their parents are much less likely to become sexually active at an early age. Also, two-parent households lower the probability of teenage girls having sex.

- Teenpregnancy.org reports that the United States has the highest rates of teen pregnancy and birth in the western industrialized world. Teen pregnancy costs the United States at least $7 billion dollars annually. The rates of both Hispanics and African-Americans, however, remain higher than other groups. Hispanic teens now have the highest teenage birth rates.[27]

TEEN PREGNANCY IS one of two areas, with school dropouts being the other, where Blacks are not the worst off amongst all racial groups.

Poverty

Poverty is yet another area where Blacks suffer more than all others.[28]

2003 People in Poverty:

Blacks...24.4%
Hispanic...22.5%
Asians..11.8%
Whites...10.5%

2003 Median Income per family:

Asian/Pacific Islanders............................$55,262
Whites..45,572
Hispanics... 32,997
Blacks... 29,689

As you may notice, percentage wise, BA has the largest number of people and families that qualify as low-income. Simultaneously, BA also has the lowest median income of all ethnic groups. And while this is true, you would never know it judging by the way many Black people place style above substance. Adorning ones body with expensive clothing means nothing without a strong education and a future, as this is what elevates a people out of poverty. Asians have the highest median income per families in relation to all ethnic groups, including whites, due to their commitment to education. Blacks and Asians are at totally opposite ends of the education spectrum. Poverty can be tamed by way of education.

Asthma

Asthma is a chronic lung disease characterized by episodes of airflow obstruction. Symptoms of an asthma attack include coughing, wheezing, shortness of breath, and chest tightness. Allergic conditions, including asthma, are among the major causes of illness and disability in the United States. Illness and death from asthma have been increasing in this country for the past 15 years and are particularly high among poor, inner city African-Americans and Latino populations.

Although asthma is only slightly more prevalent among minority children than among whites, it accounts for three times the number of deaths. Low socioeconomic status, exposure to urban environmental contaminants, lack of access to medical care, and lack of self-management skills all contribute to the increase in deaths in minority communities. Asthma claims approximately 5,000 lives annually in the United States. African Americans were 3 to 4 times more likely than Whites to be hospitalized for asthma, and 4 to 6 times more likely than Whites to die from asthma. The increasing prevalence of asthma in inner-city children underscores the need for new therapies to prevent asthma and reduce its prevalence.

Asthma is the leading causing cause of school absenteeism due to chronic illness and the second most important respiratory condition to cause home confinement for adults. One study found that children with asthma lose an extra 10 million school days each year.

A NATIONAL COOPERATIVE Inner-City Asthma Study in the early 90's revealed that high levels of indoor allergens, tobacco smoking, and nitrogen dioxide, which is a respiratory irritant produced by inadequately vented stoves and heating appliances. However, the most convincing data was that cockroach allergen were the major allergen for inner-city children.[29]

Public Housing

MINORITIES HAVE HISTORICALLY constituted 50 to 60 percent of all public housing tenants, and Blacks make up the majority of this minority contingent. The worst of these public housing units are the multiple dwelling units, a.k.a., 'The Projects'. From the one-story units that were once in Saginaw, Michigan to the high-rise complexes of New York and Chicago, they all represent the worst of places to raise children and have families. The prevalence of drugs, drugs, violence, alcoholism and all of the other negative social repercussions that are present stemming from a large number of people living on top of each other. A large part of this situation is that many, if not all, of the occupants of project housing are unemployed, underemployed, uneducated, or minimally educated. Basically, you have a great deal of people crammed together that have a lot of problems.

It is this veritable ugliness of Black Americans occupying public housing in grand numbers that make Black Americans the poster people of dysfunction. As many project communities are located in major cities along interstate highways, a simple car ride through many of these cities can be likened to going to the cinema and watching all of the Black exploitation movies combined.

The good news is that there is a national movement to demolish project-housing communities across the land, which gives Black people a real chance to make a sort of fresh housing start. Cities like Nashville, Philadelphia, Seattle, and Dallas are tearing down their projects with a purpose. This demolition project is the largest of its kind in history.

Whatever the reasons are for this demolition, this is both a victory and an excellent opportunity for a lot of Black Americans to start anew. Before this inner city refurbishing plan starting our, there were over 1 million public housing units in America.

Just about all of the project units are occupied by Blacks, so we're talking about approximately 3 million people, or roughly ten percent of the Black population. There are also other problems associated with living in project housing.

AN ARTICLE FROM the Natural Resources Defense Council dated October 8, 2003 called on The Department of Housing and Urban Development (HUD) to comply with federal law by using safer pest management practices in public housing. It also mentioned that children are particularly at risk from pesticide because their neuro-muscular systems are still developing. Exposure to pesticides both in the womb and during the first years after birth have been linked to an increased risk of cancer and brain and nervous system problems. HUD had refused to comply with the law.

It may also be true that tearing down the projects is not enough, and this is because the attitudes and beliefs of the people that ultimately leave project housing must change also. It will be up to each individual person to change their own personal attitudes and behaviors and set goals that will allow them to take advantage of this new opportunity.

It would have been nice if Black Mayors had the vision, determination and expertise to accomplish the eradication of project housing themselves in their respective cities. I know of no instance where this was the case. However, I can recall an instance where new project housing was recognized as a victorious achievement. Nevertheless, a victory is a victory.

Materialism and Vanity

DR. KING HIMSELF once said, "Black people are religious, patriotic and materialistic." How accurate this statement is. Unemployed? School dropout? No problem. Just give me that new pair of Jordan's. Materialism is the cornerstone of the value systems of our youth. They want the popular shoes – Air Force 1', Nike, Reebok, Puma, And 1, Jordan, Hirachi, and Timberland. They want the popular clothing – Lot

29, South Pole, Ecko, Fat Albert, 8 Ball, Phat Farm, Sean John, Pelle Pel, Rocca Wear, Tommy Hilfiger, Fubu, NBA and NFL apparel. Many Blacks want the popular, expensive car rims – Sprewell, Giovanna, Cabo, and Lexani, regardless of cost. If Black youth could match their thirst for material things with an equal thirst for education, this book would not have been written. Instead, many place 'looking good' above most anything else. This style without substance mindset plays a role in the death of their futures.

MANY YOUTH HAVE their self-esteem tied directly into materialism as they feel the need to wear the popular clothing just to fit in, ignoring the fact that to really fit in means to prepare for the future. Those that do not have the expensive clothing items are often ridiculed and looked down upon as though they are coming up short in life. They are looked down on as being poor, by people who are poor themselves. It also does not help when Hip Hop artists get on Black radio stations and request that kids wear the 'real' $300 jerseys when they attend their concerts and after parties. And where do the kids get the money to buy $300 jerseys? Let's just say they can get creative in a number of ways to get that jersey.

BA seems to have jumped right over appreciation and utilization of the Civil Rights era victories, and straight into celebration and demonstration through materialism. As Black youth adorn themselves with meaningless symbols and ornaments, there are other student contingencies that have their priorities in order. There are other more important ways for youth to spend money, such as travel, stocks, mutual funds, or simple savings. It is all about value systems, which is the Achilles heel of too many Black youth.

The mental condition described above is defined as Vanity, and it is quite a foolish state of mind. The outer-self is a product of the inner-self, and it is the inner-self that Black youth should be concerned with over and above the outer self. You are who you are and you look like what you look like. Materialism and Vanity may play tricks on the mind, but time will tell if those nice clothes and nice hairdos will get the nice job or swell up the old bank account. As for me, I'm going with the one who chose the education route, as this is the one with a chance to have it all in life.

Drugs

THE LOVE OF money is the root of all that is evil. This evil permeates all of society, from the ghettos to the halls of the White House. In Black communities, the biggest manifestation of this evil would be the existence of drug-dealers, these 'self-made' business people that desire to control the land. The fact of the matter is that there are businesses that are good for a community, and there are businesses that are bad for a community, and those seen hanging out on street corners like wet clothes are examples of the bad ones. As a result, Black communities suffer immensely.

Drug dealers destroy families, murder, sponsors crime, cause property values to plummet, and operate in plain sight for all children to see. Nowhere is this truer than in Black communities. Drug dealers are the pimps, players, hustlers, and death-merchants of black communities. They intimidate, hurt, and kill those who stand up against them. There are more well-to-do drug dealers in Black communities than there are legitimate, hard-working entrepreneurs and professionals, and even though the shelf life of a drug dealer is short, it is still the popular career choice for many. Invariably, these one-man drug cartels run their course, and like a cork in a fine bottle of champagne, eventually get popped. Now it's roll call in the Big House. It's time to bunk with Bubba and Big 'Toine. Sooner or later, everyone has to answer for his or her actions, and this is definitely true for drug dealers. In Black communities, it just needs to happen in a more swifter and final fashion.

Nothing drains the life out of Black communities as does drugs. The prevalence of drug sales in Black communities is astounding. Drug usage destroys lives and families; is a primary cause of absenteeism and subsequent job loss; and is a primary reason that people indulge in unprotected and ill-engaged sexual activity, which promotes the spread of HIV/AIDS. It has become a rite of passage, and continues to proliferate to this day.

THE FOLLOWING EXCERPTS from 'Race and the Drug War' highlight some of the glaring racial inequities that have been manifested as a result of drug sales and use in the Black communities.

Though their rates of drug use are roughly equal to those of Whites, African-Americans are arrested for drug offenses at six times the rate of Whites. The drug war subjects communities of color to systematic racial profiling, as well as to increasingly aggressive police tactics such as massive street sweeps, "buy and bust" operations, and other activities heavily targeted at street level drug activity (as opposed to the less visible drug activity prevalent in more affluent communities).

African-Americans comprise nearly two-thirds of all drug offenders admitted to state prison, though they constitute only 13% of American drug users. According to recent Human Rights Watch report, Black men are admitted to state prison on drug charges at a rate that is 13.4 times greater than that of White men – with rates up to 57 times greater in some states.[30]

THE EXISTENCE OF mandatory minimum sentences for crimes involving drugs has contributed to the stunning increase in the prison population. It has also resulted in longer sentences for those convicted. According to the Bureau of Justice Statistics, in 2001, 90 percent of drug defendants were convicted, with 62 percent receiving mandatory minimum sentences ranging from 60 months or less to life. The longest sentences were imposed on those involved with crack cocaine, drug crimes that involved firearms, and those with prior records. In addition, three-strike laws, parole abolition, and truth-in-sentencing initiatives have also contributed to the swelling prison population.[31]

Many look at criminal prosecution and criminal sentencing 'discrepancies' of race and walk away somewhat bewildered. I am for tougher sentencing on all drug dealers, especially in Black communities. Young children deserve to have as drug-free a world as is possible, and they should not have to see drug dealers and users in their own neighborhoods daily. And though many want crack dealers out of their neighborhoods, many are not willing to do what it takes to bring about this change.

When you consider the many sons, daughters, family members and friends that becoming addicted to illegal drugs, the decision gets real easy. If drug dealers were not dealt with harshly and decisively, there would be even more of them hanging out on street corners. Should they receive long prison sentences? I say yes, unless someone is making them sell drugs against their own free will. Drug dealers know the consequences of their actions. All drug dealers know that crack, heroine, crystal methamphetamine, and other powerful drugs destroy lives and families. And the dealers just have to know that there are other ways to make a living. If there is partiality in drug sentencing, then the moral of that story should be to not sell illegal drugs. Then they would not have to worry about it.

SOCIETY SHOULD NOT be sympathetic toward the removal of a drug dealer. For every drug dealer, there are dozens and dozens of people and families that incurred various losses. For those communities that are infested with drug dealers, there is a choice to be made: Drug dealers roaming your communities with lighter sentencing and better treatment, or your children and loved ones being safe and drug-free? – **You** make the choice.

Mental Illness

SEVEN PERCENT OF African American men will develop depression during their lifetimes, and this is an understatement due to lack of screening and treatment services. African American men are less likely to be treated with medications, especially newer medications that have less side effects. When they do receive medications, they often receive higher doses leading to more severe side effects. When mental disorders are not treated, African American men are more vulnerable to incarceration, homelessness, substance abuse, homicide and suicide.[32]

PSYCHIATRISTS INVOLUNTARILY COMMIT African Americans three to five times as often as they do whites. Psychiatrists diagnose African American men in public and private mental hospitals as having schizophrenia at a rate of up to 1,500 percent higher than white men. African Americans are given significantly higher doses of psychiatric drugs, major tranquilizers, and neuroleptics than are whites.[33]

African American women could also be added to the statistics. It can also be noted that drug use and alcoholism contribute mightily to the conditions of Black mental illness. The drug use could be prescription, or illegal. However, this is another piece to the support of the removal of drug dealers. As far as the medical under-representation in regards to mental illness, educational outreach and more Black professionals could indeed help alleviate these shortcomings significantly

Black on Black Violence

THIS IS PROBABLY the most sensational segment of Black society today, with the only exception being the HIV/AIDS situation, and it is well deserved. Since 1964 approximately half of the violent crimes committed each year in the United States is attributable to young Black males, who represent less than 3 percent of the total population. In many instances after a murder, the murderer is sort of labeled an urban legend, and usually only for a short time. "He is crazy," they will say. Then, off he goes to prison, soon to be forgotten, until the next 'crazy' character takes his place. The psyche and behavior of Black males can be quite intimidating. Most murders that occur in inner cities take place for the most senseless of reasons, and they murders do not seem to be slowing down.

The threat of violence also haunts the lives of lower-class Black women. Blacks account for more than 45 (percent) of all spousal homicides; the rates for such crimes are nearly nine times White rates. Young Black women who live in cities and have never married are also the (most) likely to be harmed or killed by male intimates, strangers, and acquaintances. Battering frequently precedes death in these crimes, and victims fight back; it is the male abuser, as often as not, who dies in the struggle.

The most troubling fact about the scourge of Black-on-Black violence is that both the killers and their victims are getting younger. Children are not only having babies they are unprepared to care for, they are killing one another with withering regularity. Inner-city public schools are already among the most dangerous sites in the United States. But in the last decade, the threat of spontaneous violence has become a constant companion to Black children of all ages, not only in school but wherever they congregate. In one study, for example, 73 percent of the eighth graders surveyed in a Chicago neighborhood reported that they had seen someone shot, stabbed, robbed, or killed. In Washington D.C., a similar survey of 1st and 2nd graders revealed that 45 percent had witnessed muggings, 31 percent had seen someone shot, and 39 percent had seen a dead body in the street.

Abundant research has shown that crowded and inadequate living conditions greatly diminish the moral, mental, and physical health of those forced to endure them. Overcrowding is associated with irritability, communicable diseases, prostitution, juvenile delinquency, and domestic violence—especially child neglect and abuse. Moreover, family controls are weakened because both adults and children who live in such stressful conditions seek relief and privacy wherever they can find it.

The ultimate victims in this war are the children who issue from the transient couplings that have replaced marriage among the black lower class. Domestic violence and abuse is having a devastating impact on children. The National Center on Child Abuse and Neglect reported that in 1992 nearly three million children had been victimized. While most victims are white (55 percent), a disproportionate number are Black (26 percent), and the pattern is found in all regions of the country. Approximately 754,000 Black children were neglected and abused that year. Current estimates suggest that probably 29 percent of neglected and abused children become adult violent offenders. That could mean that as many as 218,660 violent criminal are being turned loose in inner-city streets regularly for these reasons alone. But an unknown – and far greater – number of neglected children enter their childbearing years without having learned how to be responsible, loving parents themselves.

Finally, the extraordinary levels of violence among Blacks set them apart from every other ethnic group. Scholars have pointed out that unlike native-born Whites and European immigrants, Blacks did not go through a cycle of violent crime that declined after the Civil War. Black rates of violent crimes climbed steadily through the last quarter of the nineteenth century. With only brief reversals, they continued to climb in the twentieth century.[34]

All across this nation, Black communities to great extents comprise a broken and murderous wasteland. Murder is expected in Black communities to the point that many have become de-sensitized to it, knowing it can happen at any given moment. Ideally, the position should be to create new and effective measures to prevent Black on

Black violence from happening. Keep in mind, though, this situation is not totally hopeless. All it takes is for Black constituents to say enough is enough.

We shall now create a new moniker for those that commit violent acts – 'Viopreneurs'. Viopreneurs kill, injure, assault, and threaten people. They carjack, clothes-jack, and have a range of murder motives. Viopreneurs are usually high on drugs, alcohol, stupidity or anger, and warrant to be kept off of our streets for as long as the law allows.

Most of the time when a shooting takes place, it is because of one of three reasons: an individual is scared to take a butt whipping, they want to make a (pointless) point, or they want to get their adversary before that adversary gets him. Those reasons might explain a forgetful ten-day shooting spree in my hometown of Saginaw, Michigan in the spring of 2003.

- 4/13/03 @ 2:30a.m. – A man is shot in the back and face, then shot again in the leg when he fell to the ground. This occurred after an argument.

- 4/13/03 @ 11:30 p.m. – A man is driving alone when bullets hit his left shoulder. Left leg, and right hand.

- 4/14/03 @ 1:30 p.m. – A man is walking down the street when a gun is 'dropped' by one of a group of people he was just gambling with. The firearm discharged and struck him in the right foot.

- 4/16/03 @ 1:30 a.m. – Bullets are fired through the home of a 19-year-old woman. Police found a shotgun shell in the street and two blast holes in the home. One pellet entered the wall of a bedroom, missing the head of a 3-year-old boy by inches. Another child, 11 months old, was also in the home, as well as the woman's 17-year-old brother.

- 4/16/03 @ 2:30a.m. – A 36-year-old woman tells police that someone shot "more than 10 times" at her house. Police recovered 15 shell casings outside her home – seven .40-caliber, six 9mm and two .380-caliber – and 14 bullet holes in her home.

- 4/16/03 @ 2:40 a.m. – Three men were wounded as a vehicle with "four or five" people passed the three men, then stopped. A man jumped out of the car, fired seven times, and struck the driver in his left back, the front-seat passenger in the chin and left back, and the rear seat passenger was cut by glass on both elbows.

- 4/16/03 @ 4:15p.m. – A man attempted to take $5 from a 15-year-old teen. When he refused, a fight broke out. The man left, saying he was going to get a gun. He returned, pulled out a brown paper bag and claimed he had a gun inside. Everyone fled.

- 4/17/03 @ 1:20a.m. – Q 22-year-oldwas driving a car when three young males shot at him. Police found a bullet hole in the rear driver's door; and a rear tire was flat.

- 4/17/03 @ 11:45 a.m. – A 28-yeasr-old woman was sitting in a parked car when a man she did not know approached and began arguing with her. The man slapped her, she told police, and when she drove off the man fired several shots at her.

- 4/18/03 @ 12:30a.m. – As a 37-year-old man returned home from work and enter his home, gunshots erupted. The man was hit in the left buttocks. The man's parents, 55 and 58, and brother, 18, were home sleeping at the time.

- 4/18/03 @1:55a.m. – A man was leaving a store when he heard gunshots and ran for his car. He thought he "scraped" his knee when he dove into his car. However, the next morning he noticed that his bed was soaked with blood and his leg was swollen. He later discovered that there was a bullet lodged in his left knee.

- 4/19/03 @ 2:50a.m. – A 16-year-old girl was standing with

friends in a parking lot when a vehicle pulled up and a man yelled "Get the gun" in Spanish. The man shot twice at the crowd, took off, circled and came back, with the man firing several more times. The teen ran into the store, and later told police that another man was shot in the leg, but didn't know who he was.

- 4/19/03 @ 4:50a.m. – A 22-year-oldwoman and a 24-year-old man said the man's uncle asked the m to go along with him on a cab trip, to take care of some business. Upon arriving at his destination, the uncle got out to talk to a man. Shots rang out. As the uncle ran back to the cab, six men appeared, all shooting. The cab driver was shot, and soon could not drive. The woman pushed him to the side and drove to the hospital. Upon entering the parking lot, the uncle disappeared. The woman suffered from glass fragments in her left hand, the 24-year-old was shot in the arm and buttocks, and the taxi driver was shot in the chest and twice in the back.

- 4/19/03 @ 5:30 a.m. - Police responded to the shooting to find a 31-year-old man lying in the street with a head wound. Witnesses say they saw him fighting with another man when a red vehicle pulled up. A man got out and started shooting at them. Police recovered three .22-caliber shell casings from the sidewalk.

- 4/19/03 @ 5:30p.m. - A 49-year-old woman told police she and her husband were our driving when they heard a gunshot and the rear of window of their car exploded.

- 4/19/03 @ 11:00 p.m. – A 17-year-old man was at a service station with his girlfriend when another vehicle pulled up and a man in the rear seat pointed a handgun at them, cocked it and said, "I'll melt you right now." The couple ducked down and the other car drove off without the occupant firing.

- 4/19/03 @ 11:10 p.m. – A 19-year-old man told police he was walking down the street when a pickup pulled up and a man asked him what was "going on tonight?" The man then pulled a handgun, pointed it at the teen and told him to

"get in the truck." The teen took off running, stopped at a residence and asked to use the phone to call police.

- 4/20/03 @ 7:40 a.m. – A 26-year-old man told police he was at an after hours club when a man he knew with the street name "Monster" punched him in the face. The suspect then went back to his truck to retrieve a handgun, which he pointed at the victim and said he would kill him.

- 4/20/03 @ 2 p.m. – A 42-year-old woman told police she and a friend were out driving when they saw a red car pull over to the side of the street. The woman said two men got out and both began firing handguns, possibly at another passing vehicle. However, as the woman drove off, a bullet struck her vehicle in the right front quarter panel.

- 4/20/03 @ 4:40 p.m. – A 41-year-old woman was walking in a field when she heard five shots and felt blood running down her face, so she ran. She did not see who shot her. She was treated for two abrasions over her right eye.

- 4/21/03 @ 7:55 p.m. – A 10-year-old boy was playing in the front yard of his home when a man approached him with a BB gun and shot him, puncturing his wrist. The boy ran into his house to tell relatives. They called the police.

- 4/21/03 @ 7:55 p.m. – An 18-year-old man was drinking with friends at his house when they decided to go to a bar to play pool. When they went home, they heard "a gunshot and a car squealing away." A bullet hit the teen in the back right shoulder.

- 4/22/03 @ 1:40 p.m. – A woman told police her 14-year-old

grandson was playing football in the street nearby when a man came out of a house and pointed a handgun at the youth. The suspect is an 18-year-old.

- 4/22/03 @ 11:45 p.m. – Police responded to a "shots fired" call in an area of the city. Central Dispatch said there was a shooting victim at 1817 Tausend, but there was no such address. Police then went to the 3000 block of Glenwood and found six 9mm casings and five .380-caliber casings in a market parking lot. A 52-year-old man who was in the area told police he heard shots but did not see anything.

- 4/23/03 @ 12:15 a.m. – A 26-year-old man was out driving when a white van drove up on his right side. He heard several shots and a bullet hit his right foot. He also noticed a small, gray vehicle following him. The victim told police he believed the man who shot him is someone with whom he has feuded. The victim's wife told police the suspect shot at her a few weeks ago.

- 4/23/03 @ 12:15 p.m. – A 33-year-old woman was at a red light when a blue car and a white car came around the corner with the white car coming around the blue car to cut it off. She told police she heard some "loud pops" and the windows of her van smashed. She ran the red light to get out of the area. Police noted two of her windows were shot out, as well as her outside rearview mirror.[35]

THIS MOVIE SCRIPT from hell has since repeated itself numerous times. How in the world can a family feel safe in a city with this level of gun violence? Sadly, this is true in probably every Black community in America. This type of gunplay sent a new level of fear throughout a city that has a history of Black on Black violence. But nothing particularly effective was done to put an end to this type of violence, and as a result, people braced themselves for worse to come, as comments such as "this will be the bloodiest summer ever" and "I've got to get the hell out of here" were common. In fact, in the months to follow, Saginaw had another reduction in its police force. Just what the law-abiding citizens of Saginaw did not need, and exactly what the viopreneurs wanted.

Even my nine-year-old granddaughter at the time was fully aware of the situation in Saginaw. She is a certified viopreneur-spotter. One summer day of 2004, as we visited a neighborhood market, with a watchful eye she observed a disagreement amongst two teenagers. She hurriedly jumped into the van shouting, "granddaddy, we had better hurry up and leave because I think they are about to start shooting!" I concurred, and we fled. Be it as it may, Saginaw often makes the top ten most dangerous places to live.

A city such as Saginaw pays a huge price for its social condition. Saginaw currently has a population of approximately 62,000 people, with approximately 27,000 Blacks that reside in close to a 25-30 square mile radius. This is down from a 100,000 plus population in the 1970's. There is somewhere in th neighborhood of a dozen multi-millionaire, world famous Black superstar athletes, entertainers, and business people from the city of Saginaw, and to the best of my knowledge, not one of them has ever invested anything of substance into the city. Personally, I understand as to why they do not come back home with flowers and boxes of chocolates. This is the price that a city pays for allowing its citizens get out of control. Those that have the resources to invest in a city such as Saginaw feel that it would just be a waste of time. A dismal point of view, but still, so often true.

The phenomenal level of gun violence illustrated in this ten-day stretch in Saginaw has made it and many other cities like it across America the most undesired places to live for all people, and especially for Blacks. Violence is deeply woven in Black society. Until the decision is made in favor of the hard choices to rid Black communities of violence, there will continue to be heavy losses of life, liberty, and prominence.

IN ADDITION TO Black on Black crime that and prolific statistical numbers, there is also White on White crime, and Asian on Asian crime, and so on. Criminal activity flows like this because people tend to commit crimes where they live, and with BA, its homicide numbers painfully and shamefully exceeds those of all other ethnic groups.

Blacks and the Criminal Justice System

- In the year 2000 there were a total of 1,937,482 inmates in custody of federal, state, and local jails.[36]

- In the year 2000, there were 871,867 blacks, or 45% of all inmates, in custody of federal, state, and local jails.[36]

- There were 589,586 black inmates with sentences of more than one year in federal or state prisons, which was 45.5 percent of all inmates.[36]

- In 2002, 10.4 percent of black males, age 25-29, were in prison.[36]

- The lifetime likelihood of incarceration for African-Americans (16.2%) is almost twice that of Hispanics and more than six times that of whites (2.5%).[36]

- In 1996, African-Americans spent an average of 7.5 years in Federal prisons. That's 3.6 years longer than whites.[36]

- In counties using the death penalty in America, nearly 98 percent of the Chief District Attorneys are white, and only 1 percent are African-American.[37]

- Approximately 90 percent of those whom prosecutors seek to execute are African-American or Latino.[37]

- Historically, more than 80 percent of those executed were convicted of killing whites, although people of color comprise more than half of all homicide victims in the United States.[37]

- The Death Row population is approximately 42 percent African-American, although African Americans make up only 12 percent of the general population.[37]

- African-Americans are afforded less competent counsel, and punished more severely than whites charged with the same crimes.[37]

- African-Americans are stopped more frequently, and charged with higher-level offenses.[37]

- Defense Attorneys and Judges are "sources of potential racial discrimination in a capital trial".[37]

- Of the 500 prisoners executed between 1977 and 1998, over 80 percent were convicted of murdering a white person even though Blacks and Whites are the victims of homicide in almost equal numbers.[37]

- Judge Greg Mathis, of television fame, was a panel member on Tavis Smiley's Black Think Tank's "The Black Family". He says that 80% of prisoners have either no high school diploma or G.E.D.[22]

IT NEEDS TO be mentioned that there is a systematic, built-in racial factor at work within America's criminal justice system. That much I agree with. Poverty and illiteracy only adds to the problems of those who get caught in the system. An understanding of the criminal justice system and access to good attorneys also play a role in criminal conviction results. However, ignorance is the number one factor because any criminal knows that if you do the crime, you must do the time. The best remedy to this situation is for people to simply stop breaking the law.

More Facts

- In the year 2004, Blacks were charged with 27.1 percent of a total of 10, 021,050 offenses.[38]

- According to the U.S. Department of Justice's Office of Bureau Statistics, since 1976, 86% of Whites are murdered by Whites, and 94% of Blacks are murdered by Blacks.

• In the year 2004, Blacks were charged with 47.7% of 9,983 murders and manslaughter charges, while Whites were charged with 49.4% off those same murder and manslaughter charges.[38]

• Of thirty-one offense categories, only Driving under the Influence (9.1%), Liquor Laws (10.2%), and Drunkenness (13%) either matched or fell short of the Black population percentage (13%).[38]

College vs. Incarceration

THE FUNDING OF Higher Education and Corrections and Its Impact on African American Men, reports that while 603,000 Black men were in college in 2001, 791,600 were imprisoned.

However, there are more college-aged African American men in college than incarcerated. College age is roughly 18 to 24, but the study researched incarcerated men ages 18 to 55 plus. In 2000 there were more than 469,000 African American men ages 18-24 that were enrolled in college, which represents 24.9% of the country's 1,885,000 African American men in that age range. U.S. Department of Justice statistics from 2001 indicate that 179,500 Black men ages 18-24 were in prison and jail. Therefore, in the 18-24 age group, the college/imprisoned ratio for Black males is 2.6 to 1.

For their White male counterparts, the ratio is 28 to one. In 2000 there were 3,522,392 White men ages 18-24 enrolled in college, which represents 32.8% of that age group, while 125,700 were in prison in 2001.[39]

SINCE 1980, AMERICANS have shown a great deal more enthusiasm for locking up Black males -- including heavily investing in their incarceration – than they have in supporting their higher education to equip Black males for productive, independent, socially responsible lives. Expressed another way. For each Black male added to the higher education system, about six Black males were added to the prison and jail population in the United States.

THE TEN STATES where a Black male was more than twice as likely to be in college as behind bars are: North Dakota (11.2 times), Maine (6.3), Hawaii (5.8), New Hampshire (5.5), Idaho (4.8), West Virginia (3.8),

South Dakota (3.2), Montana (2.8), New Mexico (2.6), and Wyoming (2.4). This group of states will be referred to as Group A.

At the other extreme are those states where Black males are more likely to be behind bars than in college. Florida is the extreme case. It has 29,385 Black males in state prisons, and another 14,656 in jails, for a total of 44,041 behind bars. In contrast, Florida has 29,394 Black males enrolled in its colleges and universities. There are 14,647 more Black males behind bars in Florida than there are in college.

THE TEN STATES with more than 3,000 more Black males behind bars than in college or where a Black male is more *likely* to be behind bars than in college include Texas, New Jersey, Michigan, Ohio, Pennsylvania, Louisiana, Nevada, Florida, Wisconsin, and Connecticut. This group of states will be referred to as Group B.[40]

IT DESERVES NOTICE that in the states where most likely smaller congregations of Black people live, Group A, these same Black people are engaging in less crime and thus more success in terms of college enrollment. Montana, here I come. On the other hand, the Group B states seem to have dense populations of Black people and for some reason the criminal outcomes are more proliferate.

THE BIGGEST CONTRIBUTOR to this imbalance is the incarceration of drug offenders, which usually are young men looking to get rich quickly. The best alternative would be for young people to go to college, but most chose to eliminate that option. By breaking the law, they have chosen to put their destiny in the hands of prison officials. One law that is irrefutably fair is that we all live, and we all die by the choices we make.

Disenfranchisement

DISENFRANCHISEMENT IN THE context of this scribe means to deprive citizens of their right to vote. Almost 1.4 million African-American males, or 13% of the adult Black male population, are currently disenfranchised as a result of felony convictions. Black men represent more than 36% of the total disenfranchisement male population in the U.S., although they make up less than 15% of American males.

State disenfranchisement laws have a dramatically disproportionate racial impact. Thirteen percent of all adult Black men – 1.4 million – are disenfranchised, representing one-third of the total disenfranchised population in the U.S. and reflecting a rate of disenfranchisement that is seven times the national average. Election voting statistics offer an approximation of the political importance of Black disenfranchisement: 1.4 million Black men are disenfranchised compared to 4.6 million Black men who voted in 1996.

The racial impact in certain states is extraordinary.

- In Alabama and Florida, 31 percent of all Black men are permanently disenfranchised.
- In five other states – Iowa, Mississippi, New Mexico, Virginia, and Wyoming – one in four Black men (24 to 28 percent) is permanently disenfranchised.

- In Washington State, one in four Black men (24 percent) are currently or permanently disenfranchised.

- In Delaware, one in five Black men (20 percent) are permanently disenfranchised.

- In Texas, one in five Black men (20.8 percent) are currently disenfranchised.

- In four states – Minnesota, New Jersey, Rhode Island, and Wisconsin – 16 to 18 percent of Black men are currently disenfranchised.[41]

ALTHOUGH SOME FELONS have been legally disenfranchised, others have not. Specifically, while only four states allow felons to vote while they are in prison, 18 allow felons to vote while they are on parole and 21 allow them to vote while on probation. Only 10 states permanently disenfranchise all felons and another handful does the same to some ex-offenders, or restores the ability to vote after a time limit.[42]

Voting

VOTING IS AN area that has always received a lot of attention in black communities. The U.S. Census Bureau released voting and voting registration information on February 27, 2002. The following information shows how Blacks, Whites, Hispanic, and Asian and Pacific Islanders compare in four different categories: (1) total eligible voters, (2) registered voters and respective percentage, (3) not registered voters and percentage, (4) reported voted and percentage, and (5) not voted and percentage (numbers are in thousands). B = Black; W = White; H = Hispanics; A = Asian & Pacific Islanders. The numbers represents thousands.[43]

	1	2	3	4	5
B –	24,132;	15,348 & 63.6%;	8,784 & 36.4%;	12,917 & 53.5%;	11,215 & 46.5%
W-	168,333;	110,773 & 65.6%;	57,961 & 34.4%;	95,098 & 56.4%;	73,635 & 43.6%
H -	21,598;	7,546 & 34.9%;	14,052 & 65.1%;	5,934 & 27.5%;	15,664 & 72.5%
A -	8,041;	2,470 & 30.7%;	5,571 & 69.3%;	2,045 & 25.4%;	5,996 & 74.6%

Blacks have made gains at the polls, but not enough to be happy about. All people should exercise their right to vote because this is one way in which a person can cast their opinion. All Americans ultimately want to make America as great a nation as is possible. Getting preferred officials elected is the beginning, but not the end of the political process. Where does one start to make a difference in America? With the voting process, that's where.

Disenfranchisement and Black imprisonment are byproducts of deeper problems in Black communities. Taking guns and drugs out of our communities will take BA a long, long way towards reconciliation. With less imprisonment, there will be less disenfranchisement, which should lead to more representation and ultimately more government dollars for the people and schools in Black communities.

Loss of Jobs

THE EMPLOYMENT SITUATION is bad and getting worse with time. More and more jobs will continue to be outsourced, which is why it is so important for individuals to reassess their value systems and come to terms with the fact that education and expert knowledge is needed in

order to be competitive in the employment game. Jobs are the lifeblood
to any individual, family, and community, and if BA is to achieve any
degree of success, it must, to a person, become employable, and then
become employed.

The Washington Post said the national unemployment rate
"jumped" from 6.1 percent in May to 6.4 percent in June – the highest
level in 10 years, with 9.4 million people unable to find work. But here's
the story that the Washington Post and the rest of the media ignored:
the Black unemployment rate jumped or leaped or bounced – whatever
verb fits – from 10.8 percent in May to 11.8 percent in June -- more
than 3 times the increase in the national rate. The June unemployment
report contained even more eye-opening "news":

- Nearly half of the 360,000 people who lost their jobs in June
  were African Americans, even though Black workers are only
  11 percent of the civilian workforce.

- Black workers suffered the highest job loss (172,000) of all
  races or ethnic groups in June.

- While White unemployment inched up from 5.4 percent in
  May to 5.5 percent in June, Black unemployment, already in
  double digits, soared from 10.8 percent to 11.8 percent in the
  same month

The long-term trends are even more daunting. In the year since
June 2002:

- The number of unemployed Black workers has increased by
  approximately 214,000.

- The Black unemployment rate has increased four times faster
  than the rate for White worker. (1.2 percent for Blacks versus
  .3 percent for Whites, respectively).

- Black teenage unemployment has risen from 30 percent to
  40 percent in just one year in what economists call a jobless

economic recovery.[44]

The unemployment crisis has hit the Black worker much worse, as much as ten times worse in some instances, than all other races, and there are two other factors as well that makes the employment situation worse. The first factor is immigration. Latinos are coming into America by the hundreds of thousands every year, well beyond the net number of 184,000 Blacks that were added to the population rolls in the year 2000. The Latino contingent has passed BA by the way Carl Lewis used to blaze past his competitors at the finish line of a 100-meter sprint final. This affects jobs, political representation, and a host of other important metrics.

In the year 2000, there were over 400,00 new Latino members, not counting illegal immigrants, added to the American population from Latino countries. These people came from Spain, Mexico, Argentina, Columbia, Ecuador, and other Central and South American countries. There are immigrants from other countries that come to America, and these immigrants can also be added to the total number.[2]

THE SECOND FACTOR, unbeknown to most, and probably just as important as immigration, are the nonimmigrant visas that are issued for varying periods of time and frequency of use, ranging from a day or two, to those of unlimited entry and indefinite validity. By the end of the year 2001 more than 890,000 H-1B (specialty occupations, e.g. High Tech) workers were employed in the United States.

The following number of nonimmigrant visa entries into the United States and the respective nonimmigrant types in the year 2002: [45]

F1 (Academic Student) 646,016
H1B (Specialty Occupations) 370,490
H2A (Agricultural Worker) 15,628
H2B (Skilled & Unskilled Worker 86,987
TN (Professional Workers under NAFTA)............ 73,699

There are 47 other nonimmigrant visa categories that total million of entries into America, some being worker, some being family workers, entertainers, etc. There is a part of the unemployment equation that the average Black American is unaware of, and that is there are multiple contributors to unemployment situation amongst Black Americans. Now you know.

It is a competitive world we live in. More than ever, there are certain skill sets and educational attainment levels that are required of anyone that wants to have at least a decent standard of living. The Quality of Life Mortality Metrics and the Afflictions are enormous obstacles that stand in the way of BA and total utopian supremacy. BA's entire contingent of people deserve the opportunity to achieve a state of contentment and happiness. Instead, there exists more problems on top of problems. And just when it seems that things are probably as bad as they are going to get, guess what? It gets worse.

PART III

IMAGES, PEOPLE, &

HOPE

OPPORTUNITY

THERE WAS ONCE A YOUNG MAN whom shoveled manure for a living. Of course it was a nasty job, and as result the farm owner had trouble keeping workers. But the young man hung tough. After about a year, he had an idea. He would buy a truck, notify all of the local farmers that he would be available to pick up their manure, and their worker problems would be solved. Eventually the young man would be the owner of a very successful fertilizer business, and today he is a millionaire.

TRUE STORY.................IT IS possible to turn **Shit** into **Sugar.**

'IMAGE' AND 'THE Falsehood of Brotherhood' are the next two Afflictions. If BA were looking for a public relations firm to change its public image, there is no doubt that it would need to have a very fat wallet, as there is a huge amount of work What's on BET tonight? Hey, don't miss the best of 'COPS'. It does get pretty ugly at times, and there is never a shortage of those of us yelling, "Nooooooooo" in reference to the next infamous embarrassing moment. Here's to image control.

Image

THE IMAGE OF BA is not quite the stuff Kodak moments are made of. For many today, to be Black means to be ashamed in numerous ways. Yes, there are many who are hard working people trying to do the right thing, while simultaneously there are others who are just plain idiots, and want the whole world to know it. From mouths full of silver and gold teeth, to pants sagging below their knees penitentiary style, Black youth are sending a message to the world that they don't give a damn about what anyone thinks.

Not many people want much to do with the Black youth of today, with the notable exceptions of family members and the military. And the possibility of giving away position on the battlefield due to the reflection of the sun off the metallic grills is real, so with that said, be careful. There has never been a time when adults have so passionately disliked the culture of its young as it does now. At least this is true in BA. There is the extreme loudness, profanity and omnipresence of the music; the traffic-blocking, the sagging pants thing with the peek-a-boo bloomers; the drug dealing; the materialism, the vanity; the school is for fools mentality; Black Female Exploitation; the gun play: the spread of HIV/AIDS; the Down Low scenario; the single parent family; and the Hip Hop culture, which is something that you are either for, or generally against.

THE HIP HOP culture dominates the image of BA image more than any other influence. The 70's generation had its very own music, whereas this generation has its very own music industry, a self-serving marketing behemoth that makes tons of money off of Black youth through its music. Piles of tiles of cash are made by packaging the spoken word with sex, attitude, expletives, ghetto glamorization, rhyme and the bling-bling image. In addition to its core music business, it has spin-off profit arms in clothing lines, body scents, and reality television shows. And this phenomenon is only surpassed by the unquenchable audio-thirst of American youth to hear the uncompromising melodies of the Hip Hop nation.

The Hip Hop culture and its image certainly does not lend itself to the concept of a 'kinder and gentler' BA. Oftentimes Black youth take this marketed Hip Hop image and parlay it into real life attitude that permeates Black schools, Black homes and society in general. Worst yet is that much of the world has accepted this image to be indicative of practically all Black people. Once these images are burned into the minds of the public, it becomes an almost irreversible stereotype to some, and a never-ending story for the media.

All Black youth don't all roam the earth rapping like a Hip Hop version Cain of the Kung Fu television series of days past. All Black youth don't have mouths full of silver and gold. All Black males are not sans morals, direction, or values. All Black women do not live to shed their clothes and hypnotically grind and swerve their curves to the King Kong beat. All Blacks are not deficient intellectually. Many Black youth have an interest in finance, politics, family, service to humanity, and everything that represents something good. Many do care and want to make a positive difference in this world. They just seem to be outnumbered due to the magic mirrors trick that the media at times so deftly performs. Although there are many Black youth that are down with what is good, they rarely seem to gain just representation on American television.

Drama Shows

DRAMA SHOWS LIKE Maury Povich, Rikki Lake, and Jerry Springer give a certain segment of BA the forum they need to show the world how ignorant they can be. The format has hit home with many viewers, as programs like The Maury Povich Show, which at one time was a more mainstream talk show with respectable guests, has been transformed into the 'My Baby's Daddy Show', and is now the king of daytime television DNA testing. Can you just imagine the things that people might say upon taking in an episode? I will not dare to postulate the possibilities. It still remains that junk television is junk television, and it is hard to be critical of television networks for promoting negative stereotypes when there is no shortage of Black people that voluntarily appear on these shows. And appear they do, with alarming ghetto-fabulous skills that not only validate existing Black stereotypes, but also creates new ones, incarnating the most preposterous characters the world has ever seen. Broadcast for all to see, how can the human race not view BA as the lower echelon of people, given the disgraceful performances these drama show guests provide?

The episodes are many: Black men submitted to lie detector tests concerning how many times they have cheated on their women, with in some cases the answer being as many as fifty times; who's is the Baby's daddy; transvestites; HIV/AIDS; Black women with many kids by many fathers; Black pimps and players; Blacks who sleep with their significant other's parents; Ebonics majors; Blacks that are a drain on society; the best and the worst slime content. And whereas Blacks have almost exclusive rights to this television genre, there are some appearances by White people to balance it out somewhat. I have yet to see a Chinese, Japanese, Asian-Indian, or Native American make an appearance, though, and I suppose it has something to do with a few traits called pride and self-respect.

AND THERE NEVER seems to be a problem finding these 'guests'. In fact, they will find you. It's as if you're walking down the street and someone suddenly falls out of a tree onto your head, lands at your feet, bounces up and asks for directions to the Jerry Springer

Show. In regards to the Jerry Springer show, where is the FCC when you need them? As time goes on, the hope is that certain Black citizens can make the trip to Oz and find some self-pride in addition to a brain. And Lord have mercy, something must be done about those Drama Shows.

A Preceding Reputation

THE COLLECTIVE REPUTATION of BA precedes it. And as it goes, masses of people build and maintain preconceived notions and foregone conclusions about this enigma, the Black race. Based on what is seen daily in society, who can blame them? What can a couple from

Australia expect to see and hear as they visit a mall in America? Would they see a young Black male with a hair full braids, parted evenly down the middle with both halves tied up in rubber bands with loose ends, giving the seventies look of afro-puffs? As they enter the food court, would they witness a young Black male call a young Black woman a bitch because she tells him his conversation is weak, only to next hear one of his boys also call him a bitch because his conversation is weak? How many times would they hear Blacks calling each other nigger? Here come a couple of young brothers rapping out loud, counting the money of that recording contract that will never come to be? What about the sight of two hundred people forming a human stampede due to an overzealous, over-reaction to the grand opening of Samuel L. Jackson's new movie "Coach Carter"? What would they think? What would they tell their family and friends as they speed-dial the 'down under'? Was this what they expected to see? Do they think that all Black people are like this? As these sorts of events take place, who really is responsible for the Black image?

There are many more scenarios in addition to those above. The question that may really float your boat is at what frequency do the above events have to take place before they surpass stereotype status and actually become true characteristics of BA? In the meantime, BA will have one hell of a time earning respect around the world. In the eyes of most, BA could be faring much better in all categories of living, if it were to only decide to do so.

Image Control

THE IMAGE OF BA has suffered almost irreparable damage. Who is to blame? In the 1950's and 60's racism would have been a legitimate scapegoat. Today, the situation is a little bit different. Black people need only look inward to find the cause of their problems, as well as the solutions to those problems. BA has to work its way out of the problems it has behaved itself into, and therein lies the way to repair its image.

IN TERMS OF employment, of course Black Americans occupy many and various occupations. However, other than the entertainment industries, BA finds itself coming up short to considerable degrees. Black Americans largely comprise a workforce of union Young shop workers, inner city school teachers that happen to be mostly female, police officers, some firemen, clerical workers, administrative staff, small business owners, a short list of doctors, attorneys, and then there is the unskilled worker. A few more hundred thousand or so medical professionals, CEOs, school principals, entrepreneurs, television executives, and the like would be great additions to BA, and would do a lot in terms of image repair. Most importantly, a doubling or tripling of the number of college students would undoubtedly serve this aim well. Of course, to be able to go to college and properly compete means to go into college prepared, and that points the index finger to BA's school systems.

EVEN HOLLYWOOD, ESPECIALLY Black Hollywood, have a certain level of accountability to the Black image. Movies like 'Soul Plane' and 'Hustle and Flow' do nothing to offset the stereotype issues. Critically acclaimed? Please. If these movies have added value to your life, then you probably need counseling. Movies about pimps and rappers are the last thing BA needs, and a pimp who happens to be a rapper is as bad as it gets. If you were to take a count of Black movies on the shelves of any video store rental business, you would find a very large percentage of gun-brandishing Black males and females that are capable of burning a hole through your body with their menacing facial expression alone. As Black children see these movies on the store shelves, is there any doubt that they also see themselves in the same capacity? Black Hollywood would best serve BA by re-thinking its movies and providing more positive role models. It is the least they could do.

The Black image starts in Black communities. From there it extends in a public way to public settings. Getting rid of negative images and replacing them with positive ones would amount to a nice start. It would eventually end with a new lesson in honor and pride.

Gag Order

TO MANUFACTURE A healthy recovery from its personal war, BA must first become honest with itself. BA has done just as much, if not more, to contribute to its present societal state as anyone. Withstanding, it is only natural that people will formulate not favorable to Blacks, and that is okay, as people are entitled to their own opinions. On the other hand, many Blacks do not see that way. If a person of another nationality were to voice a negative opinion of Blacks, many Black people tend to get highly upset. Out comes the race card. In the world of comedy, Black comedians can joke about other races but other races cannot joke about Blacks. Blacks can put skits in movies mocking Whites but Whites cannot do it to Blacks. There is no honor in that.

The fact that members of other races are not 'allowed' to speak their minds constitutes a gag order of sorts. In some ways this is good, as what is not needed are aimless and senseless derogatory racial statements made just to inflict emotional pain. However, if Blacks can dish it out, then Blacks should be able to take it in. Blacks should not speak ill or comical of others in offensive tones and then cry foul when it is reciprocated. I just believe that it makes Blacks somehow weaker as people. Does BA miss out on constructive criticisms and helpful knowledge because others are fearful to speak their minds or offer opinions that are actually constructive criticisms that sting as bigoted opinions just because they come from White America? It is a possibility.

For Blacks to go through life thinking have some sort of invisible cloak of protection that lets their criticism flow out but blocks criticisms of others should not be expected. There has to be a better form of restitution. At the same time, Blacks should not 'endearingly' call each other nigga' in public, on stage, or in movies, yet become filled with rage if someone of another ethnic group chooses the same names. How can Blacks demand respect from others when they don't give respect to one another other? This image thing is really about respect, and self-respect is the best place to start.

In a USA Today article dated August 15, 2005, Tom Joyner was interviewed and made the following comments about Black people: " Black people love to fly and love to fly cheap." After a Washington D.C. Tom Joyner Morning Show affiliate and a local car dealership reached an agreement to waive credit checks for local Blacks, Tom stated, "Blacks do have bad credit. You can have bad credit by having a certain zip code. We need some credit." Now, if a White person had made those same comments, Blacks would have demanded his job. The point is that an insult should be an insult, regardless of who says it. There is a double standard that exists which sometimes misleads people. Pride is pride, and honor is honor. Let us stand proud against all that would diminish our being, and let us be fair to all people. That is living with honor.

The Falsehood of Brotherhood

BLACK PEOPLE AT times have a tendency to support the wrong people Black people, just because they are Black, be they businessmen, politicians, or church pastor. One ill-conceived mantra says that, 'Blacks should support any Black person whom has made it, just because he or she is Black'. This is the Falsehood of Brotherhood. And if someone does not become successful, it is because 'they' (the white man) does not want him or her to make it. Neither of these paradigms is to be subscribed to. The success of Black people, just like the success of people of all colors, should be earned by great service, providing products of value, and through positive and meaningful business and personal relationships. Whereas it is definitely in the best interest of both BA and America for Black people to succeed, it is very important that any success is earned the right way.

Most of the Black leaders of today seem to be more interested in maintaining the status quo of today's state of affairs, versus dishing out tough love, so as not to fall out of favor with the masses. Speaking the truth and providing 'tough' love, as the one and only Dr. William H. Cosby Ed. has done of late, does not go over too well. Instead of requiring that each man and woman look inward at themselves for reasons of failure, BA continues to blame others for its problems. The problem with that is as long as people look outward to blame someone for their problems, they will not look inward at themselves. Positive change comes from making truthful and positive change from within.

THE FALSEHOOD OF Brotherhood allows phony people to be brought into your lives just because that person happens to be Black. The Falsehood of Brotherhood disallows Dr. Cosby from getting upset and speaking out on the problems of BA, because other popular and famous Black leaders do not agree, and sometimes censor those who would speak out. BA is better served by judging its relationships with Blacks by the value that is brought into its communities and its people.

The truth is, everybody that is Black is not BA's brother or sister. Do not feel sorry for the drug dealer who has been sentenced to twenty years because he is Black. Just think of the damage done by the dealer to the people he sold to. Do not fail to boycott Black radio stations just because they are 'Black'. BA doesn't need to see anything fart, and to tolerate and support "junk" programming, no matter the source, is stupid.

BA has spent billions of dollars on goods and services that do more harm than good to Black people. If the goods and services, and the leaders and politicians, and the business people and music artists do not uplift and strengthen Black people, then it need not be supported, whether it is Black or not. And that strategy ends the Falsehood of Brotherhood, and gives birth to genuine Brotherhood, which is planted in love and the uplifting of BA.

Heroic Causes, People, & Places

ON THE BRIGHTER side of things, there are a number of organizations and people that dedicated their lives to making the world a better place for other people to live in on a daily basis. Many of these people and organizations were born to serve. They may rarely be the topics of conversation at the department water coolers, and unless one has been personally blessed by these entities or lucky enough to be in the company of someone that has been touched by them, their good deeds often go unnoticed. Some of them are world famous, some are housed in small offices that are barely encroached by sunlight. They plug the holes, seal the cracks, and are the glue that holds together the American way of life for many people. Whether providing assistance, offering a helping hand, or speaking words of encouragement at just the right time, for them, it is truly all about giving.

People of all colors, and especially our White brothers and sisters, are in the business of giving, and this is a beautiful thing. There is not nearly enough celebration of the spirit of giving and its melting-pot makeup of America charity. There are many people and organizations offering wonderful examples of how people of varying backgrounds and races work together to supply not only goods and services, but also love and compassion. And as Black people are the recipients of many of these services, it becomes clear that peace and goodwill are still at work.

The following short list comprises some of those who are dedicated to making this world a better place:

The Victorian Hands Foundation (TVHF), launched by Nadia Campbell, now age, 20, strives to make the elderly feel loved and appreciated, as well as to make sure that they have not been abandoned by the communities that they served for so many years. Through youth volunteers, TVHF enhances intergenerational relations. Youth volunteers of TVHF learn how to interact with elders as well as help elders learn about the youth generation. The Victorian Hands Foundation was started in memory of Nadia's late Aunt Victoria who was very kind and loving towards everyone. TVHF is a group of students and adults who cherish the elders of our communities and the world. Our founder started this organization after watching a 20/20 special on elders who got abused and neglected and felt that something needed to be done! It's sad but true that many elders don't get the treatment they deserve and we at TVHF believe that it's up to us to change that. Through the organization, youth volunteers work to make seniors feel loved and appreciated through programs like "Adopt a Grandparent."

TVHF doesn't just help the elderly, we help everyone. Our founder and volunteers also participate in various events such as breast and liver cancer walks. We participate in church, school and, community fundraisers. We don't just go to nursing homes we also touch the elders of our community. With a grant from Youth Venture an organization who also specializes in teens changing our community one step at a time, TVHF has been helping senior citizens for seven years and we don't plan to stop now. Everyday we get new volunteers who help us achieve our goal, which is: That no elderly person will ever have to feel lonely or depressed as long as TVHF is an active organization. Even though we work hard to serve our communities, our schoolwork doesn't lack. Our volunteers have good grades and have risen to the top of their classes.[46]

Do Something! Do Something was founded in 1993 by Andrew Shue and Michael Sanchez, childhood friends from New Jersey who wanted to make a difference. They had a very simple dream: what if making a difference became just as cool and important to American education as athletics? What if community service became like physical education during the day and team sports after school? Kids would develop not only their minds and bodies, but also their souls. Every school might have a math teacher, football coach, and a community coach. American youth would learn leadership, citizenship, and character – and our democracy would be stronger for it.

The first community coach began work in Newark (N.J.) Public Schools in 1994. Do Something! began certifying community coaches nationally in 1998. In keeping with Do Something's youth-centered leadership philosophy, he organization utilizes the energy and idea of a coterie of smart young people. This group of 15 gathers several times during each semester to review program vision, marketing materials, and language choices of the "old people" on the staff and board.[47]

Dr. William H. Cosby has, for what seems like an eternity, provided all of America with many memorable and positive television characters that still remain amongst the all-time favorites. This is very important in today's times because the majority of the images available to youth, and especially Black youth, are shallow, selfish and dysfunctional.

Every success starts with a dream and The 'Cos' can always be counted on to provide wholesome, loving, and intelligent characters that are safe to be admired are copied. As of late, Dr. Cosby has created a new television audience – students who need help with their homework or a reason to study. *Dr. Cosby: School of Life* began airing in December of 2004 on the Philadelphia School District's local-access cable television station. There will be brief episodes that will air daily and feature inspirational messages about study skills, classroom participation, and making education part of everyday life.

Lori Tsuruda says people can make a difference in the world just by committing one or two days a year to community service. The same people could transform the world, she believes, if they learned to do good deeds every day of the year.

Ms. Tsuruda, who earned the SB degree in biology from MIT in 1989, has made community service the center of her life. The founder and driving force behind the Boston nonprofit People Making a Difference, she said she spent years studying for a career in science, only to discover her true passion was making the world a better place. Now, almost 10 years later, her organization runs 50 community service projects a year, recruiting people for one-day jobs ranging from painting floors at public housing projects to collating Braille books for children.

Ms. Tsuruda has also learned about what charities do and don't need. "When we go to the Greater Boston Food Bank, I'm struck by how much food is donated that isn't nutritious at all," she said. "Now, when PMD volunteers organize food drives in their communities, they try to be very specific about the protein products or other nutritious foods needed. After a day of community service, Ms. Tsuruda said she's sometimes chagrined to hear volunteers say, "This is a great experience; everyone should do it." "I try to help people understand that it would be even better if we never had to feed people at a shelter at all," she said. "If we wore our social awareness hats 365 days a year, maybe we could make that happen." [48]

The Reverend Jesse Jackson is more than just a Reverend, Social Activist, and Community Leader. He is also a Hero, hope personified, and an exceptional man in many ways. Just his presence in situations of oppression and calamity instantly instills conscience, faith, and resolve. With his mighty and eloquent voice Mr. Jackson has led or assisted in the resolution of many sensitive and dangerous ordeals that range from clarification of racial injustice to the release of prisoners of war.

As one who once walked with the great Dr. Martin Luther King, Mr. Jackson has continued the dream to create equality for all and he has never failed those whom he has assisted. His legacy is one that will never be forgotten and although his many accomplishments could easily fill all the pages of this book, it was still necessary, if only in short form, to summarize this remarkable individual and what he means to America.

KidPower TeenPower FullPower International is a community based non-profit organization founded in Santa Cruz, California in 1989. Our mission is to help people of all ages and abilities learn how to stay safe, act wisely, and believe in themselves. We are committed to providing high quality services to those most in need. We teach self protection, self confidence, and violence prevention skills through workshops which emphasize success-based practice. We have trained over 140,000 people worldwide. Our programs have been created with the help of experts in education, mental health, child development, martial arts, rape crisis intervention, child safety, and law enforcement.

Why we do what we do...Violence and abuse are among the leading health issues of our time. Statistics from law enforcement and crime prevention agencies in the United States estimate that:

- More than 100,000 children each year will become victims of reported attempted kidnappings by strangers in the U.S. alone!
- 1 out of 3 girls and 1 out of 6 boys will be sexually abused before the age of 18.
- 1 out of 7 school children are harmed by bullying or some other form of aggression.
- 85% of today's 12-year-olds will be victims of a violent crime in their lifetime. Their risk of being assaulted is greater than their risk of being in a serious car accident.

People from all walks of life often feel helpless in the face of physical and verbal confrontations. Survivors of assault, abuse, bullying, or harassment have to overcome damage to their sense of power and self-worth. Too many people find their freedom limited by fear and their joy in life diminished by loss of self-confidence. The simple, effective skills taught by KIDPOWER will work to deter violence and abuse most of the time. The majority of these skills can be used on an every day basis to prevent most trouble before it starts. Practicing skills tends to reduce anxiety, raise self-esteem, and build competence. By making the learning and practicing of these important skills a priority for ourselves, and our loved ones, we can improve the safety and quality of our lives.[49]

Mr. A. C. Green is a retired NBA great who was the consummate NBA professional during the course of a career that spanned 16 seasons. He was a tough player who consistently gave 200 percent effort on the court. However, a play that he made off the court deserves as much attention as anything he did on the court, and that was that A. C. lived

a life of abstinence up until his marriage to Veronique Green in April
of 2002.

It is a lifestyle that he continues to advocate, especially to young people.
The fact that he is a living example to do what is right in spite of all
the trappings a young professional athlete encounters is a testament in
itself. The message that A.C. spreads is that everyone can lead healthy
and dedicated lives by making the right choices through self-discipline
and proper decision-making. Life is what you make it, and A.C. Green
has shown us how to get the most out of life – the right way.

In addition to being a committed Christian, A. C. is dedicated
to working with youth. Through his A. C. Green Foundation, he has
created two abstinence-based curriculums – "I've got the power" and
"Game Plan" – to help today's teens deal with the incredible pressures
to become sexually active.[50]

Band Aid is a relief effort that originated in 1984 by Bob Geldof, Midge
Urge, and various artists. They recorded the hit Christmas song "Do
They Know It's Christmas?" which immediately went to #1 and raised
$18 million dollars for famine relief in
Ethiopia. Eighteen months later, Bob organized a concert entitled
"Live Aid" which went on to raise over $70 million dollars for famine
relief.[51]

On Saturday, July 2, of 2005, Mr. Geldof put together another
production for the benefit of Africa. Through Live 8, he now wanted
to organize the voices of thousands and thousands around the world,
as they demanded justice for Africa. Thousands gathered in Edinburgh
to spearhead the call to make poverty history. Later that day, millions
echoed that call as they took part in Live 8 – concerts in London, Paris,
Berlin, Rome and Philadelphia. The Live 8 event was free as some of the
world's greatest acts took stage, including U2, Robbie Williams, Scissor
Sisters, alongside legends Sir Elton John and Sir Paul McCartney.

Said Bob Geldof: "These concerts are the starting point for the
long walk to justice, the one way we can all make our voices heard in
unison. The G- leaders (Britain, Canada, France, Germany, Italy, Japan,
Russia, and The U.S.A.) have it within there power to alter history. They
will only have the will to do so if ten of thousands of people show them
that enough is enough. By doubling aid, fully canceling debt, and

delivering trade justice for Africa, the G-8 could change the future for millions of men, women, and children.

Sean "P. Diddy" Combs is a world famous Hip-Hop artist and actor who created Citizen Change, which is a national, non-partisan and non-profit organization with the mission to educate, motivate and empower the more than 42 million Americans aged 18-30, which is twenty-five percent of the population.[52]

The Innocence Project was founded by Barry C. Scheck and Peter J. Neufeld in 1992. It is a non-profit legal clinic and criminal justice center. It is a non-profit legal clinic & criminal justice center. It works to exonerate the wrongfully convicted through post-conviction DNA testing; and to develop & implement reforms to prevent wrongful convictions. The project has revealed that things such as mistaken I.D., poverty, race, poor defense lawyering, false confessions, junk science, and other harmful practices have all resulted in innocent people being imprisoned. To date, The Innocence Project has resulted in 123 exonerations.[53]

The Bill & Melinda Gates Foundation. In the year 2000, The Bill & Melinda Gates Foundation merges with the Gates Learning Foundation. The goal of the merger is to increase efficiency and communication between four main initiatives: Global Health, Education, Libraries, and Pacific Northwest. The foundation supports grantees in all 50 states and the District of Columbia. Internationally, we support work in more than 100 countries. In 2005, about 70 percent of our grants went toward global efforts; the rest was dedicated to improving lives in the United States. The Bill & Melinda Gates foundation has committed $11 billion in total grants since its inception. The total benefits the public has received really cannot simply be measured in dollars and cents. The hope for cures, the thrust of worldwide social and scientific improvements and the lives touched will all tell of the legacy of this marvelous foundation.

The East Lake Community Foundation was established in 1995 to lead the revitalization of the East Lake neighborhood in Atlanta, Georgia.

Working in a series of strategic partnerships, the Foundation has developed The Villages of East Lake, an award-winning mixed income community; the East Lake Family YMCA; the East Lake Sheltering Arms Early Learning Center; the Charlie Yates Golf Course; and a new Publix grocery store, the first grocery store in the community in 40 years. East Lake had been home to a 50-unit public housing project called East Lake Meadows, but was better known as "Little Viet Nam" because of the violence that was endemic to the community. It was soon demolished and in its place was built The Villages of East Lake, a 542-apartment community that serves families across a very broad range of incomes.

Other startling positives that have resulted from this act of giving:

- Opened the first charter school in the city of Atlanta – Drew Charter School.
- East Lake Sheltering Arms child development center.
- The 18 hole Charlie Yates Golf Course which is open to the public.
- The East Lake Junior Golf Academy – a cornerstone program of the Foundation.
- Chaplaincy – For residents of the Villages who want to build a healthy community.
- Home Ownership Program – An opportunity for public housing residents to own a their own home.
- The Golf Club's caddie program has employed 700+ local high school and college students and have awarded 35 caddie college scholarships.
- Numerous donations, awards, corporate golf memberships, and tournament hostings.
- A tremendous increase in jobs attained by the community residents.
- Since the inception of The East Lake Community Foundation, crime in the village of East Lake is down 94% compared to East Lake Meadows; crime in the surrounding neighborhoods is down 77% since 1994; property values have increased more

than 20% per year.[55]

Midland, Michigan & Plymouth Elementary School. This particular story has a very personal side to it because it involves the loss of my beloved son, Emery Mario Young. While crossing the street, Emery was struck by a car, in June 1996. A few days later he was pronounced dead. His death was, and remains to this day the single most devastating event in my life, and never in a hundred lifetimes could I sustain a greater loss. However, my family and I were the recipients of as great an outpouring of love that we could have ever thought possible. And to this day, that love still remains in my heart.

You see, Midland, Michigan is a city of approximately 40,000 people and is about 99% Caucasian. When my children and their mother relocated there, I had some serious apprehensions as to how they might be treated. I would soon come to realize that there would be no need to worry. My children were adored in Midland and never had one bad moment while living there. Living in neighboring Saginaw, Michigan, which is some twenty miles away, I visited my children at least three times a week, and as time went on I developed a great appreciation for the city of Midland. I would soon learn that Midland is one of the best-kept secrets in the State of Michigan, if not the nation.

Emery was very much liked at Plymouth Elementary School and when Emery was killed, his schoolmates were sent reeling. His memory lives on as actions were taken to ensure that the memory of Emery would never be forgotten. A tree was planted on his behalf and has since grown beautifully. Giant get-well cards were made by his schoolmates and laminated that I still have to this day. They made sure that we knew, from the entire school staff of teachers and administrators on down to each and every student, that they loved Emery, missed him, and that we were in their prayers.

The degree of love and support we received was unbelievable. While we spent our last days with Emery in the hospital, dozens of people, total strangers, streamed in and out of the hospital, almost around the clock, to pray with us, hold us, talk to us, and cry with us. People brought food and did whatever they could to soften the blow of losing our precious child. The vast majority of them were Christians, and the cumulative effects of this life-changing event taught me that our world is so much better because of our Christian brothers and sisters who show no restraint when it comes to supporting those who are in need. It was a lesson that I will never forget.

THE OTHER INDIVIDUALS and programs that were mentioned are not alone. There are more programs and organizations that play an important role in society. They may be local, regional, or national in size and scope. Organizations such as The Boys and Girls Clubs of America, 100 Black Men, The United Way, and The Growth and Afro-centric Program are staples in communities across the U.S.A., and they are all appreciated. Local church arms, youth centers, computer training programs, and sports programs all provide great value to society.

Today, it is necessary that all people transcend politics, race and religion for the common cause of helping one another. Stress, materialism, cultural and racial differences are among many realities that make our co-existence in America a more difficult than perhaps it should be. A better understanding of the mutual blessings we all have in common and a stronger appreciation of the opportunities available to us as human beings to make our country greater can make a big difference in a common peace.

However, with that said, the problems of BA still exist. All of the aforementioned angelic people and organizations are doing their part to make America great, and hopefully, there will continue to be a new influx of people to keep the effort strong. Next on the to do list is a laser-like focus by BA to strengthen itself. This could prove to be its greatest gift.

PART IV

INSTITUTIONAL

RACISM

LIVE

It is inconceivable that an entire race of people can live so badly, in so many ways, for so long. Once amongst the greatest, now on track to be the latest, major catastrophe in human history.

Created to succeed, not to fail. Blacks have instead succumbed to murder, disease, decrepit health, prison occupation, drugs, alcohol, poor academic achievement and carnal pleasures. These conditions loom over **B**lack **A**merica as most ominous spirits.

In the midst of a battle supreme that must be won. One people. One breath. One destiny. Only one acceptable outcome.

Let courage write the book that will chronicle the victory, lest idleness be the author of the epitaph of **B**lack **A**merica.

Prelude to the survival of **B**lack **A**merica.

PART IV TOUCHES thirty-seven more Afflictions that all play a role in the demise of BA. Many of these 'Afflictions' have their origin, method of operation and their futures based on the manipulation and exploitation of both the poor and minorities. The relationship between Blacks and the institutional racist Afflictions can be compared to a societal shotgun wedding between a reluctant groom (BA) the bride (dismal societal success), and the shotgun- wielding bride's father (Institutional Racist Systems and Industries).

The voodoo that these racist institutions do is powerful, lucrative and deeply entrenched in American society. There are no meaningful expositions made into the inequities produced by these institutions either, as these racist institutions are shielded by laws they pay for, utilizing lots of booty, attorney posses and intricate webs of influential players. Covering everyday activities from a-z, virtually every aspect of daily life is either unfairly regulated or heavily penalized as it relates to Black America. The price that is paid for being the prey of the rich and the greedy is dually disheartening and expensive.

As fair play is not found in the 'Minorities Handbook of Dealing with Industries and Governments', the result is a status quo within BA where poverty and peasantry insidiously restrain those who are already struggling to make it. The source of their power is not a secret. Their domination lies in the fact that the conquest of any people occurs because the governments of the day allow it to happen, and in fact are a part of it. .

Racism

IT IS ONLY natural that people attribute the problems that have befallen the Black race to racism, and this is true to an extent. Film footage, diaries, and first-hand memories by those who endured the cruel racist times of the past are just some of the ways to look back on a forgettable period in American history when racism was at its peak. Many eyebrows still drop and blood still warms just by thinking of the events of the Civil Rights era. A closer look, though, will allow one to differentiate racism of today from racism of yesterday. Racism is still there, but not to the extent that it once did within the everyday citizen, and definitely in a different manner. Yes, people are biased and always will be. But the primary practitioners of racism today are corporations and their practices connected to their fiduciary concerns and buildup of wealth and the governments that are in fact partners with these corporations. Together, they have chosen that the rights of American citizens are exploitable, that there health is malleable and there lives expendable. What makes racism of today different of yesterday is that the targets are not just Blacks, but the poor and people of all color. If you do not have the money, education and necessary resources to fight back, then you will be taken advantage of. It is not just about black and white anymore, but the dominant color today is green.

Racism of Yesterday

AN EXCERPT FROM the political magazine *The Nation* entitled "Masters of Their Universe" provides a graphic picture of true, unbiased racism: Beginning in the fifteenth century, Africa, Europe, and the Americas came together to create new economies, new cultures, and new societies. At the center of those societies was the plantation, a radically new unit of production that employed slave labor to grow exotic commodities for sale in distant markets. At the top of the plantation were men of enormous wealth who chose to go by the moniker "master", and their rule extended to all corners of the Atlantic world.

These were wicked, evil, contemptible men, and their treatment of their slaves was nothing short of the incomprehensible. There was the time when a slaveholder severely whipped a runaway slave and then rubbed limejuice and salt into the open wounds. If an unfortunate fugitive died, his head was cut off, stuck on a pole, and the body was burned. Some slaves were given as many as 300 lashes. And of course, many were hanged.

There were more gruesome, inhumane treatments than these though. One slave was forced to defecate into the mouth of another slave, who was then gagged. Bottles were forced into their private parts, and they also were forced to urinate into the mouths of other slaves. Many women were kept as mistresses. Many other demoralizing practices were conveyed onto the slaves, and it was a time when slaves were worked, sold, bought, hated, denied, raped, killed, maimed, and anything else that could be done to a people who were thought of as being nothing, dispensable, and worthless.[56]

AND SO, A look back is taken at the times of a savage past, when racism in the north was social custom, and in the south it was law. Racial integration, in terms of marriage, children playing together, education, shopping, and practically all forms of social interaction was disallowed. There were few exceptions, such as servitude or sexual gratification. And as the horrors endured are recalled, the goose bumps cover the bodies of those who would take this peek at the past as swiftly as the filaments of a light bulb brighten when the switch is flipped. The de-humanization process was wicked, and assuredly should serve as motivation enough to empower BA to the extent that this will never, ever happen again. However, it seems that a great deal of that motivation died off over time just as did the warrior generation that endured those times.

Although Blacks amassed some important victories behind the leadership and vision of Dr. Martin Luther King Jr. and company, it remains puzzling to witness how Black people continue to enslave themselves within their own minds through a lack of educational progress, self-destructive behavior and lack of love for family, friend and neighbor. Some say that the hatred slavery spawned has turned inward amongst Black people. Who is qualified to say that? What can be said is that the position of BA is envied by no one, and the same spirit that got Black people through the worst of times of decades past would be more than enough intangible power to uplift BA from its present state.

THE RELATIONSHIP OF Blacks and slavery in America goes back to the year 1619, when a Dutch slave trader exchanged his cargo of African slaves for passage into America. In 1862, President Abraham Lincoln signed a bill ending slavery in the District of Columbia. Nine months later, President Lincoln issues his Emancipation Proclamation, which basically set all slaves free. From there, history showcases the Civil Rights Era, the Brown Decision in 1954, the Civil Rights Act in 1964, and the Voting Rights Act of 1965. Today fathers an existence that has not been officially named by historians, intellectuals, nor the people. I think that 'chaos' will suffice.

Racism Continues

TODAY, RACISM IS not manifested by White people that openly and publicly spit, curse, and assault Blacks for entertainment, as was the case of past times. Today, racism is facilitated for the most part by certain individuals that sit behind the desks of governments and corporations. The Holy Bible states in Ephesians 6:12 that " For we wrestle not against flesh and blood, but against principalities, against rulers of the darkness of the world, against spiritual wickedness in high places". If you look around throughout America, this wickedness is right there in plain sight to see. We just seem to have trouble either understanding what we see, or the thought of feeling helpless to do anything about it manifests itself into some sort of denial mentality.

However, the big two, corporations and corporate-unfriendly governments, carry on, and they take no prisoners. Many people are collateral damage of the cash expansion activities of this tandem. They have a special talent of using the taxpayer money to do whatever they want to do whenever they want to do it, no matter what the general public thinks or feels. In the meantime, society is left preoccupied with media reports on politics, religion, sports and sensationalist stories of everyday American citizens, when coverage would be better spent on the inner workings of the activities of corporate America and how the are to be so corrupt and manipulative. Of course, every corporation is not in the business of making money by any means necessary, and every government official is not apathetic to U.S. citizens while being empathetic to corporations. However, there is more than enough of both to create enough havoc to send practically the entire nation reeling from their government policies and intertwined harmful corporate activities.

America: In Name Only

BIG CORPORATIONS, OLIGOPOLIES, media conglomerates, political action committees, lobby groups, greedy politicians and governments at all levels are the real shot-callers in America. These entities have transformed the 'Greatest Country in the World' into one gigantic, cutthroat marketplace. The power brokers and governments of the world are buying and selling America everyday in wholesale fashion. Low and middle-class Americans gets very little inclusion in American policies and services these days. With the exception of healthcare for children, what America offers Joe Citizen today pales in comparison to what it is capable of offering. If dissenters to this opinion were to comprise a list of blessings per American gratuity, at number one with a bullet would probably be the ability to be able to continue to live in America. I say that is not good enough, and that the number one item on that list should be the honest and zealous effort of everyone, including politicians, to sincerely work together to elevate America to the land of the free and the home of the brave, something that is fast become a myth.

Many will say that Americans still have it better than all other countries, and to some, that may well be the case. However, I get the feeling that Americans are incrementally losing both their rights and recourse. At the same time, other countries are gaining on America in terms of quality of living, even if only by default due to the fact that America is regressing. Do Americans measure their quality of living by electronic gadgets, television entertainment, and material items? If so, then America is doing swell.

Is IT RIGHT to have American views shaped by the conservative-owned newspaper, radio and television media outlets? I do not think so, because the vast majority of Americans never get their points of views heard. I don't know what people are continuously sampled for the various surveys and polls seen on the CNNs and MSNBCs, but they rarely, if ever, include BA and lower income America. Does it feel like your vote at the polls and opinions at city hall meetings are irrelevant and your appearances at these town hall meetings are just for show? That is because they probably are, as the powers that be do what they want, regardless of what the sentiment of majority America may be.

The feeling is that one can only watch as more and more jobs are outsourced, reciprocity of tax dollars is no more, and taxes go higher, broader and just plain ridiculous. You will see that as the political terms of politicians get ready to expire, then the media will criticize and discuss the inequities and immoralities of those same politicians much more than they have in the early term years. And just when collective America finally develops a clear understanding of the truth, it's déjà vu all over again, as re-election campaigns begin anew, the politicians dust-off those tired, redundant, smokescreen, election platforms, and the bull-crap has hit the fan again. In the future, Americans have to find a way, and put forth the effort, to change the American political process and if America is to truly be the "Greatest Country in the World".

Black Cash

OFTENTIMES, THERE WILL be statements made, magazine articles, and reports as to the impressive combined gross income of BA. BA has more money than this small country, and more potential buying power than that small country, and because of this, Black voices should be heard and respected, and no one had better mess with BA. Some estimates put the collective spending power in the $600 billion dollar range. But all of that spending 'power' sort of crumbles in the face of one question. What does $600 billion dollars mean if Black people continue to be the largest per-capita consumers of harmful, wasteful, zero-value products such as legal and illegal drugs, alcoholic beverages, cigarettes, excess and overpriced clothing items such as tennis shoes and athletic jerseys, new cars, video games, car rims, excessive cable and satellite television channels, junk food?

DOES BA NEED to be the ultimate consumer in America, spending valuable primary and discretionary dollars on depreciable, useless material possessions, while overlooking the more sensible spending decisions such as savings, personal, business, and community investment? How long does Black America feed its self-devouring beast? BA is not up to par in terms of wealth creation and business development, and comes away with an image of incompetence, unworthiness and lacking discipline in economics and personal finances. The "you sellin', I'm buyin'" mindset continues to crush BA, and a much more productive and intelligent mindset needs to take its place.

Do not look at how much buying power collective BA has. Rather, pay close attention to what the individual has. What is more important is what you and your family have, and what you and your family do with what you have. That is what will play a big part in turning BA around. A radical change with just $200 per month, per family would change the landscape of any family's financial future. Spend no money on video games, and buy no DVDs, television sets or personal DVD players for the kid's bedroom. Do not waste money on digital cable television or even new cars that will spend most of its time either in your parking lot or that of your job. Consider that type of spending unnecessary. Instead, invest in education, savings, a business, a home, or even vacationing with the kids. Remember the saying, "a fool is easily parted with his money". That has been true of many an individual, and surely true of collective BA.

As 'HINDERED' HAS discussed BA, remember that the reference is to collective BA. However, collective BA is made up of one person, one family at a time. One by one, we have gotten ourselves into the fix we are in, and one by one, we have to get ourselves out of this fix. Like clothes, we all wear certain statistics, and there is no way to tell which statistic each person wears. BA will become successful and prosperous one person, one family at a time. Taking care of yourself and your own family will be all you need to do to assist BA and ensure that its future will be safe. We have just to find enough people to understand that, and so far, that has not been the case.

In regards to the other social failures in America by Blacks, many may want to blame it on the "Man". Who can blame the man, or anyone else for that matter, for taking a fool's money that is intent on parting with it? If you play the fool, you get taken to school. There are also 'brothers' trying to get paid at the expense of Blacks also, causing one to wonder, just what color is the 'Man"? Actually, the man is anyone trying to get paid at the expense of another. Black and white is not the true color of the man, but rather, it is green. But the broad sense of the 'Man' is the concept of the White man, and the practices of the 'Man' hold down the Black man. Actually, it gets broader than that, as today's version of the 'Man' is one who is out to make a dollar, and as many as he can, at the expense of anyone who is there to be had, and his victims are Black, White, the poor, and anyone else he can exploit.

Manomics

MAKE NO MISTAKE about it, there is indeed this bodacious, scheming, greedy individual known as the 'Man'. He is not always White, but legend has it that the vast majority of them are. And sometimes, albeit usually overlooked, the 'Man' can sometimes be a woman. It's just that the title, the 'Woman', when coupled with the goal of world domination just does not sound right. Anyhow, the 'Man' does exist, and there is a name given to his works. The business sciences gave us Economics. The decade of the eighties gave us Reagonomics. The nineties gave us Ebonics. I now give you Manomics.

LISTEN TO WHAT one of republican leaders said in the December 15, 2004 issue of the USA Today newspaper in the 'News' section, page 10. He was the then outgoing Heath and Human Services Secretary Tommy Thompson: 'For the life of me, I cannot understand why the terrorists have not attacked our food supply, because it is so easy to do." [57]

Thanks Mr. Thompson for that Blue's Clue. If the terrorists do someday attack our food supply, we will owe it all to you. Is this the stuff that American leaders are made of? I hope not. I prefer to think of this type of individual as someone that should be doing anything but leading America. He needs to keep his thoughts to himself, and it is my hope that he never gets another chance to speak into a microphone again.

Retiring Representative Billy Tauzin, a republican from Louisiana, pulled a very large rabbit out of his butt. First, he acknowledged that the U.S. drug manufacturing industry had suffered a "black eye" in public perceptions because of high prices and profits, safety concerns on the recalls of big-selling drugs, and other issues. He would then go on to successfully negotiate and pass a bill that prohibits the federal government from negotiating lower prices for medicines and also continues a ban on importation of identical but lower-cost drugs from Canada and elsewhere. After that, he went on to become the head of the Pharmaceutical Research and Manufacturers of America, one of the most powerful pharmaceutical trade groups in America. He paved his own streets with gold, and then laughed all the way to the bank. [58]

THE FOLLOWING IS a list of works of 'The Man':

- The elimination of overtime for millions of workers who depend on overtime to pay bills, accumulate savings, finance holidays such as Christmas, and pay for their children's college expenses.
- A freeze on the minimum wage at the federal level, while

consistently blessing themselves with raises and perks.

- Seeks to protect big corporations from product liability, while their products injure and kill people.
- Allow corporations to pollute our minds and bodies by easing restrictions on air, water and food pollution.
- Man the post as corporate corruption reaches an all-time high. Corporate officers steal from pension funds and manipulate stock while raking in tens and hundreds of millions of dollars in salaries for themselves.
- Allows the existence of a corrupt and unbalanced traffic ticket system that preys on the poor and people of color.
- Start wars for profit.
- Raises taxes on the middle class, while creating tax credits and loopholes that disproportionately favor the rich.
- Put politicians above the law by making them inaccessible and unaccountable.
- Sponsor complex and intricate partnerships between government and big corporation.
- Tamper with the voting process enough to make millions feel that their vote has been minimized and the entire election process crooked.
- Build professional sports stadiums for the billionaire owners with taxpayer money, also making money on the back end, as many of these stadiums are built in inner-city neighborhoods, which causes property taxes go up, which stuffs the coffers of the government even more, with no real benefit to the citizens.
- Allow corporations to push healthcare costs so far out of reach that record numbers of adults and children have no healthcare overage. The same corporations that complain about healthcare practically serve as institutional investors in the stock of these same healthcare companies.
- While serving as CEOs of corporations, the bless themselves with salaries and bonuses that can be easily be as much as 1,000 times the salary of the average worker, while their best work oftentimes amount to benchmarking what other CEOs are doing around the country, changing the way business is done with new processes best know by their catchy names,

and sometimes even, poor performance and depreciating stock prices.

American politicians are a scary bunch of fellows. They turn it on during election time, and then turn us out once in office. The methods and platforms of politics are ancient in design yet eerily effective, primarily because of media control. They persuade people of lesser cynical stock to not be able to see that ethics in government, political action committees, Washington lobbyists, special interest groups, government-big business alliance, and truth and honesty from politicians are a future mega-trend that begs for reform. Instead, the American public is pre-occupied with the words that come out of their mouths during election time. In the end, the election results often do us more harm than good.

MANY YEARS AGO, the federal government ended its cheese program. What many Americans do not know is that in its place began a new food program, the government hash browns program. They are served up daily because the actions and words of today's politicians can be likened to the hash browns of one world famous restaurant chain. Government hash browns are:

- Scattered about, and very hard to access.
- Smothered with all kinds of ##?*^%$**@!!
- Covered with cloaks of secrecy, privacy and seclusion
- Chunked with the speed of a Roger Clemens fastball – you'll never see it coming, and the next thing you know, you're out
- Layered with rhetoric and untruths
- Diced like a Las Vegas slot machine – the odds are always against you
- Topped with a nightcap at a professional sports stadium of their choice
- Peppered with cash payouts to every 'honorable' politician and businessmen written into their deals
- Grilled just right to toast your tiny, little buns
- Steamed – the way you feel as you helplessly watch them

manipulate America.

At the current pace, America may never be able to recover. A co-worker of mine, Don Herron, put it like this: "When you look at how we are losing jobs, wages, benefits, and human rights, you can see the time is coming very soon when we will all be living just like those in third-world countries. The pace of these losses are hurried, and the actions of our government officials are at the very least both questionable and suspicious." Undoubtedly, there are many whom would agree with Mr. Herron.

Killer Racial Systems & Industries

THERE ARE A number of industries and social systems that make their fortunes off of the inability of people to fight back against them. These fortunes can be referred to as "misery money". Somewhere behind every one of these institutions and social systems is a police officer, judge, doctor, CEO, lawyer, politician, or entire government body. They are devastators of the minds, bodies and spirits of everyday people that are simply trying to make a living. They exploit people either in the name of the law, or just simply because they can. The symptoms of their invasion is a big pinch in the wallet, an extraction of government dollars from your inner city schools, an increase in Black students labeled special education, increased revenue for drug companies, greater problem indexes with Black foster children, and a host of other indicators of that go on and on and bear testament to the presence and power of these omnipresent entities.

The works of these industries and social systems is skewed, as tens of thousands of people will have some segment of their day negatively affected by their iron hand of control, and almost incessantly, the majority of their victims will be Black, Hispanic, or poor, and usually in that order. And when these industries bring it, they bring it hard and heavy. The stakes are getting higher and higher, as they have set their sights on bigger and bigger prizes, as the present eminent domain debacle can attest to. They are large, intent on staying in charge, and are quite the formidable opponent.

There are nine such Killer Systems & Industries that need to be reformed. In spite of media apathy and government/corporate collusion that work together to disarm those who would care and fight for change, the people must never give up the fight. It has to be BA that takes the point in the fight against these behemoths, and this is only logical, since it is BA that bears the brunt of their force.

Black Foster Care

OVER 500,000 CHILDREN in the U.S. currently reside in some form of foster care, and placements have dramatically increased over the past ten years. African-American children make up approximately *66 percent* of the foster care population, while making up only 15 percent of the child population. African American children, when compared to other children in foster care, generally remain in care longer.

Being removed from their home and placed in foster care is a difficult and stressful experience for any child. Many of these children have suffered some form of serious abuse or neglect. About 30% of children in foster care have severe emotional, behavioral, or developmental problems. Physical health problems are also common.[59]

There are additional problems with the foster care system in addition to the aforementioned ones. Statistical facts tell a part of the story, and there are some concerns that do not show up in statistics as well. There are also problems in relation to the adoption process. The adoption process can be difficult and disheartening for aspiring parents-to-be. There are hoops and hurdles that can leave one wondering exactly what the intentions of the adoption agencies really are. In the end, however, the thing that matters most is that those who can, should continue to try and rescue those who can't help themselves for being caught up in an imperfect system that manipulates God's perfect creation - children.

Drugging Foster Children

DR. MARK SIMMONS, medical director and professor of Pediatrics at the Medical College of Wisconsin in Milwaukee, has written a report, *The Crisis in Health Care for America's Foster Children*, which documents serious health concerns for foster children.

Key points of the report include the following:

- Mental health surveys of children in foster care have found extremely high rates of depression, conduct disorder, oppositional defiant disorder, attention deficit hyperactivity disorder, and attachment and anxiety disorder;

- Given the high prevalence of psychological and behavioral symptoms among these children, the overuse of psychotropic medication has become a significant concern.[60]

- Nearly 1,900 children under the care of Florida's welfare system are taking antidepressant drugs, despite the increased risk of suicidal thinking amongst the children. One in four Florida foster children are taking at least one mood-altering drug, and one in ten are taking at least three.[61]

On Wednesday, 11 August, the Boston Globe reported that two-thirds of children in state care in Massachusetts are being treated for mental illness with psychosomatic drugs.

In her first national act since beginning her run for Senator of New York, Hilary Clinton announced a new program to examine the overuse of psychiatric drugs in young children. The initiative is based on a study published in the Journal of the American Medical Association (JAMA) that showed dramatic increases in the use of drugs to deal with behavioral difficulties in young kids between the ages of 2-4 years old. The study reviewed three regions between 1991-1995, and found that the use of Ritalin and other stimulants increased over 200%, while the use of psychoactive drugs such as Prozac increased by 150%. "Some of these young people have problems that are symptoms of nothing more than childhood or adolescence," said Mrs. Clinton.[62]

Is it not amazing how the 'Great States' of America, in conjunction with the pharmaceuticals, use American children as guinea pigs? And by the way, the disparity dilemma continues, as the majority of these unfortunate 'experimental' children just happen to be Black. For children to be pharmacologically inundated from ages as low as two years old is criminal. We are talking about pre-teens and toddlers here people. It is no small wonder that some of these kids have the behavioral, societal, and educational problems that they do, and to think that it is all done with the blessings of our government. The fact that there are over four million children on Ritalin speaks volumes about what is happening to Black children. And guess who benefits from this massive drug program? The pharmaceutical companies, that's who!

THIS SYSTEMATIC INSTITUTION of medical mistreatment brings to mind another sad saga of American history, one spearheaded by a psychiatrist named Walter Freeman. From 1946 to 1967, Mr. Freeman performed gruesome, ten-minute lobotomies on over 2,500 'patients'. Some of his patients were adolescents. These people were supposedly 'mentally ill', however new evidence shows that this was not true of a great deal of his patients. They all had one thing in common though, with the foster children of today. And that is, all of these medical shenanigans are being conducted against the will of the people being experimented on. Those whom Mr. Freeman 'operated' on did not ask for a lobotomy, just like America's foster kids are not raising their hands and volunteering for drugs. The government has gone too far in this instance, and its partnered practice of medicating children is appalling, and needs to be stopped.[63]

AT THE UNAWARES of society, and in particular Black society, when these kids are unleashed, they will bring a set of very complex problems with them. The chances of these kids being chemically dependent on either pharmaceutical drugs or street drugs well into their adolescent and adult years are indeed great. These children yearn for love, but instead receive drugs. Their stories simply fill the diaries of what has gone wrong with the America.

With so many Black children in foster care, the need to strengthen Black families needs to be one of the top priorities for BA. Foster care should be an option of last resort, not of the first. It is imperative that BA does not forget about this important segment of its society.

Contaminated Schools

VOLATILE ORGANIC COMPOUNDS, or VOCs, are volatile toxins in the sense that they easily evaporate in the air. There are certain VOCs that exist in certain schools, mostly older schools that usually can be found in inner-city neighborhoods. Some VOCs are:

- Mold – Sometimes called the new asbestos, looms as a tremendous problem. Exposure to molds or mold spores can trigger a wide range of reactions, including headaches, breathing difficulties, skin irritation, allergic reactions, aggravation of asthma symptoms, bloody noses, and eye irritations.

- Polyvinyl Chloride (PVC) are petroleum-based plasticizers and stabilizers used in piping, flooring, carpet fibers and backing, blinds, door and window frames, vinyl siding, electrical cables, and wall flooring.

- Chromated Copper Arsenate (CCA) I a wood preservative made with Arsenic, Chromium, and copper and is intended to reduce damage from insects, mildew, and fungi. This pesticide mixture is 22percent pure arsenic and is forced into wood under pressure. It bleeds off into the air, and may continue to bleed for years. Children absorb it by putting their hands to their mouths, or by eating off of it.

- Other toxins of concern are lead, carbon monoxide and carbon dioxide, dust, and carpeting, which collects these toxins. HVAC systems, which circulate these toxins, can be offset by opening windows and letting fresh air in whenever possible. Inner city children run the risk of being exposed to abnormal levels of these toxins when their schools are outdated or improperly maintained. Children move through several stages of rapid growth and development. Growth is most rapid from conception to age 7. The ensuing years, through adolescence, bring continued growth as crucial systems, such as the reproductive system, mature. Insulation of brain nerve fibers is not complete until adolescence. Similarly, air sacs in the lungs, which is where oxygen enters the blood stream, increases in number until adolescence.

During these critical years, as structures and vital connections develop, bodily systems are not suited to repair damage caused by toxins. Thus, if neurotoxins assault cells in the brain, immune system, or reproductive organs, or if endocrine disruption diverts development, the resulting dysfunction will likely be permanent and irreversible, depending on the organ damage, consequences can include lowered intelligence, immune dysfunction, or reproductive impairment.

THERE ARE NO federal laws governing the environmental health conditions in schools. Federal initiatives, as most federal assistance aimed to support inner-city causes, have had funding either cut or withdrawn. It is for this reason that parents, community members and school administrators work together to protect our children from toxic poisons that are present in schools.[64]

There does exist other forms of help. Green Seal is the pre-eminent environmental certification body in the U.S. that strives to achieve a healthier and cleaner environment by identifying and promoting products and services that cause less toxic pollution and waste, conserves resources and habitats, and minimizes global warming and ozone depletion. Green Seal has become "The" authority for many public and private organizations, including public schools.[65]

IT IS NOT surprising that spending decisions are made with taxpayer money that the taxpayers would not agree with. Oftentimes these spending decisions are painful, especially when the victims are children. Old inner-city schools are often refurbished, at the expense of building new schools. As a result, the students spend one-third of their lives in schools that have been bombarded with the previously mentioned chemicals such as PVC and CCA, and as noted, these chemicals been proven to be extremely toxic to the development of the children. The condition of old schools in inner city communities, coupled with under-funding and slighting by state governments comprise severe obstacles for the inner city that deserve more respect, and certainly, better schools.

The Environmental Waste Industry

Environmental racism can be defined as the intentional siting of hazardous waste sites, landfills, incinerators, and polluting industries in communities inhabited mainly by African-Americans, Hispanics, Native Americans, Asians, migrant farm workers, and the working poor. Minorities are particularly vulnerable because they are perceived as weak and passive citizens who will not fight back against the poisoning of their neighborhoods in fear that it might jeopardize jobs and economic survival.

The Landmark Study, "Toxic Waste & Race in the U.S.", described the extent of environmental racism and the consequences for those who are victims of polluted environments. The study revealed that:

(1) Race was the most significant variable associated with the location of hazardous waste sites.

(2) The greatest number of commercial hazardous facilities were located in communities with the highest composition of racial and ethnic minorities.

(3) The average minority population in communities with one commercial hazardous hazardous waste facility was twice the average minority population in communities without such facilities.

(4) Although socioeconomic status was also an important variable in the location of these sites, race was the most significant even after controlling for urban and regional differences.

Bullard points out that, "many of the at-risk communities are victims of land-use decision making that mirrors the power arrangements of the dominant society. Historically, exclusionary zoning has been a subtle form of using government authority and power to foster and perpetuate discriminatory practices.

SOME REAL-LIFE EXAMPLES of hazards facing minority communities in the United States:

- The largest hazardous waste landfill in the U.S. is located in Emelle, Alabama, a poor, predominantly African-American community. It receives toxic material from forty-five states and several foreign countries.

- Over 30,000 Hispanic farm workers and their families, including a large number of women of child-bearing age, are seriously affected by pesticide-related illnesses.

- An industrial toxic waste site is located in a predominantly Hispanic neighborhood on the south side of Tucson, Arizona. The air and water are polluted with toxic chemicals, which have caused a high rate of cancer, birth defects, genetic mutations, and other illnesses among the inhabitants of the area. The community is tainted with twenty times the acceptable levels of trichloroethylene.

- Waste disposal companies have been attempting to convince Native Americans to permit dumping on the reservations under the guise of improving the economic conditions. High rates of lung cancer and poisoned land have occurred on Navajo reservations as a result of uranium mining.

- The south side of Chicago, which is predominantly African-American and Hispanic, has the greatest concentration of hazardous waste sites in the nation.

- The portion of minorities living in communities with existing incinerators is 89% higher than the national average.

- Pharmaceutical companies, oil refineries, and petro-chemical plants are responsible for making Puerto Rico one of the world's most heavily polluted places.

- Radiation exposure is a major health problem in the Marshall Islands, Bikini, and other Pacific Islands, which have been used as test sites for nuclear and atomic weapons.

- Six of the eight incinerators and five of the municipal landfills in Houston, Texas are located in predominantly African-American neighborhoods.

- Communities where incinerators are proposed have minority populations 60% higher than the national average and property values 35% lower than the national average.

Studies suggest a clear relationship between a high concentration of minority populations and a low average income, with an unhealthy environment. Poor people do not have the economic means to leave their neighborhoods for resettlement elsewhere. Housing discrimination often makes it difficult to find alternative dwellings at affordable rates. Industries that pollute are attracted to poor neighborhoods because land values, income, and other costs of doing business are lower, and political power and community resources to fight back are weak or lacking. Higher income areas are usually more successful in preventing or controlling the entry of polluting industries to their communities.[66]

THIS INDUSTRY IN particular is one of the most dangerous. The Environmental Waste problem serves up a multi-faceted attack on those that inhabit the affected areas, often manifested as death in children and adults, and also affects unborn children. Cancers, child deformities, asthma, learning disabilities, mental retardation and general declining health are just some of the many major health problems that result due to the placement of environmental waste disposal systems near people.

One ironic twist related to this killer system is that Black men have no problem obtaining jobs as 'sanitary engineers', a.k.a. garbage truck workers. These ambassadors of the environmental waste industry fearlessly go about their jobs as a means top provide for their families. My observation of them is that they usually are not the drivers of the trucks, but instead are left to make direct contact with the unclean and unsafe contents of the waste in al its forms. In this world of ever-increasing viruses, diseases and drug activity, it can actually be a death sentence, instead of just a way to pay the bills. The sanitation engineers of America probably do not know that theirs is one of the most dangerous occupations in America.

On a positive note, at least these sanitary engineers were given a choice as to whether or not they wanted to be exposed to the unsanitary conditions of their jobs. The citizens that live near environmental waste systems were not given that same choice, as their lack of information rendered them unaware of the poison that lives amongst them.

Government

The Members Only Club

THE U.S. WORKFORCE is made up 228 million employees who earned a total of $6.7 trillion dollars last year. The rich one percent took away a whopping $1.8 trillion, or over 26 percent of America's national income. One percent of Americans have incomes in excess of $373,000 a year. There are 243 billionaires in America and over 5,000,000 millionaires. [67] These people are movers and shakers, which means if they are not moving something around, they are shaking it up. Many are decent and respectable people, and not all are republicans. By any means, they are to be commended for their accomplishments, in the very least because acquiring wealth was their goal, and we all want to be able to reach our goals.

Often the word is power is used to describe the very rich and their organizations. When I think of power, I think of God, a volcano, or cartoon superheroes. Well, at least I did when I was a kid. It's difficult for me to refer to a mortal as powerful because he or she has a lot of money. The reality is that wealthy individuals can buy things a lot of other people cannot, and that is that. In addition to rich Americans, there are many super-rich individuals from around the world who are in this mix also. These are the shot callers and the big-ballers of planet Earth, and together they comprise what I refer to as the exclusive 'Members Only Club', or M.O.C.

According to a 1998 Human Development Report, the top 10 percent in the US own 71 percent of all private wealth. Another version has the top 1 percent of Americans owning more than the bottom 90 percent. And yet, there is another group of millionaires and billionaires that do not always show up on the traditional lists of the rich. They are the Mayors, Senators, and Governors that have access to public tax roll monies and budgets. These are the people that run our country politically. Some have already amassed small fortunes, while others have not. Regardless of their tax bracket, what they do have is access to American taxpayer money, which cumulatively adds up to millions and even billions of dollars. It is American tax-roll money that puts these politicians in the money game. At times, they spend it as they wish, and their decisions increasingly favor the M.O.C. In fact, it seems that just about every decision that the politicians of today make is somehow tied into Corporate America. Putting the people first is like a thirty-cent loaf of bread, a thing of the past.

Southern Hospitality in Nashville, Tennessee

By the year 2020, the Nashville metropolitan area could be the 15th-fastest growing metro area in the United States. Of the eight counties in the Nashville Metropolitan Statistical Area, Davidson County finished seventh. Davidson County, which houses Nashville, has a projected population growth of nearly 32 percent from 1995 50 2020. Its population is expected to grow from 530,796 to 699,564.[68]

One of the benefits to increased population comes in the form of increased state revenue, where each new resident results somewhere in the neighborhood of $115 per resident, with bigger cities getting more of this state-shared cash. These dollars are so important that many cities pay tens of thousands of dollars on special censuses to prove that there has been an increase in their populations.[69]

Since 1995, Nashville has been very generous with its revenue increases, whether from state revenue, increased public fees of various sorts or increased taxes levied on the general public, in regards to spending. The catch is that it usually goes to millionaires, billionaires, and big business. Some cases in point:

- In 1995, Nashville lavished the Houston Oilers and owner Bud Adams with a $28 million dollar 'relocation fee', new stadium with 120 luxury boxes, 9,600 "premium seats", and 42,700 seat licenses, the proceeds of which will go to Adams, and consequently, Mr. Adams not only would not have to pay a dime to build the new facility, but he would also garner 100 percent of stadium related revenues. The state would kick in $55 million in construction bonds and $12 million more for road improvements. Nashville kicked in $144 million and had to guarantee $70 million in net sales of personal seat licenses.[70]

- In 1997, The Nashville Predators were given an 18,500-seat arena built in 1996 at a cost of $145 million. The arena, The Gaylord Entertainment Center, was re-modeled to add luxury boxes, at additional cost to the city of $14 million. Because the Predators needed a place to practice, the city built that as well for $6.5 million. The city contributed 25 percent of the $80 million expansion fee. The team also gets to keep all the revenue, all the board advertising revenue, all the scoreboard revenue, all the luxury-box revenue, all the parking revenue, all the revenue from the sale of team merchandise, and all the revenue from the sale of the arena's corporate name. In return, the team is committed to paying a whopping $50,000 a year in rent.[71]

- Before the Predators came to town, The Gaylord Entertainment Center hosted about 145 events a year and had an operating deficit of less than $500,000. Now, the arena hosts fewer events and has an operating deficit of over $5 million.[72]

- In 1999, Dell Computer received $166 million dollars in the form of land, tax incentives, relocation incentives, property tax exemptions, city services, and free land to sublease back to its suppliers significant employee training and recruiting incentives, and a $500-per-year credit for every employee on its Nashville payroll. To date in 2006, Dell primarily employs temporary workers at eight to ten dollars an hour.[73]

- In 2005, Nashville has put together its largest case of corporate welfare to date. It has put together a deal to give Nissan North

America close to $200 million in incentives over 20 years to lure the automakers headquarters from California. The deal includes $23 million in 'site' incentives; $6 million for temporary office space; $80.3 million for enhanced jobs tax credits; $5.5 million for headquarters tax credits; $175,000 for industrial machinery tax credits; $63.75 million for relocation of its employees; $2.97 million for recruitment, screening and training; $1 million for FastTrack job training; and a $14.8 million government payment in lieu of taxes. There will not be many jobs for local residents.[74]

- In the year 2005, the city of Nashville announced the closing of seven schools Along with the cutting of 490 jobs, including 200 teachers and 26 principals, in the Metro school system because of a decrease in the school budget. All of the schools are in the inner city. The state of Tennessee has also made headlines for its callous cuts in healthcare for its citizens, again most of who live in the inner-city.[75]

- The city of Nashville has also put together lucrative deals to accommodate Columbia/HCA Healthcare, Dollar General Headquarters, Ingram Industries and publishing operation Thomas Nelson.

THE PARTNERSHIP OF government and private industry provides the means to how the M.O.C. expands its national playground. A corporation will announce plans for a new factory, relocation plans, or an expansion. During the course of negotiations, the corporation receives tax-breaks, immense sums of incentive money, and praise beyond belief. The city announces how good it will be for the citizens, and how lucky everyone is to have a new corporation locate in its city. And then, the new corporation falls short of its promises. The new dollars that were to be pumped into the community, it turns out, actually requires a smaller pump. The full time jobs with benefits in fact proved to be part-time jobs with no benefits. The lawyers that represented the corporation were eventually discovered to be much smarter than the city's lawyers. And it is the citizens who are left footing the bill. In the end, the only people that benefit from these ventures are the members of the M.O.C. There are chapters in every city in America, and if by chance there is not one in your city, rest assured that one is coming to a theatre near you.

Government Expansionism

IN THE LAST 30 years all governments – federal, state, and local – have gone on a buying spree, gobbling up land everywhere to protect and preserve which is not one of the purposes authorized by the Constitution. In two separate sessions of Congress, these same environmental organizations promoted legislation to set aside $3 billion each year for 18 years, expressly for the purpose of buying private property. Opponents were able to seriously weaken these efforts, but each year, more and more local, state and federal tax dollars are being used to buy private property. Simultaneously, increasingly restrictive land-use planning, zoning and regulatory control laws have also been adopted by every level of government.

Increasing property tax is one of the first consequences of excessive government ownership. The cost of government does not decrease, but the number of property owners who must pay the costs does decrease, thereby forcing the remaining property owners to pay a higher rate, in both taxes and fees. Even more important is the long-term consequence. Currently, governments own about 42 percent of the total land area in the U.S. In their world, people will have to live on property that is owned by the government – or a land trust. Farmers will have to farmland that also is owned by the government or a land trust, and industry will have to operate using resources that are publicly owned. Get the picture? He who owns the land controls its use – and gathers its wealth. Sadly, many people are eager to sell their land or the use of their land through easements to the government or to a land trust. These buyers have no shortage of money and can offer tax breaks that private buyers cannot. Consequently, America is being sold out. Every new land-acquisition appropriation in Washington or at the state and local level moves America closer and closer to that socialist utopia described in the 1976 U.N. document, Conference on Human Settlements

(HABITATI), which declares that "public control of land use is therefore indispensable, and it is the common citizen that loses. " [76]

Another Boondoggle

THE OFFICE OF Homeland Security was created to protect America from terrorists, in spite of the fact that we already have the CIA, FBI, DEA, ATF, Customs, Border Patrol and the IRS, in addition to other protectionist groups well. These agencies, which have protected us for decades, have now more or less been deemed ineffective. As a result, The Office of Homeland Security was created, using billions of dollars. This was to be the supreme being of all American law enforcement agencies, and America would be, from the day this new office was created, forever safe.

However, that was not to be, and everyone would soon find out. Eventually, it became clear to the 911 Commission, newspaper reporters, government officials and the general public that America is not one bit safer than before the deadly tragedy that rocked our soil, the attack on New York on September 11, 2001. American borders, harbors, and streets are not protected anymore now than before 911. Except for aggravating the hell out of us at airports and creating a national color code game, The Office of Homeland Security seems to just barely exist. It might still be around, but it seems to have fallen short of its much-ballyhooed purpose.

There is one more important note regarding The Office of Homeland Security. Of late, a tremendous amount of money has been deemed unaccounted for. Even I saw this one coming! Did not you? On July 28, 2006, CNN reported that The Office of Homeland

Security has wasted $34 billion dollars on 32 contracts in just its first two years of existence. Problems such as a shortage of contract managers, abuse, fraud, and mismanagement were cited. [77] This is in addition to the billions wasted in Iraq the same way. Never to worry though, America. Trust me, nothing much will be doe about it, as this is how the M.O.C. operates. Besides, what are we to do? We're just the voters, and it isn't election time, so who will listen?

Government Incentive

ONCE A NEWLY elected government official is hot off the campaign and election trail, they immediately get down to the real business at hand, and that is to make deals with taxpayer money. They leave the day-to-day operations of government to their department heads and staff, and this allows the elected official to be free to make money for The M.O.C. With the media on their side and short of making any glaring missteps, they are poised to make deals of the century behind closed doors at the expense of public citizens. In short, the politicians drop the soap, and we pick it up.

Often times, fellow politicians will rubber stamp bills and laws without even reading any material on these prospective bills and laws. Bill King, chief editor of *Expansion Management* magazine, states that it is common for states to write laws for a specific economic development project. The laws are usually written in conjunction *with* the prospective company and are written in such a way that few companies could qualify for them.[78]

As GOVERNMENT OFFICIALS and business executives expand their national playground, they can be found traveling the country attending any of various dinners, meetings and sporting events. All across the country politicians and business executives get together to spend tax dollars on corporate plants and buildings, sports stadiums and other enterprises that are supposedly 'good' for both the general public, their respective cities and business entities involved. The real winners in this expansion game are the politicians, business executives, contractors, family members and friends of the M.O.C. They get to make some huge sums of money, party together, have lavish parties, attend black-tie dinners, and corporate appointments, get talk show appearances, ride in limousines, make and receive campaign contributions, appear on talk shows, and exchange favors of cash, credit, jobs. They are indeed true stars that have arrived.

What role does the general public play? Why, it gets to finance it all, what else? The general public gets rewarded in the form of higher gasoline prices, increased gasoline taxes, increased cable prices, increased sales taxes, increased property taxes, increased FCC taxes, increased motor vehicle fees of all sorts, increased license renewal fees, increased water, electric and gas bills, increased traffic ticket prices, increased specialty taxes, and increased taxes across the board. On the flip side, it also get less healthcare, less money spent on education, many children left behind, less public services, less fire and police services, and less of everything, except for deceptions and campaign promises.

Why? Because when it comes to false promises and deceptions and American politicians, they 'gotta' million of 'em'.

Pharmaceuticals

As the health of Black people has deteriorated, the pharmaceutical companies have been right there to capitalize. Whatever drugs the people need, the pharmaceuticals are right there to supply it. With the help of the federal government, the pharmaceutical companies make up the most profitable industry in the world, raking in billions on top of billions of dollars. And the American public is the cash cow that gives them fresh milk. Americans are a self-replenishing pool of sick people that dearly depends on the drugs the pharmaceuticals produce. And they help themselves by maintaining certain 'minor league' teams, if you will, of customers, such as the all but forgotten foster care children.

Understand that the average 'sick' person afflicted with a serious medical conditions such as diabetes, cancer, HIV/AIDS, etc., is worth hundreds of thousands of dollars in terms of income to the pharmaceuticals and medical professionals. This takes into account prescription drugs, doctor visits, surgeries, and hospital visits. As a result, the medical profession – which consists of the pharmaceutical companies, hospitals, doctors, medical laboratories, nurses, and clinics – makes hundreds of billions of dollars, in effect, more than any other industry in the world. And it is in the best interests of the pharmaceuticals and medical professionals to keep their customers hopes up and drugged out, lest they cease to stay in business. This is the state of the business in the industry of pharmaceuticals, in spite of the fact that their goods and services cause as much harm, if not more so, than good to the people that receive their drugs.

The following companies sit perched atop the pharmaceutical industry. Their names and revenues for the year 2003:[79]

(1) Pfizer - $28,228,000,000 in revenue. Leading drugs are Zoloft, Zyrtec, Lipitor, Cardura, Celebrex, and Viagra.

(2) GlaxomithKline - $27,060,000,000 in revenue. Leading drugs are Seretide/Advair, Levitra, and Flonase.

(3) Merck - $20,130,000,000 in revenue. Leading drugs are Zocor, Vioxx, and Fosomax.

(4) AstraZeneca - $17,841,000,000 in revenue. Leading drugs are Prilosec, Crestor, and Nexium.

(5) Johnson & Johnson - $17,151,000,000 in revenue. Leading drugs are Procrit/Eprex.

THE FOLLOWING INSURANCE companies are world leaders in their fields of accident and health insurance. They, too, profit inequitably off of minorities, the poor, and African-Americans in particular. Take a look at their considerable revenues from the year 2004:

(1) Blue Cross & Blue Shield - $162,800,000,000

(2) United Healthcare - $28,566,000,000

(3) Wellpoint Inc. - $18,600,000,000

(4) Cigna – 18,808,000,000,

(5) Aetna - $17,976, 000,000

(6) Aflac - $13,200,000,000[80]

HOW MUCH OF these revenues is BA responsible for? How many of those dollars can be attributed to Latino-America? BA is the largest contributor, per capita, to the total revenue of these industries. As a way of saying thanks, the pharmaceuticals provide more drugs. In fact, all of the Killer Industries and Systems make the majority of their money off of minorities and the poor. Because minorities are the most sick, drug-addicted and under-educated customers that they have, they do not receive much of a fight against their practices. However, that can all change.

Privatized Prisons

WELCOME TO ONE of America's growth industries – private sector, for-profit prisons. Under the direction of the Reagan administration and it "toughness" on criminal offenders, prison populations soared through the 1980s and into the 1990s, making the U.S. the unquestioned leader in jailing its own populace. While incarceration statistics have skyrocketed, crime rates have increased much more slowly. The number of people sent to prison is actually determined by policy decisions and political expediency

Politicians of all stripes have sought cheap political points by being "tough on crime." They throw oil on the fire of public panic by portraying the urban underclass (read: young, black males) as predator. Ignoring the broad context of economic policies that have effectively abandoned large segments of the population, they have instituted mandatory minimum sentences, tighter or no parole schedules, and tougher "good time" regulations. The number of people in jails and prisons on any given day tops 2 million, up from fewer than 400,000 at the start of the Reagan era.

Adding to the overpopulation these putative measures wrought is the War on Drugs, which aimed its frenzy in the inner city, and stuffed the nation's already over crowded prisons with a large crop of mostly African-Americans and Latino nonviolent offenders. The last time the U.S. faced such an influx of prisoners was after the Civil War when freed Blacks, who were previously punished and controlled within the slave system, were sent to formerly all-white prisons.

Companies that profit from crime have an incentive to imprison more inmates for longer sentences – even when violent crime rates are on the decline. Longer sentences mean more profits for corporation. Since 1991, the number of prisoners has increased 50 percent, while the violent crime rate has decreased 20 percent. Society would benefit more by having these people working and paying taxes instead of living off our taxes. No one should benefit from crime.

THE BUSINESS OF punishment is vast and profitable. The prison-industrial complex rakes in tens of billions of dollars. The public sector imprisonment industry employs more than 50,000 guards, as well as additional tens of thousands of administrators, and health, education, and food service providers. Especially in rural communities where other employment is scarce, corrections assume huge economic importance as a growth industry, which provides stable jobs.[81]

In contrast, the North Carolina Department of Corrections runs a program that pays for itself and puts $1 million dollars a year in the general fund and $500,000 into a restitution fund for crime victims.[82]

The following corporations lead the way in private prison profits in America in the year 2005:

- Corrections Corporation of America (CCA) – CCA had $1,192.4 million in total revenue and $50.2 million in net income. CCA operates more than 60 correctional, detention, and juvenile facilities with a capacity of some 70,000 beds in about 20 states and Washington, DC. Federal correctional and detention authorities account for more than 35 percent of CCA sales.

- The Geo Group – The Geo Group had $612.9 million in total revenue and $7 million in net income. The Geo Group operates about 60 correctional facilities with some 48,000 beds. Geo expanded by buying smaller U.S. rival Correctional Services Corporation.

- Cornell Companies, Inc. – Cornell Companies, Inc. had $310 million in total revenue and $300,000 in net income. CCA runs more than 80 adult and juvenile facilities with some 80,000 beds in about 15 states and Washington, DC.[83]

THE PRIVATIZED PRISON industry is yet still another example of big business exploiting American citizens for the sole purpose of making money. Prisons are the factories and the poor are their raw materials. The finished product is a man or woman viewing the world from behind bars for a long, long time. These privatized prisons did not create this 'need' all by themselves, as they had help from politicians. Having and needing prisons is one thing, but letting Corporate America control it and profit from it is another. As prisons have become privatized, there came an explosion of long-term prison sentences being routinely handed out to non-violent offenders?

Private prisons have their customers handed to them on a platter from American government. If your business is putting people behind bars, then finding ways to increase the value of your stock value is a priority, and increasing the prisoner count is the best way to address that priority. It all adds to increased job security for prosecuting attorneys, defense attorneys, and judges. As long as the big house remains full with a waiting list of prisoners, err guests, waiting to get in, consider the mission accomplished.

Another piece to this is that prisoners are counted by the national census as residents of the towns in which they are imprisoned, leaving their hometowns with diminished political power and government funding. Since voting representation and the distribution of government resources are determined by population count, convicts bring a transfer of public funds and electoral influence from their home communities, which are generally urban and poor, to the mostly rural towns in which they are imprisoned. And so, urban communities are de-powered, while rural communities are empowered. And the sweetest part of the deal is that those of the rural communities will never see their new neighbors in their malls or supermarkets. However, they will leave the lights on for you.

Special Education in the School Systems

SINCE ITS PASSAGE in 1975, the IDEA has brought tremendous benefits: today, approximately six million children with disabilities enjoy their right to a free appropriate public education. The benefits of special education, however, have not been equitably distributed. Minority children with disabilities all too often experience inadequate services, low-quality curriculum and instruction, and unnecessary isolation from their non-disabled peers. Moreover, inappropriate practices in both general and special education classrooms have resulted in overrepresentation, misclassification, and hardship for minority students, particularly black children.

In 1998, approximately 1.5 million minority children were identified as having mental retardation, emotional disturbance, or a specific learning disability. In most states, African American children are identified at one and a half to four times the rate of white children in the disability categories of mental retardation and emotional disturbance.

Once identified, most minority students are significantly more likely to be removed from the general education program and be educated in a more restrictive environment. For instance, African American and Latino students are about twice as likely as white students to be educated in a restrictive, substantially separate educational setting.

Additional Findings

- In wealthier districts, contrary to researcher's expectations, black children, especially males, were more likely to be labeled mentally retarded. Native American children also showed this unexpected trend, but to a lesser degree than black children. Usually, poverty correlates with poor prenatal care, low birth rates and other factors and therefore an increased risk for disabilities, while wealth usually correlates with a decreased risk.

- Minority children with disabilities are under-served: Black children with emotional disturbance often do not receive high quality early intervention and received far fewer hours of counseling and related services than white students with emotional disturbance. The lack of early intervention for minority children may exacerbate their learning and behavior problems and contribute to racial dis-proportionality in our juvenile justice system

- Black identification for mental retardation is pronounced in the South: Southern states constituted nearly three quarters of the states with unusually high incidence levels; where between

2.75 and 5.41 percent of the blacks enrolled were labeled as mentally retarded. The prevalence of mental retardation for whites nationally was approximately 0.75 percent in 2001, and in no state did the incidence of mental retardation among Whites rise above 2.32 percent.

These issues are compounded by a dwindling number of African American educators, who have traditionally played an important role in creating a positive learning environment for African American students. The diminishing number of African American educators may have a direct impact on the sensitivity of the school climate to African American children.[84]

The Traffic Ticket System

TRAFFIC TICKETS ARE a pervasive and perennial component of life in the United States because the traffic system justifies, supports, and rationalizes a multi-billion dollar slice of the national economy.

State and local governments learned long ago that traffic ticket financial sanctions he little deterrent effect on motorists. In reality, large fines increase motorist resistance to paying high fines and instead, they demand trials, which take all the profit out of the system. Eventually the "point system" was developed which further penalized motorists and put money into the pockets of one of our government's watcher industries, the insurance industry.

The reason that the traffic system has survived all these years is in one word, "money". Traffic tickets virtually fund many court systems. Traffic tickets justify the existence of entire police agencies (state highway patrols). Traffic tickets are the measurement criteria for enforcement budget requests and personnel performance ratings. Traffic tickets are used as an excuse to raise the insurance for otherwise safe drivers to the cumulative total of billions of dollars each year. And, in some instances, traffic tickets virtually fund local units of government.

Not including parking tickets, we can only estimate that somewhere between 25 and 50 million traffic tickets are issued each year. Traffic tickets average about $150.00, which means that the up front cost nationally is between $3.75 and $7.5 billion dollars. If just half of these tickets result in insurance surcharges (typically $300 over a period of three years), you can add another $3.75 to $7.5 billion dollars to this blatantly immoral and unethical system which amount to a $15 billion-dollar annual income stream just from fines and insurance surcharges. We haven't even considered the money siphoned off for "traffic schools", and attorney fees. That's more money than a fair number of states take in just from taxes alone![85]

This is a system of legalized extortion that should be changed, and minorities should lead the charge! Why? Because, as is the case of every other "Quality of Life" metric, BA suffers more than any other group of people. Let's take a look at five of our most popular cities and see just what happens to minorities:

Boston, Massachusetts:

A BOSTON GLOBE analysis of more than 750,000 tickets from every police department in the state showed a wide disparity in traffic tickets and vehicle searches. Although Blacks and Whites are more likely to be searched, whites are more likely than any other racial group to face drug charges following a search, which supports a claim by minorities that they are searched with less reason.

Blacks and Hispanics are ticketed at about twice their share of the population. Although Blacks account for 4.6 percent of the population, they receive 10 percent of the tickets. Hispanics make up about 5.6 percent of the population, but get 9.6 percent of the tickets. Once ticketed, they were 50 percent more likely than whites to have their cars searched. Blacks and Hispanics driving a new car are especially searched more than whites in a new car. Once searched, more of the whites were apparently found with drugs.[86]

Cincinnati, Ohio:

CINCINNATI POLICE OFFICERS issued 108,132 traffic tickets containing 141,132 citations between March 1, 199 and December 30, 2000. Blacks received 41.3 percent of the tickets and 46.8 percent of the citations.[87]

Justice Department Report:

A 2002 JUSTICE Department report concluded that, nationwide, "Police were more likely to conduct a search of the vehicle and/or driver in traffic stops involving black male drivers (15.9%) or Hispanic male drivers (14.2%), compared to white male drivers (7.9%)." [88]

Maryland:

DATA FROM 1995 and 1996 studies found that while Blacks represent 17% of Maryland's driving population and can be observed to drive no differently than Whites, 72% of those stopped and searched were Black. Fully one-half of Maryland's State Police traffic officers stopped Blacks in at least 80% of their stops; two officers stopped Blacks in 95% of their stops, and one officer only stopped Blacks. Race is also useless as an indicator of criminality. Where 70% of those searched were Black, the rate at which searches produced evidence of a crime was about the same for Blacks as for whites -- 28.4% and 28.8%, respectively.[88]

Milwaukee, Wisconsin:

FROM OCTOBER 1998 to October 1999, minorities received 70% of all traffic tickets and 75% of municipal non-traffic tickets. Blacks accounted for 58% of all traffic tickets and 58% of all non-traffic tickets in the downtown area, and 65% of all municipal non-traffic stops. Blacks make up roughly 37% of Milwaukee's population.[89]

Nashville, Tennessee:

IN NASHVILLE, TENNESSEE, 2003 traffic shows that there were 121,838 traffic stops that year where the race of the driver was indicated by police. Of these stops, Blacks represented 34% of the total, whereas the Black share of drivers was 23 percent. This equates to the fact that Blacks are 48 percent more likely to be stopped by police when compared to their actual driver makeup.

What makes the findings even more glaring is that data suggests that white drivers average more trips per day in their cars than blacks--roughly 4.4 as compared to 3.9. Figured over the course of a year, this amounts to about 183 more individual car trips for white drivers each year compared to blacks, or roughly 183 more chances annually to break a law, be caught, and be ticketed *for each white driver in Nashville.* Multiplied by the city's white driving population, this amounts to literally millions more opportunities for whites collectively to be stopped or ticketed relative to blacks.[90]

Additionally, The Tennessean reported on May 28th that Mayor Bill Purcell of the city of Nashville proposed a 33%, or $1.5 million dollar, increase in ticket revenue for the year 2007. This comes on the heels on a $42.00 traffic ticket increase announced in April of 2006. Statistics indicate that for all of the newly written tickets, and there will be many of them, Nashville's minority population will be in for the roughest ride. Those car seats just got a lot more uncomfortable.[91]

Dateline:

ONE RECENT STUDY suggests that rates of disparity like those found in Nashville between Black and White drivers may be somewhat obscured by a failure to disaggregate moving violations from less serious types of infractions (busted taillights, missing rear view mirrors, expired tags, darkened window tint, being illegally parked, etc.).

According to the study in which researchers at Dateline NBC examined over 100,000 police stops over a three-year period, Blacks were three times ore likely to be stopped than Whites for non-moving violations.[90]

New Jersey:

IN 1999, THE New Jersey Attorney General's Office issued a report showing that during two previous years (1997 and 1998), 40% of motorists stopped on the New Jersey Turnpike and 80% of those searched were minorities. While Blacks and Latinos accounted for 78% of those searched at the south end of the New Jersey Turnpike during the year 2000, evidence was more reliably found by searching whites: 25% of whites searched had contraband, as compared to 13% of Blacks and 5% of Latinos.[88]

North Carolina:

RESEARCHERS WITH NORTH Carolina State University found that in 1998, Blacks were 68% more likely than Whites to be searched by the North Carolina Highway Patrol. The study also found that 26% of those Blacks searched, and 33% of the whites searched, were found to possess contraband.[88]

Seattle, Washington:

IN JUNE OF 2002, a statistical analysis by The Seattle Times of some 324,000 citations issued between June 1995 and May 2000 shows that while Blacks make up 9% of the city's population, they account for 18.6% of tickets given during that time.[89]

It is estimated that Blacks and Hispanics are contributing anywhere from 25 to 40 percent of the total amount of traffic fines to government coffers all across the nation. That equals $1.5 to $3 billion dollars annually. It is hard enough as it is for many Black people to make ends meet, and this type of financial penal system certainly makes the problem worse. The traffic ticket system will be one of the toughest systems to fight, as one police department after another deny any knowledge of injustice, traffic departments owe it their jobs, insurance companies profit from it, and sheriff and highway patrol departments are directly paid from its proliferation.

Many companies and industries practice deception on the American public. Combating the big corporations and the government is definitely a difficult task for some, and an impossible task for most. Wrongful policies and practices will never be overcome until BA finds a way to get smart about it, and to bring change about it. Although it is David versus Goliath all over again, history can repeat itself, if BA makes it so.

Staring Doom in the Face – Even More Afflictions

THE PREVIOUS TEN Afflictions dealt with problems that originate outside of the psyche of Black people. However, the following Afflictions are mostly self-imposed, sprinkled with some effective discriminatory mechanisms that ensure minorities have even more difficulties and disadvantages in dealing with them.

Abortion

SINCE 1973, MORE than twice as many blacks have died from abortion than from heart disease, cancer, accidents, violent crimes and AIDS combined. Blacks make up about 13 percent of the population in the United States but account for about 35 percent of the abortions. About 1,450 black infants are aborted every day in this country.

Between 1882 and 1968, 3,226 Blacks were lynched in the United States. That number is surpassed in less than three days by abortions. Three out of five pregnant Black women will abort their child.

Planned Parenthood operates the nation's largest chain of abortion clinics and almost 80 percent of its facilities are located in minority neighborhoods. About 13 percent of the American population are black, yet black women submit to over 35 percent of abortions. **Black people are the only people in America that is on the decline in population!**[92]

Abortion clearly is a contributor to the de-population issue within BA. It is a sorry state when so many people believe it to be okay to discard unborn children in such great numbers, especially when they were given the chance to live.

Autism

THERE ARE OVER 1.5 million Americans affected by Autism Spectrum Disorder (ASD). An estimated 50 children are diagnosed with Autism everyday. Autism affects black children at about the same rate as others, at a rate of about 3.4 per 1,000 persons. But there are some areas of concern with this Affliction. Some researchers think that the rate of Autism may be increasing, while at the same time feeling that the current estimates may be too conservative.

Black autistic children receive more misdiagnoses than White children. Black children are more likely to be misdiagnosed as having organic psychoses, mental retardation, or selective mutism. Studies also show that Black children with autism are diagnosed nearly two years after children of all other ethnic groups. Another concern of note is that Black parents may be more concerned than White parents about the consequences of reporting their child's behavioral problems. A recent study suggested that under identical conditions in the home, Black children are more likely than Whites to be taken away from their parents.[93]

There is an environmental factor at work here also. Although researchers believe that several genes may contribute to the Autistic condition, there is also concern that viral infections and exposure to environmental chemicals play a major role also. These same environmental hazards are believed to contribute to mental retardation, ADHD, learning disabilities, and other neurological behaviors. Black children disproportionately suffer from these conditions.[94]

Of course, Contaminated Schools and The Environmental Waste Industry come to mind when talking about adverse effects on Black children due to chemicals and toxic materials.

Black Child Maltreatment

EACH YEAR 2,000 black children die at the hands of their parents and caretakers. Abuse and neglect in the home are considered one of the leading causes of death for children four years of age and younger and the largest number of child abuse fatalities is due to severe head trauma. Near fatal abuse and neglect account for more than 18,000 permanently disabled children and 142,000 serious injuries. Black children account for 12 percent of the U.S. children population, yet in some regions of the country they represent 30 to 70 percent of all reported cases of child abuse.

Historically, intervention and treatment of Black children in the child welfare system have been plagued by inequitable policies, insufficient services, and inadequate intervention.[95]

THERE ARE A number of different types of child maltreatment.

- Physical Abuse
- Neglect
- Medical Neglect
- Sexual Abuse
- Psychological Abuse
- Maltreatment

- Other Abuse
- Unknown

IN THE YEAR 2004, there were 809,582 cases of substantiated child maltreatment. Out of those, 442,340 (55%) were White, 207,476 (26%) were Black, 139,994 (17%) were Hispanic, 10,398 (1%) were American Indian, 7,676 (.9%) were Asian, and 1,968 (.2%) were Pacific Islanders.[96]

Again, and in repeat fashion, Black people endure the greatest disproportional effect in relation to a detrimental facet of society. Some research suggests that Doctors and authorities are much more likely to suspect child abuse in minority children with certain injuries than in white children with similar injuries, and that they're also far more liable to refer the case to child protection officials when treating minorities than they are when the patient is white.

Are Black children over-reported or underreported? If the reporting of child maltreatment is fairly accurate, then that, and only that, is a good thing. It is good in that at least the authorities and families become aware of what is going on in terms of abused children, yet it is terribly bad in knowing that there are so many Black children that are being abused.

Black Child Sexual Abuse

ROBIN STONE, AUTHOR of ' No Secrets No Lies', writes : "Sexual Abuse affects women's sexual choices. Survivors are more likely to engage in risky sexual behavior that leads to disease and pregnancy. In one study, 66 percent of pregnant teens reported a history of abuse, and 66 percent of all prostitutes were sexually abused as children. Sexual Abuse statistics on Blacks:

- Blacks are sexually victimized in childhood at about the same rate as Whites. In one survey, they report being more severely abused and with greater force.

- Black women were more likely to have withheld reports of attempted rape from authorities.

- Black women tended to be the victims of repeated assaults slightly more than Whites." [97]

In Los Angeles, Philadelphia, Atlanta, in cities across the United States, young Black boys are being abused and assaulted in foster homes, government-run prisons, and detention centers in a shocking national problem that nobody wants to talk about. The statistics are explosive. One out of six boys is abused before age 16, and the rates are dramatically higher in Black areas marred by systematic poverty, broken homes, high unemployment rates and sociological problems.[98]

With the hope that all sorts of Black Child Maltreatment will one day be alleviated, one must also realize that this situation stems from the same inertia of other Afflictions. Too Much Television, Radio Sell-Out, Teen Sex, Foster Care, Alcohol Advertising, Black on Black Crime and other societal realities encompassing BA happen to the extent that they do simply because BA is not protecting its children, nor loving its children enough, and because of that, BA is perishing.

Drug Addiction

- From 1993 to 2003, treatment center admissions versus the U.S. population numbers breakdown as follows: Whites – 59 percent of admissions versus 71 percent of population; Blacks – 24 percent of admissions versus 12 percent of population; Hispanics – 13 percent of admissions versus 12 percent of population.

- In 1999, alcohol or cocaine abuse accounted for almost two-thirds of the 366,000 Black treatment admissions.

- More than a decade after the introduction of crack cocaine, 14 percent of all adult female admissions to substance treatment centers were for the primary use of crack cocaine. About 58 percent were Black, 32 percent were White, and 5 percent were Hispanic.

- More than 120,000 admissions to substance abuse treatment centers in 2000 were homeless at the time of admission. Blacks were most likely to be admitted for crack cocaine (37%), alcohol (37%) and opiates (15%).[99]

Crack cocaine seems to dominate this statistical forum. If BA could rid its communities of the crack effect, then its families and communities can become stronger.

This is why, regardless of sentencing inequities and other drug dealer concerns that bother some folks, BA needs to rid its communities of crack cocaine and drug dealers. You see there are many individuals that have never been unjustly or too harshly sentenced to a prison term for selling crack cocaine. Why? The answer is because they have never chosen to sell crack cocaine. It is that simple. Others need to make the same choice.

Homelessness

WHILE REPRESENTING ONLY 12% of the U.S. population, African-Americans make up about 40% of the homelessness population.[100]

The National Law Center on Homelessness and Poverty estimates some 3 million men, women, and children will be homeless for at least some part of 2002 (and the years to come).

Homosexuality

THE 2000 U.S. Census reported that there are 1,202,418 gay individuals in America. When that figure of 1,202,418 gay people is multiplied by the percent makeup of Black Americans in America of 13 percent, we now have 156,314 Black Gay Americans.[101]

So, what's the fuss? Okay. First of all, it is unholy. Second, it is the leading cause of the spread of HIV/AIDS amongst Black people. Third, The Center for Disease Control reported that a new five-city study found that 46% of all Black men who sleep with men are HIV positive.[102]

Illiteracy

THE 1965 ELEMENTARY and Secondary Education Act was intended to allow teachers to quickly identify and assist children who needed extra assistance in school. The result was the creation of Chapter I classes (classes of six to ten students).Ten years later, Congress passes the Individuals with Disabilities Education Act, commonly referred to as Special Education. It is surprising that today four million of the five million Special Education students in our schools have no mental or physical disabilities. About 2.5 million of those are in the Learning Disabled category that by definition, are students with average or above-average intelligence who –for some reason—can't read.

Rolls show that nearly half of Special Education and Chapter I students are in grades six through twelve. Though overall school population are 70 percent White, 12 percent Black, and 13 percent Hispanic, the combined enrollment in these programs are 58 percent White, 25 percent Black, and 11 percent Hispanic.

IN 1930, 20 percent of Blacks over age 14 could not read. By 1990, 44 percent of Blacks over age 14 could not read.[103]

By tabulating the rate of an additional 6 percent per decade since 1930, by the year 2000 some 50 percent of Blacks over age 14 will not be able to read and some 56 percent of Blacks over age 14 will not be able to read by the year 2010.

Data from the 1998 National Assessment of Educational Progress (NAEP) show not only the often-cited fact that 41 percent of fourth grade boys and 35 percent of fourth grade girls read below the basic level, but also reveal disturbing facts about high school youths. For instance, in 8th grade, at a time when all students are expected to be able to acquire information through the reading of textbooks and other materials, 47 percent of Black, 46 percent of Hispanic, and 39 percent of American Indian 8th graders and 43 percent of Black, 36 percent of Hispanic, and 35 percent of American Indian 12th graders read below the basic level.

APPROXIMATELY 1.4 MILLION students drop out of school between grades 9 and 12. Achievement varies among ethnicities and economic classes, with large differences between whites versus Latinos and African Americans. A majority of incoming ninth graders in high-poverty urban schools read two to three years below grade level.

Reading disabilities persist over time – they do not go away. Research has indicated that as many as 74 percent of children with early reading disabilities have reading deficits at follow-up several years later. There is also evidence that some successful early readers develop substantial difficulties with reading at older ages. Thus, research illustrates that the long-term implications of low literacy levels among pre-adolescents and adolescents are serious.

Many high school graduates enter college unprepared in reading. Approximately 25 percent require remedial reading courses. In community colleges, that number ranges from 40 to 60 percent of freshmen, and 25 percent of these students leave school without America graduating. Many drop out because they cannot read well enough to do the course work. About 56 percent of Hispanics, African Americans, and students with disabilities do not finish with a diploma four years after they start.[104]

If Black people who cannot read would only learn to read, their ability to curb the affects of many of the Mortality Metrics and Afflictions would be significant. As it stands right now, those who cannot read have to depend on television, radio, and other people as a way to ascertain information. To be able to read at will about health issues, mortality, education, finance, usury, politics, and so on would be so empowering for those who cannot read. As it stands now, the inability to read is proving to be deadly.

With statistics showing that upwards of 80% of juveniles and prison inmates are illiterate, it is easy to conclude that Black school systems are breeding grounds for future prison inmates, with Privatized Prisons being amongst the biggest benefactors. Piecemeal tactics, strategies and tactics will not work. Change is definitely needed in the form of a total and immediate transformation of school systems that serve BA.

Missing Persons

OF THE NEARLY 47,600 active adult cases tracked by the FBI as of the beginning of May, 53 percent were men and 29 percent (13,804) are black. (About 12 percent of the U.S. population is black, Census data show.) About 62 percent of those missing are white, but that figure includes Hispanics. This category comprises a large number of people that probably should be added to the death tolls, but it is not 'official' yet. In all, there are more than 100,000 active files on missing adults and children currently tracked by the Federal Bureau of Investigation.[105]

Pornography

PORNOGRAPHY BROUGHT IN $57.0 billion revenue worldwide. $12.0 billion of this is US revenue, more than all combined revenues of all professional football, baseball and basketball franchises or the combined revenues of ABC, CBS, and NBC (6.2 billion). $2.5 of the $12 billion is related to internet porn.

Pornography has a very deep and serious affect on children. There are 100,000 websites that offer illegal child pornography. Child pornography generates $3 billion annually. 90% of 8-16 year olds have viewed porn online (most while doing homework). Average age of first internet exposure to pornography is 11 years old. Largest consumer of internet pornography is the 12 – 17 year age group.[106]

As I was unable to ascertain statistics that relate to the race and gender makeup of this industry, a guesstimate would say that we are most likely amply, if not overly, represented to the point that it would sound off alarms, as is the case of almost every statistical category within this book. The situation of the disproportionate numbers of Black children in foster care and Black missing persons also lends credence to that assumption.

Prostitution

FORTY PERCENT OF street prostitutes are women of color. Fifty-five percent of those arrested are women of color. Eighty-five percent of prostitutes sentenced to jail are women of color. In addition, one million women and girls work as prostitutes. 500,000 to 1,200,000 children are involved in child prostitution.[107]

Redlining

REDLINING IS THE practice of denying or increasing the cost of services, such as banking or insurance to residents of certain areas. In the United States, the practice is illegal when the criteria are based on race, religion, gender, familial status (if there are children in a family), disability, or ethnic origin. ....billions of dollars in mark-up costs or not allowed altogether to purchase homes, insurance policies, and the like.

School Dropouts

HIGH SCHOOL DROPOUT rates in the year 2000 are as follows: Whites – 6.9%; Blacks – 13.1%; Hispanics – 27.8%. The high school dropout rates are greatest in cities versus other localities, and is highest in the West and South. This is one of the only areas where Blacks do not fare the absolute worse amongst other groups of people. It is my estimation that the language barrier has a lot to do with the Hispanic dropout problem.[108]

Smile

DENTAL DISEASE IS a "silent epidemic" of oral diseases afflicts the nation's most vulnerable populations -- its children, elderly and many minorities. Just one-quarter of U.S. children and adolescents suffer 80 percent of all cases of decay in permanent teeth. An estimated 4 million to 5 million children have dental problems severe enough to impair their ability to eat, sleep and learn.

Many people would love nothing more than to flash a big, beautiful smile. However, this is extremely difficult for many, as eighty-five percent of Medicaid insurance recipients no longer receive service. Dental disease is the most prevalent disease in our society, as it is five times more prevalent than asthma. And the sad part is that it is 95% to 85% preventable.[109]

- Tooth decay (dental caries) is the most common chronic disease of childhood. For example, 5 times more frequent than asthma.
- Tooth decay interferes with routine activities in millions of children living in poverty. The suffering of these children includes chronic toothache, searing pain from dental abscesses, disfigured smiles, dysfunctional speech, and eating difficulties.
- Over 51,000,000 school hours are lost each year to dental related illness. Poor children suffer almost 12 times more restricted

activity days than children from higher income families.
- The high cost of health care virtually prohibits impoverished families from receiving quality dentistry.[110]

Unemployment & Union Membership

FOR A WHILE in the 1980's, one out of every four Black workers was a union member; now it is closer to one in seven. This helps to explain why blacks are doing worse than any other group in the current recovery. Overall, in 2004, union membership fell by 304,000, and blacks accounted for 55 percent of that drop, according to the Bureau of Labor Statistics, even though whites outnumbered blacks six to one in unions (12.4 million to 2.1 million).[111]

Usury Law Discrimination

RACE AND GENDER discrimination pose problems for minorities in the housing, cars, and employment markets, to name a few. Both the purchase price for homes and cars and the financing of these items have been affected by the practice of consumer law discrimination. In fact, a 1997 survey revealed that 86% of African Americans believed that they were treated differently in retail stores on the basis of their race and a 1999 Gallup poll reported that 50% of black men believed they had been subjected to race discrimination while shopping, dining out, using public transportation, at work, or with police

First, we found that discriminatory behavior results in either an outright denial or a degradation of the products and services the customer seeks. Second, our analysis revealed that discriminatory behavior can be either overt or subtle. Overt discrimination is obvious and direct whereas subtle discrimination is more ambiguous and indirect. Third, discriminatory behavior can betray an individual's belief that consumers of color are predisposed to criminality. These beliefs result in billions of dollars in mark-ups of both prices and finance charges.[112]

If you think that this is not a big deal, then just remember that many American families live paycheck to paycheck, often in the red, and this especially true for Black family units and senior citizens. The difference between six percent interest and eighteen to twenty-four percent interest can amount to a couple hundred dollars more per month, depending on what is financed, and this is huge. Usury Discrimination, as well as all the other Killer Industries and Systems, definitely contributes to inter-generational poverty in Black communities.

Other Afflictions

THERE ARE STILL other crippling Afflictions that disproportionately affect Black people. Afflictions such as deaths due to kidney disease, multiple sclerosis, tuberculosis, burglary, robbery, violent-assault, rape, alcohol addiction and gang involvement, with even more Afflictions not mentioned in this book. Blacks have lost, and continue to lose, an incomprehensible sum of people to the powerful Quality of Life Mortality Metrics and Afflictions.

A Startling Statistic to Ponder

IN AFRICA, 23 million HIV-positives now generate per year about 75,000 AIDS cases, or 1 AIDS case per 300 HIV-positives. **But in the U.S., 0.9 million HIV-positives now generate per year about 45,000 AIDS cases or 1 AIDS case per 20 HIV-positives. Thus the AIDS risk of an American is about 15-times higher than that of an African!** Do you still think that the message of condom use is working?[113]

Diminishing Returns – The TFR Theory

MR. BEN WATTENBERG is the author of "*The Birth Dearth*", and "*Fewer*", with both books discussing the depopulation of the Earth. He takes a look at the "Total Fertility Rate," or TFR. Simply put, the TFR represents the average number of children born per woman over the course of her childbearing years. If the average woman in a given country bears three children, the TFR for that country is 3.0. The "replacement" level in modern countries is a TFR of 2.1 children per woman. This is the number of children that are required to be born to "replace" a population.

The TFR of the Less Developed Countries (LDCs) averaged 6.0 children per woman as recently as 1965-1970. In the 2000-2005 time frame, the TFR in the LDCs has fallen to 2.9 children per woman.

The countries that qualify a LDCs are China and India, the two most populous nations in the world. China's rate has fallen to 1.8 children per woman. Other LDCs are all of Latin America, Africa, an Asia (with the exceptions of Japan, Australia, an New Zealand). Southern Europe is at 1.32 children per woman, South America's TFR is at 2.45 and falling quite rapidly.

The More Developed Countries (MDCs) TFRs have fallen below replacement level as they averaged out at 1.85 children per woman. America's TFR is 2.01; Canada's TFR is 1.5; Europe's TFR is 1.38; Germany's TFR is 1.35; and Russia's TFR is an almost unbelievable 1.1.

IN 1965, THE Black TFR in America was 3.8. By the early 1980s it was 3.2. Today the TFR for Blacks in America is 2.04. As is the case for most other countries, the TFR for Black America is on the decline. The TFR is a natural indicator for the forecasting of population growth. Per Mr. Wattenburg's expert opinion, the global population will not go much over 8 billion people and then begin contracting. The global population is now at approximately 6.5 billion.[114]

According to Mr. Wattenburg's theory, the TFR of BA is shrinking, and this means that there will be a **natural** depopulation of Black people, just as there will be amongst all races of people the world over. This natural depopulation of Black people, when combined with the almost unnatural depopulation due to the Quality of Life Mortality Metric and Afflictions, further posit that the future for Blacks looks extremely dismal, and together they both basically guarantee and extinction of BA.

Accurate Information

TO HAVE ACCURATE and truthful information also plays an important role in getting a grip on the many problems facing BA. The following report came out of the 11/25/02 issue of Multi-Channel News, which is a magazine dedicated to the cable television industry. 'At a recent International AIDS Conference in Barcelona, Spain it was reported that in the United States, an estimated 91 percent of African-American, 75 percent of Hispanics, and 74 percent of Whites ages 16-22 years old are infected with the HIV/AIDS virus and don't even know it.'

So, what is wrong with that report? Well, back in Part I, the USA Today newspaper is shown to have reported that 'only 25% of Blacks do not know that they are infected with HIV.' This is an important discrepancy, and if it can happen in this instance, then it can happen in other instances.

Accurate information is crucial in that the degree of concern and the accompanying public reaction to a given problem is tied directly to what is reported in relation to that problem. The degree of concern and public reaction will be much different if it is reported that 1,000 Blacks are infected with HIV/AIDS versus the reporting of 100,000 Blacks having HIV/AIDS. Because of this potential quandary, I choose to maintain the 'glass half empty' attitude concerning BA's problems. I choose to react in a manner conducive to the worst-case scenarios, with the option to accept the 'good news' of a more favorable scenario later. The objective is to not be caught off-guard with inaccurate information concerning a matter so important as that facing BA.

BA JUST MAY be a medical aberration or two away from sending both BA and America into sheer panic and utter despair? Imagine an announcement goes out saying that a mistake was made in terms of reporting HIV/AIDS facts in BA. This announcement states HIV/AIDS carriers are spreading the virus at a rate that is three times faster than originally thought. How would that announcement affect BA? How would the country react? Would there be widespread panic? Would Blacks be purged from American society? Imagine the situation if three to five million of Blacks were infected with HIV/AIDS. That would amount to 10 to 16 percent of the Black race, and 1 to 2 percent of the American population. Who would want to share bathrooms, or get in the same pool, as Blacks? There are already a significant number of people with that mindset already. If BA does not find a way to change its fate, it will definitely be looking at these types of scenarios in the next few decades.

WHAT I BA does not want to become is an old folk tale that people a hundred years from now will tell. The tale would start like this: " Once upon a time Black people walked the earth..........." and then you see an ugly picture of me to the left of 'Cro-Magnon Man', with a name like, 'Blackus Homey Sapien'. And you don't want to see that because, guess what, your picture might be right next to mine.

The Gloom of it All

AS SHOWN BACK on page 11, in the year 2000, the U.S. Census shows an addition of 608,000 black people added to the U.S. population. When a total of 126,000 immigrants are subtracted from the 608,000 people originally reported, the numbers show that 482,000 black people were added to the BA population. At that point, another 328,000 that died due to the Quality of Life Mortality Metrics, leaving a paltry 153,000 people that were added to the BA population from the year 1999 to the year 2000.

It is a beautiful thing indeed to add 153,000 new lives to the Black race and to America. One would like to think that the chance for success is great. The reality is that as time rolls on, it not be easy to succeed by any means, and the prospects for success will actually worsen over time, one day at a time, for those 153,00 newly added angels. Their prospects to have prosperous and fruitful lives will decline with virtually every breath they take, and this is based on facts.

The Quality of Life Mortality Metrics and the powerful Afflictions will make sure that the vast majority of those 153,000 people will either die or fall victim to life-crippling conditions. When coupled with Mr. Wattenburg's TFR theory, the conditions for race-replenishment are bleak. The sweet fruit of life such as good educations, strong families, good health, entrepreneurship, employment with medical benefits and simple happiness are just some of the desirables that will be extremely difficult to obtain for the average Black citizen in America.

BECAUSE OF THE long and varied list of problems that BA faces, and the continued proliferation of our Latino brothers and sisters, there will continue to be a shift of power amongst minorities. The year 2000 net population increase of 153,000 people to BA pales in comparison to the estimation of the United States Immigration Office of as much as 500,000 illegal immigrants that come to America each year, and of course that figure does not include those Latinos that come to America legally. There will be a continued shift of power in terms of political clout, jobs, entrepreneurial growth, educational opportunities and synergies of all sorts. This is yet another situation that BA should not fall asleep on. This notice of transfer of power is not to speak ill of Latino America, but just to make a point of what is at stake in regards to the future of BA.

In closing, let me state again that racism still exists today. Those that would rob, steal, manipulate, and even kill do so today behind the chambers of governments and the walls of corporations. Which institution is worse? Both, as they are one in the same, with the main difference being their respective form of business, ala corporation versus government entity. They both do provide services, but in their course of doing business people are hurt physically, mentally and financially, as well as the environment, inner city school systems, and the future of BA. The Killer Systems & Industries are doing a number on BA.

Remember that all colors of people are manipulated by the processes and systems in place in society today, as racism targets probably the poor more so than anything else. It just so happens that Blacks are more inept and unprepared than others in this battle. Because of educational dis-achievement, BA has not enough specialty doctors, attorneys, environmental specialists, and professionals of all types to put up the good fight. This is how BA contributes to its own mess. BA has to fix its own schools. BA has to address its own Black on Black crime dilemma. BA has to address its own illiteracy, health, and voting issues. Foster care, physical health and education have all deteriorated to varying levels of embarrassment and dysfunction. And possibly the most important areas are the decision-making processes, personal choices and behaviors of BA youth. They all must be addressed if BA is to stop staring doom in the face.

WITH ALL OF that said, is there anything BA can do to put itself in a position of confidence and control? How about get educated!

PART V

THE PLAN

PERSERVERANCE

SHE DONNED HER CAP. ADJUSTED IT just so. Then Grace Strobel joined her classmates in the processional and walked to the podium to collect her Metropolitan State University diploma.

LIKE EVERY GRADUATE, she overcame the obstacles of exams and balancing her life with schoolwork. But the 77-year old Anoka woman stood out for more than her age. Two years into her psychology program, Strobel's vision began to fail. She developed Maculae degeneration – a condition that results in the loss of vision in the center of the eye. Despite not being able to read letters smaller than five inches, she maintained her 4.0 GPA.

"IT WAS NOT hard work and I loved doing my papers and every page I turned in." After putting her former husband and four children through college, Strobel decided in 1999 that it was her turn. "Every time I drove by the University of Minnesota, I felt exhilarated," she said. And now she is a shining star for all to see.

(www.anokacountyunion.com/2002/may/30strobel.html)

A New Beginning

THERE IS A core of problems within BA from which all other problems emanate. To borrow from the classic baseball movie 'Field of Dreams', "If you eliminate the problems, prosperity will come". The removal of these core problems will allow for the positive reform that BA desperately needs. There are three doors that must be unlocked, and once unlocked, BA will be free to proceed to greener pastures. By way of fortune, BA holds the keys to the doors of its own self-imposed prison. Understand that behind these doors lie common sense, purpose, passion and vision, all necessary tools to remove the shackles of aimlessness, materialism, and selfishness. These tools will help build a new solution-based infrastructure that will allow BA to rise above its present cellar-dwelling state and ultimately soar like eagles.

The acceptance and recognition that a problem actually exists is necessary before a solution has a chance to be found, as denial is the precursor to inaction. Much of BA has given up hope, and this shows in the fact that BA's living conditions get worse day by day. A great percentage of BA is guilty of inaction, and to an extent this is understandable, when taken into consideration that the problems in Black communities are so numerous, so inter-connected, and have been around for so long that most Black people have simply become accustomed to them, immune to them, and thus accepting of them. The tendency to blame the others, as in the White man, is the soother of any guilt the conscience could ever muster up. The quick-money fix of drug trafficking, self-medication with drugs and alcohol, and pimpin' women all serve as unhealthy ways to deal with BA's problems, and only amplify them while making the elimination of them even more difficult. But before the solution stage can ever be reached, there must be a broad acceptance and recognition of the depth of BA's problems, and then action is required.

THERE ARE THREE fundamental elements of a society in particular that bring about positive change in communities: the creation of new jobs, the passage of new and effective legislation, and strong, visionary effective school systems. These three components allow communities to be strong and vibrant, and can positively affect residents, communities, families, schools, property values, and community investment. However, without jobs, effective laws that work for the people, and effective school systems, those same attributes sidestep Black communities like Barry Sanders avoiding would-be tacklers on the football field. The results are a people consumed of hopelessness and disrupted communities filled with desperation. When Black communities do not thrive by way of the three fundamental societal elements of new jobs, legislation and schools, they then become sitting ducks for detrimental external elements such as the Killer Systems and Industries and the other Afflictions.

Problem Solving

THERE ARE THREE methods in which to confront and deal with problems. The first method I will call Motivational Phrasing. Motivational phrasing involves the use of motivational phrases such as "Each one, teach one", or "We must all love one another", or "It takes a village to raise a child". Motivational speakers and public leaders use phrases such as these, and sometimes make a pretty good living using them. However cool sounding they may be, motivational phrases do not save lives, and their effects are temporal at best on most people. It takes action on the part of the person or persons listening to the phrase, and with the problems BA is enduring, a lot of action.

The next problem-solving technique I refer to as Temporary Intervention Measures. These measures serve their purpose well and are adequate in bringing smiles to the faces of their recipients and purpose in their lives sometimes for a considerable length of time. There are others that are over-rated, ineffective and do little more than bring media attention to its target cause. Private foundations, tutoring programs for students, sports programs, church activities, counseling services are all examples of effective intervention with awesome intentions. And yet, as warm and as well received as their services may be, their effects still do not last forever. They do provide long lasting memories though. However, marches, rallies, panel discussions and the like will not work if there are no accompanying actions behind them. However, they can bring attention to the given cause. How fleeting the attention is correlated to the action plan behind the Temporary Intervention Measure. Riots are destructive. I know of no lasting effect of the million-man march. The church is the church and cannot take the lead in every single matter BA is engaged in. The search for solutions must be ratcheted up a notch.

The third problem-solving technique is Action Plan Implementation. This is where the treasure is. It is here where an actual plan is formulated, the people get prepared to put in the work, and the mission can be subsequently carried out. Actual Plan Implementation is precisely what BA needs, a clear plan that will allow BA to navigate itself into a more favorable co-existence on planet earth. That can all change now. A new, comprehensive vision will now be put before all of BA, one that can certainly create a line of winners and change its course of history, and one that everyone, at all levels, can be a part of.

BEHIND THE THREE doors mentioned earlier are three areas needing total and dedicated reform. These three areas are: Public School Reformation, Community Action, and Pursuit of Educational Excellence. All three are extremely crucial components to the survival of BA. They are the targets of the rebuilding process that must be undertaken so that BA might be renewed. There are simple and practical ways to bring about this reform within the three components. Once commitment to these changes is made, BA will manifest itself from the bottom of society, which is where it is now, all the way to the Promised Land, which is where it wants to be. A practical and possible action plan is the vehicle that can drive BA to the three doors. One by one the doors can be opened, and when this is done, the process to make the critical changes that BA needs can begin.

Community Action

When internal problems such as gun violence and drug trafficking are thrown into the mix, the path to community success becomes exponentially more difficult to navigate.

But with a national plan of recovery, the ship can be righted. Addressing the disruptions to the learning process in public schools, providing better menu items for the children while they are in school, and restoring pride and value to the educational process all are beacons of light for BA. Remember, the goal is to become a more educated, success prone, and visionary people. And yet still, it doesn't stop there.

Next comes the task of cleaning up the neighborhoods. Certain changes have to be made in communities that result in more opportunity, increased safety, and pride. Removing anti-role models, drugs, and gun violence from Black communities should be the top priority of BA. Replacing the images of drug dealers, pimps, and hustlers with a fresh, new push for college attendance and educational achievement by both young and old should be high on the list also. And finally, the creation of new Black entrepreneurs in Black communities is necessary as well. Black children deserve an environment that will decrease their odds of becoming zeroes and increase their chances of becoming heroes. Making the lives of the citizens of Black communities better through the creation of laws and the utilization of resources can help bring about the social change BA so desperately needs and deserves. Alleviation of the pain and suffering that most Black Americans take to bed with them night after night is the end, and pro-action by BA is the means.

Urban Law

MARTIAL LAW IS a temporary government and control by military authorities of a territory or state, when war or overwhelming public disturbance makes the civil authorities of the region unable to enforce its law. In most U.S. states, martial law may be proclaimed when deemed necessary for the public's safety.

There is a need to have the law better enforced in Black communities from the negative elements within. A spin-off of Martial Law, called Urban Law, is the type of new law that can better allow Black communities the ability to protect itself from the throngs of gunplay, guns and violence. Urban Law is a way to create new and effective legislation, and is an Action Plan Technique. Urban Law would provide a tool in which to clean up the streets, and send a message that, yes, Black lives and communities are important; that Blacks indeed want safe communities; and that Blacks truly care about both their and their children's futures. Leaving police departments to deal with the problems in a business as usual manner is reactive, and is not getting the job done. Proactive changes are required, and new measures and attitudes that are capable of bringing about positive results are high priorities.

Martial Law is ordered whenever civil disruption *first begins,* regardless of whom the perpetrators are, be it war, peacetime, or national disaster. When Hurricane Katrina destroyed the city of New Orleans in the late summer of 2005, Martial Law was declared and the National Guard was called to stop looting and restore order in business and residential districts of New Orleans. In the case of New Orleans, we are talking about looting. In the case of Black communities, we are talking about saving lives! I would like to think that saving a person's life is still more important than preventing the theft of a television. New Orleans was protecting its business interests. In similar fashion, Black communities need to protect its citizens by fighting against the many problems that exist within its own communities. Urban Law can do that.

Black communities suffer incessantly from killing and drug dealing. Killing in Black communities rocks, and the drug dealing seems to never stop. The two of these evils combine to form a plague of sort that pushes away business investors and government dollars. Up to this point, BA has dealt with these problems through tolerance and funeral attendance. However, enough is enough, and courageous change must now find its way as Black people slowly become more and more scarce.

URBAN LAW WOULD work like this: According to their size, cities would have Urban Law activated after a certain number of deaths were to occur. For example, take my hometown of Saginaw, Michigan. After a predetermined number of say, five murders occur, Urban Law would kick in. There would be a curfew enacted. After the curfew hours, cars would be randomly searched with the intention of only looking for guns and drugs. If drugs were found, certain pre-set amounts would be established as personal use quantities, and the drugs would simply be destroyed, right on the spot, with no arrest. If the amounts of drugs exceeded the 'personal use' amount, then local drug possession laws would go into effect. If guns were found, local laws would also go into effect, as this is the intent of Urban Law, to get guns and drugs off of the streets.

There would not be truckloads of people hauled off to jail as a result of Urban Law. Any arrests would only occur as a result of the possession of guns, quantity-specific drug possession, or existing warrants that are of a violent nature, such as homicide or violent assault.

Only the driver would be asked for identification, and only the driver would have his/her name ran through the system by the police, but everyone in the car would be searched, including the car itself. The only way others in the car would have their names ran through the system or asked for identification would be if guns or drugs were found in their possession. Pre-existing violations such as child support warrants, outstanding traffic violations, suspended licenses, etc. would result in the handing out of another citation. Any new citation that is not responded to by the citizen that receives it would have to deal with the court systems.

Another aspect to this new law would be a cessation of plea bargain. Plea-bargaining basically tells criminals that, "regardless of your crime or how much damage you have inflicted, your punishment will be minimal. Your rights are just as important as those of the victim". This would not be the case with Urban Law violators. There would be no plea-bargaining under Urban Law, only maximum penalties handed down. In the long run, crime and murder would significantly drop. Ideally, as long as a person is not illegally handling guns or trafficking drugs, that person would not have a problem with

Urban Law. However, those who were to realize newfound protection and less violence and drugs in their communities would experience victory.

The intent of Urban Law is to get guns and drugs out of Black communities, and to do this, BA has to become much more proactive, versus remaining reactive. As it stands right now, those who break the law by use of guns and drugs eventually do their time, and this is sometimes followed by an uproar concerning disproportionate prison sentencing and 'more Blacks being in prison than college', which statistics testify to. This 'double dose' problem publicly overlooks those many lives of law abiding Black citizens that are lost. It does not have to be this way any longer. The loss of lives can be mitigated through a system of zero-tolerance for the bad guys. By getting tough on criminals in Black communities, the lives of many outstanding and promising Blacks can be saved. The alternative is to continue to let others handle the business of BA. That has been the method up to this point, and clearly does not work.

'I'm Shot'

THOSE WERE THE last words of nine-year-old Marquise Hudson,
who was shot in the chest and the leg from gunfire of a mysterious
perpetrator that showed up on the doorsteps of the home of Marquise's
aunt and uncle. Within seconds, Marquise was dead. There were also
other children were present in the house whom fortunate. In addition,
Marquise had a sister and two other brothers. Because of a vicious act
by a stranger with a gun, the precious lives of all these children have
been violently changed.[121]

Another story reports the sister of freshman guard Jessie Sapp of
the 2006 NCAA Basketball Champion Florida Gators shot in the back
of the head while at a playground in East Harlem, New York as the
Gators were en route to winning the National Championship. Another
thirteen-year old girl was shot as well. Recent times have seen a shooting
at Vanderbilt University, five Duquesne University basketball players
shot, and a University of Miami football player, Bryan Pata, shot and
killed. The list is long, furious, and unimpeded, and this is so primarily
because BA is not taking care of its own business. In BA, no one is
immune from death by the bullet as infants, famous actors, college and
professional athletes, men, women, teens, and practically every category
of citizenry seem to endure shocking deaths by gunfire. And it happens
often, and no one is given a pass.

The level of lawlessness that prevails in Black communities is
appalling, and there is no need to allow the madness to continue on until
it is too late to make a meaningful change. On the other hand, there
is a tremendous need to take additional measures to save BA citizens
from excessive criminal and violent behavior, and nothing epitomizes
that more than the loss of a life such as that of young Marquise, or the
gruesome shooting incident involving Mr. Sapp's sister, as well as the
thousands of other shooting incidents across the country that rob BA of
any sense of control and self-respect. As the thought of Marquise's last
words cause us all to ponder, there will hopefully be a mass conclusion
that enough is indeed enough.

Time to Get Tough

URBAN LAW REPRESENTS instituting tough measures in tough times. The results would be fewer deaths, fewer drug dealers on the streets, fewer drug addicts, and safer neighborhoods. Urban Law would instill a sense of pride amongst citizens and city officials, and make the streets safer for law enforcement officers. Urban Law would open doors to much-needed financial investment in Black communities, which would result in more success-conducive environments for Black children, thereby increasing their chances to lead fuller, more productive lives. How many George Washington Carvers, Martin Luther Kings, or Carol Mae Jemisons has BA lost to gun violence? How many lives and families have been destroyed due to drugs? The sum answer to these questions is staggering, and also one that BA should not dread to answer when asked.

Getting tough with criminals is the best way to put a stop to criminal behavior. As long as criminals are tolerated or punished lightly, they're not going anywhere. It is for that reason that criminals flourish in Black communities. What would happen if ten Black men attempted to set up a drug business, or hang out with guns, on the White side of town? The citizens would take action, and the attempted drug business would be squashed in a New York minute. What would happen if ten Blacks attempted to do the same thing on the Black side of town? Well, just look around. It is already there, and many of the individuals that are selling drugs or brandishing guns are not stopped until they take someone down with them, no matter whom it is. Black communities can do better than that. Black communities deserve better than that. Black communities can become safe and protected the same way any other community are safe and protected. A law such as Urban Law can help facilitate that protectionism.

Getting Tough on Criminals

AN INVESTIGATIVE STORY by 'Al Roker Investigates' highlights an example of changes made together by community members and local law enforcement that decided to get tough on crime and bring about positive change. In Durham, North Carolina, an escalation in gang activity prompted citizens and officials to say enough is enough. After realizing that 60% of all murder suspects are gang members, they put a plan in effect. In conjunction with Professor David Kennedy, The Head of the Center for Crime Prevention and Control, the city of Durham took action. The following highlights the actions taken:

- They gathered intelligence on gang members for a period of three to six months
- They made a list of all known gang members and identified the worst ones
- The police make an effort to give them a citation for any and all offenses that they could
- They informed the gang members that the revolving door of justice was about to stop
- Prosecutors through the book at these gang members every chance they got with lengthy sentences
- Police and community resources were utilized and gang members were offered rewards for good behavior. Gang members were now being targeted for success. At the same time, they informed gang members that any future jail visits would be one-stop visits

Within a year, there was a 56% reduction in violent crime in West End. The neighborhoods were a lot safer, and the children were a lot happier.[122]

Tulia, Texas

FROM 1999 TO 2000, Tulia, Texas, a town of approximately 5,000, went on an arrest spree of its residents for alleged drug dealing. In all, 46 people were indicted, and all received swift convictions. The first defendant was given 90 years for allegedly selling 3.5 grams of cocaine. The others received sentences ranging from 20 to 300 years for selling approximately the same amount of cocaine, which generally was termed in street language as an 'eight ball' of powdered cocaine.

All 46 people were arrested unwashed, half-dressed, hair uncombed, in front of family and friends. In every single case, there was no wire worn by the undercover agent, there were no eye-witnesses, there was no back-up, and there were no tape recordings of any conversations, there were no drugs found on their persons when arrested, there were no guns found upon arrest, there was no money on their persons upon arrest, and none were caught in possession of cocaine. All 46 were arrested and found guilty based on the testimony of just one undercover officer.

One of the defendants picked up cans for a living, and had no electricity at home. He was accused of selling two grams of powdered cocaine. Another man who had never sold or used drugs was accused of selling a few grams of powdered cocaine and was sentenced to 29 years as a first time offender. Yet another man was accused of selling a few grams of cocaine to this same undercover cop, even though he was completely misidentified. The crime report pertaining to his arrest was conveniently changed so that the suspect description now matched the man arrested. Still another person, this time a woman, was accused of selling 3.5 grams of powdered cocaine to this same undercover officer, even though she was at a bank 350 miles away at the time of the alleged buy and sell. All of the defendants were black, with the exception of a few others who had ties to the black community. The arresting officer was later proved to be a liar and a racist.

Early in the year 2003 all 46 Tulia residents had their cases reviewed by the Texas Appellate Court and were released on bond. Later that same year, the Texas Governor signed a pardon against all 46 defendants. In all, this ordeal took more than three years to make right.[123]

THE TWO CITIES of Durham, North Carolina and Tulia, Texas are examples of how a city and its citizens can take the initiative to clean up their streets. However, it must be noted that the two cases are polar opposites of each other ethically, socially, and legally. One city took action for all the right reasons, and the other city for all the wrong ones. Regardless, the lesson is that the legal systems of both municipalities threw the book at its defendants, and got the results it wanted. In the more legally correct case of Durham, the measures undertaken worked, and rightfully so.

There has to be a love of family and community that compel people to do whatever it takes to make their lives safe. It also takes a concerted effort by parents, residents, local governments, teachers, businesses, and everyone else that has a stake in BA to make it happen.

The rewards can be likened to a heaven-on-Earth existence for BA, and an existence that BA has very little experience with.

One of the beautiful elements of the Durham example is that there were no excuses by local government as to what they could not do, just action to get it done. When you hear justification of non-action, such as the need for money to pay for judges and prosecuting attorneys that specialize in gun crimes or gang crimes, be assured that the officials involved have little or no desire to help its constituents. Oftentimes the goal is to get their bread buttered, and sometimes it may be to leave the status quo untouched for other unknown reasons. In any event, it is what it is, and what is most important is that BA no longer intends to allow hard-core criminals to feast on its communities.

URBAN LAW PROVIDES a sort of "Extreme Makeover: Urban Law Edition". Keep in mind that there are homes for people who sell drugs and kill people, and these places are called jail and prison. Those that choose to sell drugs and kill people need to be shown their way home. There are places for children, families, schools and businesses that decide to strive for success and achievement, and these places are called residences, schools, and communities. Those people that choose to strive for success and achievement deserve to have a place to call home also. Just think, if Martin Luther King was growing up today in the inner-city, he not only would have a good chance of being killed by a Black person, but also an even greater chance of being derailed by drugs, gangs, internet pornography, violence, and other vices. In the fifties and sixties, the enemy stood out and was easily recognized. It is not so in Urban America today. Today, the enemy often goes by the names 'friend' and 'neighbor'.

Gun, Drug, & Gang Hotlines

LIKE BURGERS AND fries, peanut butter and jelly, and bacon and eggs, guns and drugs are popular combinations, of which many Black youth have deemed tasty. Guns and drugs play a starring role in the decimation of Black communities. The losses that accompany guns and drugs numerate like stars in the night sky. Gangs continue to proliferate, and are one of the main vessels in which guns and drugs flow.

Gun, drug, and gang hotlines can be very important in the mitigation of these vices. These hotlines are needed to serve both the school systems and Black neighborhoods. Although hotlines are nothing new, they are both simultaneously under-deployed and underused. When citizens report criminal activity, effective measures can be instituted as a means of keeping communities safe and free of guns, gangs and drugs. Citizens and police departments need to work hand in hand in combating the criminal element and hotlines act as an optional means to that end.

ART O'NEAL, CHIEF of Security for the Saginaw Public School District and a 21-year police officer/detective for the city of Saginaw, Michigan, believes that it is tantamount for law enforcement agencies to get the confidence of the communities in which they serve in order to make a difference.

Whether it's the school campuses or the various neighborhoods of the city, Art believes in a "community" approach to law enforcement. At schools, everyone, including school faculty, staff, parents, and even janitors, play important roles in curbing drug, gang, and gun activity. In the communities, parents, friends, and neighbors play those same roles in providing safety to the communities. At his schools, custodians wear radios to relay problem situations to the proper individuals, and are also trained to provide encouragement and guidance to the students.

Says Art, " When people see law enforcement doing something to bring about change, they then began to report criminal activity even more. This may bring about a 'spike' in criminal activity, but actually this activity has always been there. It just now is being reported. Now that it is being reported, something can be done, and this usually results in a decline in criminal activity in these respective communities.

Taking action across the nation with both public schools and inner city communities with a more prolific use of drug, gang, and gun hotlines will produce positive change. Moving forward, positive changes such as increased academic performance, rising property values, the gaining of respect, and prouder parents can, and will, happen. Heck, we just might see our senior citizens walking the neighborhoods and sitting on their porches again, and that, people, would be an awesome sight to see.

Who 'Dose Cities That Need Urban Law?

THERE ARE MANY cities in need of an "Extreme Makeover: Urban Law Edition". Many are familiar with these cities, and most would not be at the top of anyone's travel list. Nevertheless, these are all places of stratospheric danger levels. In order of first to worst, they are: Detroit-area, MI., New Orleans, LA., Memphis, TN., Sumter, S.C., Miami-Dade County, FL., Stockton, CA., Las Vegas, NV., Florence, SC., Hot Springs, AR., Myrtle Beach, SC., Pine Bluff, AR., Flint, MI., Saginaw, MI. (my hometown), Little Rock, AR., Tucson, AZ., Modesto, CA., Albuquerque, NM., Jackson, TN., Charlotte-area, NC., Baltimore, MD., Wichita Falls, TX., Houston, TX., Phoenix-area, AZ., Tallahassee, FL., and finally, Los Angeles County, CA.[124]

These places are the modern day Tombstones, Dodge Cities and O.K. Corrals of America. Most, if not all, have made the list by the ruthless choices and asinine behavior of a relatively small percentage of its residents. Most, if not all, of these places are hurting socially, economically, spiritually, and mortally. And most, if not all, of these inner cities receive little empathy, sympathy, or meaningful investment in its Black communities. The Red Cross could not be blamed for setting up satellite offices right in the hearts of these 'metropolis hoods'. Who can blame the casket maker for setting up shop on the sidewalks of these cities to promote his craft? These are the cities that have opened up and swallowed Blacks in large numbers, and in doing have sucked the proverbial life right out of those same communities, destroying the livelihoods, dreams, and loved ones of the families that reside in them. The viopreneurs number too many, and they have peddled death for too long. There is no need to accommodate them any longer. Their checkout time has arrived.

New Opportunities in New Communities

MAKING BLACK COMMUNITIES safer allows for new opportunities for BA. Significant and meaningful change has to be present for all to see. The prevalence of guns, drugs, and gangs in Black communities must be greatly diminished. People have a need to feel good again, and the Black pride that James Brown sang about needs to come alive. Next are the matters of capitalism, and the procurement of community investment.

And guess what? As a result of hard work and bold measures pointing towards a new destiny, the world will change its outlook on BA, and a new infrastructure can be built.

BA needs an economic renaissance. Black communities all across the country needs to be able to roll out the red carpet for new community investment, and this is something that is long overdue. BA has never achieved any sustained level of entrepreneurial achievement that has touched all of the United States zip codes. As every other ethnic community in America has its own distinct brand of entrepreneurial makeup, Black communities should be no different. As a result of making the right changes to make Black communities safer and strengthening Black schools, the climate can be right for success in regards to businesses and financial investment in Black communities.

By way of a new direction, BA can be both ready and able to build a new commercial infrastructure of viable businesses built by Black citizens from within its own communities. The practice of outsiders coming in and setting up businesses can become a thing of the past, at least on a wholesale level. BA can now able time to intelligently and loyally build and support its very own business infrastructure, accepting or rejecting services and products based on the quality provided of those services and products, and the Black entrepreneur is now reaching unparalleled levels of economic success, right in its very own communities. The infrastructure of BA will get stronger every day, and this is because crime will be significantly diminished, property values will increase, educational achievement will head north, and everything is beautiful. And this is the way it could have been all along

STATISTICS BEAR THAT Blacks do have the potential to create successful businesses. The report, "Survey of Business Owners: Black-Owned Firms: 2002," says that between 1997 and 2002, the number of Black-owned businesses in the United States rose 45 percent to 1.2 million, while the combined revenue increased 25 percent to $88.8 billion. In the Pittsburgh area alone, there 4,363 Black-owned firms in 2002, which is up 38.8 percent from 3,142 in 1997.

Both local and national figures show the greatest numbers of Black-owned businesses in the fields of health care and social assistance. Other categories with a strong presence of black-owned businesses include retail; professional, scientific and technical services; and transportation and warehousing.

New York City had more black-owned firms than any other city at 98,076, followed by Chicago (39,424), Los Angeles (25,958), Houston (21,226), and Detroit (19,530).

Among states, New York had the greatest number of black-owned firms with 129,324, followed by California (112,873), Florida (102,079), Georgia (90,461), and Texas (88,769). These five states accounted for about 44 percent of all black-owned businesses in the United States. Pennsylvania had 24,757.[125]

CRIME, DRUGS, AND guns have been prevalent in Black communities for decades, and all have played a part in the stunting of Black entrepreneurial growth. There is an enormous amount of economic potential within BA, and the amazing thing is that *this potential has always been there.* BA has always had the means to be increasingly successful business-wise in its own communities, but never the proper infrastructure in which to make it happen. And if the right measures are not taken, it never will happen. BA can canvass America with successful businesses and corporations like spreading jam across bread, if it only chooses to do so. But it's going to take change. To move forward, BA must improve its schools, clean up its neighborhoods, and create the type of social infrastructure that can breed success on all levels, be it personal, scholastic, business, or family. BA has the power to succeed.

Economic Immunity

ECONOMIC IMMUNITY PROVIDES another tool that can help to jump-start Black communities. Much like Diplomatic Immunity, which exempts both diplomatic officials and their dependents from taxation, searches, and arrests, among other things, Economic Immunity would allow individuals to invest monies to start businesses in Black communities without strict audit as to where the money came from. In other words, if money has been made in, let us say, not the most ethical of ways, then those monies can still be used to invest in the Black communities in which the people that have the money live. What this means is that although there will be no questions as to where the money came from, the new business has to be legal, of value, built in good faith, and in short, one that momma can be proud of. The person taking advantage of this new tool would be best served to leave his iniquitous past behind him, and this of course a requirement of Economic Immunity.

Economic Immunity would serve as a way for certain individuals to make a fresh start, to abstain from illegal business ventures, and instead create economic growth and jobs in their respective communities. It is a legitimate and practical component to building healthy and prosperous communities in BA. It must be remembered that in attempting to take BA where it needs to be, every little bit counts.

The Fantastically Wonderful 70's

IN RETROSPECT, THE 70's unequivocally had to be the greatest decade of all-time for Black people. There was safe radio, safe television, and safe games. The music was incredible, and will never, ever fade away from our memories. Friends seemed to be truer, and people in general were friendlier and not quite in a constant rush as people are today. Clothing styles, and hairstyles, were awesome and creative. School aged kids hustled money by buying boxes of blow-pops and selling them individually in school. The girls extracted juice out of lemons through over-sized peppermint sticks, and they just loved the over-sized dill pickles.

Before school, on weekends, no-school days, and all summer long, kids would spend the days playing football, baseball, softball, basketball, and popping wheelies and riding bikes, sharing food and drink, and generally just having good times. Summer recreation cites across the city were hours of four square, foot races, jumping rope, and playing board games. I can hear Mrs. Sidney, as if it were yesterday, calling my friend, 'Hound-dog', in for lunch or dinner by his first name, "Gradyyyyyyyy", in a funny and exaggerated fashion that still invokes laughter to this day. This was because we would play until being forced to come in and eat. Homework was not a chore, we had good relationships with our teachers, and school was both appreciated and a joy. College and professional sports would become totally integrated, thus allowing kids all over to dream of becoming the next Walt Frazier, Gale Sayers, or Frank Robinson. This made sports a little more important to us than they are to the kids today.

Of course there were those who would mess up sometimes, but that was cool too. The 'cats' that hustled selling weed did not have turf wars, and did not have nor cause all of the problems that the cocaine kingpins of today are responsible for. Drug dealers and drug addicts did not hang out in communities in the numbers that they do today. Jobs were more plentiful and more students were graduating from school.

I OFTEN TELL my children how wonderful the times were then. I tell them of my childhood friends I still have to this day, and how I love them like real brothers. I tell them that the 70's were so good to me that I would not have traded my childhood with anyone. I also play the 70's music often, hoping that there is some sort of connection that would cause them to want to know how it really felt to be a part of a truly wonderful era.

It seemed that BA was doing okay, fresh off the triumphs of the Civil Rights era and all. In hindsight, it can be seen that the gains from those triumphs have been wasted, and now BA is in a fight for its collective lives. BA appears somewhat clueless as to how to win this fight, and yet, it can be won by, among other things, taking it back to the way it used to be. The times were simpler than, versus the maddening times of today. The 80's laid the foundation for the 90's, and the 90's pushed BA to where it currently is, on the ropes, about to be knocked the you-know-what out!

The 70's provide a sort of template for success that BA can achieve. The Black social culture of today is not working, and needs to be re-evaluated, and then replaced. The system is broken, and needs to be fixed. BA needs to take it back to the way it was in that wonderful era of the 70's, when Black citizens were not mental guinea pigs to the technological gadgetry of the present time, instead relying more on brains, social skills and personality. It is not quite the novel concept, but taking it back would work miracles for BA.

Taking it Back

THE 70's. THE old frontier. A place where BA has been before. The era where old-heads thrived, and the young heads of today have only heard about. A time that was not quite captive of today's corporate behemoths with its quest to control the minds and precious time of young people.

When paralleled against the chaotic state of the new millennium, it was a tranquil time. The 70's were a fabulous, free-spirited, innocent period that represents the best of memories for many of those born into that era.

BA can get better by taking it back to the 70's. BA can boycott any 'Black' radio station that would even think about airing sex-laden and profane music for Black children to listen to. BA can take it back to the safe television days by strongly pushing for a la carte cable television options and getting the mentally destructive, sexually suggestive, shallow, materialistic television shows and channels out of Black homes. BA can take it back by ridding its homes of video game systems such as xbox, playstation, and game cube, and teach its kids how to use their time in a healthy and productive manner, with books and physical exercise, versus 'entershamement' video games that glorify guns, violence, sex, money, materialism, and inadequate personality traits. BA can take it back to when the children had to wait until Saturday to watch cartoons instead of addicting them as infants to Cartoon Network, the Disney Channel, and other 'junior varsity' television channels that graduate the children into the 'varsity' channels such as BET, MTV and VH-1.

BA can take it back to when kids would stumble across pornographic material by mistake, versus clicking a computer mouse that allows children to see as much pornography as they can, whenever they want to see it. BA can take it back to when homework was both challenging and fun, and the children would do it in groups, urging one another to stop talking so that they would be able to finish and be able to go outside to play. BA can take it back to when society and its offerings really was 'all good'. BA can take it back to when being polite, respecting the elders, and doing for parents was okay. BA can take it back to when Black families were not vulnerable to the vast array of vain, substance-less electronic gadgets of today which Black youth deem more important than education. BA would simply do much better without the crap that the corporations of today are selling. BA can take it back to the time when homes were places of love, and not pit stops for refueling while running the streets. Simply put, BA needs to go back in time and borrow from the greatest era of all for Black people, a time when families did not surrender the minds of their children to the time consuming gadgetry of today's corporations.

Reformation of Public Schools

Transforming public schools into top-notch institutions of learning is priority number one. This is an Action Plan Implementation technique, as well as a component to help create strong, effective and visionary school systems. The Reformation of Public Schools requires new procedures, new processes and systematic change in schools all across America; in short, it requires action. The recovery of BA has to start with the schools. Education has to be established as a right, a privilege, and luxury. Education is the one commodity that must not be taken for granted anymore. The attitudes, behaviors, and mindsets of Black youth today do not lend themselves to educational excellence. Purpose, discipline, and excellence have been replaced by educational disinterest, illiteracy, and a lack of vision. The children of BA need to have positive goals, critical thinking skills, and laser-like focus to become leaders endeared with the idea of mastering education and learning for the rest of their lives. In addition, the many behavioral and respect issues that exist in public schools must be addressed as well.

The National Center for Family Literacy reports that:

- The richest school districts spend more than 56 percent more per student than do the poorest; and schools with large numbers of poor children tend to have fewer books, supplies, and teachers with less training and experience.

- Too many of today's teachers in our nation's public school system are not formally trained in the classes they are now teaching. Students at public schools in poor communities were more likely than their wealthier counterparts to be taught core subjects by a teacher who had not majored in that subject matter.

- In addition, 2.2 million new teachers will be needed to replace retiring teachers and those leaving the teaching profession as well as to accommodate population increases and the movement to reduce class-size.

- In 1999, lack of discipline was cited as a major problem 18 percent of the teacher population; fighting, gangs, and violence was cited by 11 percent; and lack of financial support was cited by 8 percent of the population.

- In 1999, 20 percent of Hispanic teens were high school dropouts, compared to 7 percent of white kids and 13 percent of African-American teens.

- The amount of homework done by students is positively related to achievement. Students who read eleven or more pages each day for school or homework have higher average reading proficiency scores than those who read less than five pages a day.

- Among 13-year-old students doing homework two or more hours a day, the United States ranks eleventh out of 15 countries.[115]

Zero, Teensie-Weenie, and A Whole-Lotta Tolerance Policies

IN THE NAME of keeping order and control, school districts utilize their very own discipline system. The most prominent element of a typical school district's discipline system is the use of the "Zero Tolerance Policy". This policy punishes offenses such as bullying, fighting, drug usage, drug sales, gang activity, weapons possession, sexual touching and sexual assault, with possibly more infractions that can be added to the list. The penalties for these types of behavior can range from one-day suspensions to permanent expulsions from school. This is understandable, and this is the way it should be, provided it has been proven the student is actually guilty of the charge. Zero Tolerance means to not be tolerated at all, with the penalty extremely dire. The purpose is to protect both the students and the learning process, and that concept is a good thing.

However, there is another type of behaviors that are tolerated more than they should be, and addressing these behaviors and making the necessary tolerance adjustments could make a world of difference in public schools. This class of behavior disallows the vast majority of students the opportunity to learn, while simultaneously allowing the perpetrators to stay in the classroom, thus continuing the destructive process of learning disruption. As a result, most students have a difficult time paying attention in the classroom and being able to learn. This state of non-learning begins in elementary school, the formative years, all the way to high school, the college-ready years. Unfortunately, by then it is too late for many, if not most, of the students, and educational statistics of today attest to that.

Classroom disruptive behavior is the most prevalent, disruptive force in the public schools today. While simple in nature, its damage on Black students is not so simple. Classroom disruptive behavior is the single most fundamental reason many students endure so much trouble within the learning process. As those who disrupt the learning process are allowed to stay in the classroom playing the role of disruptor, the remainder of the class pays a dear price: they cannot learn! As the years go by, the list of classroom disruptors grows, and this is due to the old axiom: "If you can't beat 'em, join 'em". Over time, the sheer numbers of class clowns and disruptors are too much for teachers to bear, making their jobs extremely challenging, and almost impossible. Dropout rates increase, test scores decrease, and many of those that can enter college not nearly as prepared as they should be. Ultimately, the popular recourse is to blame someone. It is not the 'Man' that is blamed, but the poor teachers.

WHAT IS NEEDED in public schools is a simple respect for the learning process. Teachers need to be allowed to teach, and students need to be allowed to learn. This is why Black children soak up knowledge like sponges in their early elementary years with eagerness that overflows, only to have the educational bottom fall out around the late elementary-early middle school years. By the middle school years, the primary purpose of school for too many students is to have fun and look good, instead of facing and accepting academic challenges and educational excellence. It is nearly impossible for a student to reach his or her intellectual potential if there is a classroom disruption every couple of minutes or so.

The students incur an intellectual harm that can follow them for the rest of their lives. The tolerating of classroom disruption is, and has proven to be, very dangerous to BA. Some schools off behaviorally and educationally that they would almost be no worse off in there were no school at all.

And so we create a new category of offenses that will serve to protect the rights of both the teachers and the students, including the classroom disrupters themselves. Classroom disruption is tolerated a whole lot, whereas it should be tolerated just a teensie-weensie bit. Inner cities schools need to convert its "Whole-Lotta Tolerance Policy" into a 'Teensie-Wensie Tolerance Policy'. When that is done, the respect for the learning process is in place, and the learning process takes place unimpeded. By doing so, the inner city schools will begin the transformation of going from under-achieving embarrassments to prideful palaces of educational excellence. When that happens, the children will then be transformed from potential societal and educational losers to feeling like educational royalty and bona fide winners.

I HAVE A very personal example of this classroom disruption scenario. When my son Emery was in the first grade, I would stop by his classroom about twice a month to sit in with him for the first half of his school day. With each visit, I would see the same few boys acting out, and as always, the other kids would lose total concentration with each disruption. At times others would briefly join in and disrupt the class also, but usually would snap back in line at the teacher's insistence. However, the same cannot be said of the original few. They would continue to disrupt the class, only stopping when they were tired. And this would go on for the entirety of the time that I would sit in the classroom, every couple of visits, every month. These bi-weekly visits became frustrating even for me.

After hearing the same complaints from other parents that I knew, and just generally knowing that a high percentage of students from my former high school and the entire school system of my hometown were constantly getting suspended, flunking classes and flunking school, I realized that this is most likely a national problem. National education statistics bears witness to this, as math,, reading, and science achievement, along with national Black graduation rates, reveal a pathetic and alarming pattern across the country.

Now, the term 'Whole-Lotta Tolerance Policy' and 'Teenswie-Weensie Tolerance Policy' were just used for fun. However, the intent is dead serious and the situation needs to be completely addressed. BA needs to stop being concerned about those that tears down its schools and communities and protect those who strive to succeed and build up its schools and communities. BA needs to raise the standard of living within its borders and in doing so, elevate its constituents to a higher standard of living and success.

School Suspensions

THE CIVIL RIGHTS Project at Harvard University has accumulated some important information in regards to school suspensions as they relate to minority youth. They have found that:

- In 2000, Black students constituted approximately 17% of students enrolled in public schools, but 34% of all students suspended.

- Black students are 2.6 times as likely to be suspended as white students.

- Since the early 1990's, many school districts have replaced a system of graduated sanctions with a "zero tolerance' approach to wrongdoing. The result has nearly doubled the number of students suspended annually from school since 1974 from 1.7 million (570,000 Black students) to 3.1 million (1 million Black students)

- In America's 100 largest cities, 58% or more of ninth grade students in high minority schools do not graduate four years later.[116]

This is a situation of the Killer Systems & Industries making a bad situation worse. What is happening here is some schools and their officials are engaging in the Zero Tolerance Policy with added seasoning. One scenario is that that these officials go into the school year from day one with the intent on not taking any you-know-what from those students that start trouble. Be the schools inner city schools, or suburban schools with a minority of Black students, they have taken on the view that any problems whatsoever out of Black students will not be tolerated. The result is that these students are often guilty before being proven as such, and they are denied due process.

Getting inner city schools in order not only brings back respect to the learning process, but also helps to quell the myth and preconceived stereotypes about Black students. It helps to dispel the myth of being troublemakers and uncaring about school. It could very well be that the intentions are good in some of these suspension situations, but the due process is not there, along with a genuine care and concern about Black kids. However, many times these suspensions are justified, but the art of separating the justified versus non-justified may be a difficult one to master, especially if an entire community is on uproars concerning statistics alone without true accountability.

THE REFORMATION OF Public Schools concept can address the problems of classroom disruptions and high achievement in school together. Of course, there are other factors that play a vital role in educating, such as parental involvement, school funding, and quality of teachers, but the protection of the learning process is the place to start. Public schools can do much better with what they already have. There just has to be a healthy respect for learning, academic goals, and a clear vision in which to make it happen.

One thing that clearly has to happen is that parents need to be held more accountable for the actions of their children. It is to easy for parents to blame the school systems for the behaviors of their children. With that said, the parents themselves need to gain a more healthy respect for the learning process, also.

Whether it is the Zero Tolerance Policy of the public school systems, or the police making arrests or issuing citations, the prosecuting attorneys of American cities pressing charges, or the judges of the land handing out lengthy sentences and punishments, BA seems to be content with letting others police the rights of its communities, but is much less adept at doing the same thing itself. Dose there always need to be someone else that takes the steps to correct BA? When that happens, it is more costly and certainly more punitive. BA needs to handle its own business by taking charge of its own schools and communities. This requires a self-derived initiative on the part of BA if success is of the order and the goal is to change the status quo of today's BA.

Transition Classes and Transition Schools

TRANSITION CLASSES IN elementary and middle schools are classrooms that are set up for the children that consistently interrupt the learning process for other children. If the anti-classroom behaviors of these students exceed pre-determined levels and in repeated fashion, then it's off to the transition class they go. In the transition classrooms, children can be taught the importance of listening, learning and respecting the rights of others, while also completing their regular class work. Additionally, the parents can participate and help come up with solutions as to how to change this behavior. Most importantly, though, the learning process is not destroyed for the other children.

Transition classes will help at the high school level also, although they may ultimately result in a transfer to a different kind of classroom setting such as an alternative school, which already exists in many, if not all, school districts. If that is the option they choose, then so must they be accommodated. Everyone has to live by his or her own choices, as that is the way of the world. Again, the learning opportunities of those that want to learn must not be comprised, and that is what is most important.

IN ORDER FOR anyone to have a future in BA, there has to be a strong and genuine concern for the academic success of Black children. The Transition Class and School concept would be an effective addition to public school systems. If it needs funding, then that need would have to be met. If it meant that classrooms would need to be set aside, teachers and necessary materials provided, and a certain level of support from all involved parties at every level in order for the concept to flourish, then so be it. The cost is very minimal compared to the returns it will provide.

Black children are already being expelled from school, at a disproportional rate, for Zero-Tolerance reasons. Black children can be intervened well before that expulsion point by teaching respect, demanding effort, and putting value back into the learning processes in inner city schools. Teaching children is what school is all about, and I believe that BA students can be amongst the best and the brightest students in the world, if only the proper focus and effort is allocated in that direction.

Cognitive Clubs and Organizational

PROVIDING OUTLETS AND resources for cognitive and educational growth is also very important in building top students. By initiating clubs and organizations that stimulate the minds of children, allow for friendly competition, and provide alternatives to the counter-productive activities that are currently popular, BA can create a new and exciting educational culture that can last throughout the lives of all involved. Chess, science, geography, math, spelling and travel clubs can all be achieved through a volunteer network, along with the support of the parents and the schools.

There are thousands and thousands of young students wasting their minds, talents, and time everyday throughout the inner cities of America via watching too much television, excessive video gaming, wrongful and excessive internet usage, and a host of other time wasting activities. Black students cannot wait for the world to come to them. It never will for most. Black students have to go and claim a piece of the world. Black students have to take the initiative to be someone who at full potential and throttle go out and make their mark on this world. Opening doors by providing Black our youth with challenging, meaningful and fun cognitive clubs and organizations is a big step in the fight to right the wrongs and eliminate the shortcomings in urban schools.

Teaching Healthy Lifestyle Choices in Schools

AFRICAN-AMERICAN CHILDREN EAT less than half of the amount of fruits and vegetables recommended for good health. They also have high rates of overweight, obesity and Type 2 diabetes. When our kids eat fruits and vegetables, combined with physical activity, it promotes good health and can help reduce their risk of obesity and Type 2 diabetes. As parents, we have to make sure our kids eat a healthy diet.[117]

Black America is engulfed in a healthcare crisis. Sedentary lifestyles and bad choices are sending many to the grave prematurely. A good way to ensure a healthier future for Black America is by educating Black youth at an early age to incorporate healthy choices into their lives so that productivity and fruitful living is the norm versus inactivity and high mortality. There is every reason to believe that inner-city schools can make the changes necessary to help facilitate healthy lifestyles amongst Black children. Numerous school districts have made their marks in assisting their students to become proactive and to lead healthy lives. The following are examples:

- In western Kentucky, a Tobacco Belt city named Owensboro was nicknamed "The Fast Food Capital of the World" in the late 1980's, when it was found to order more food-to-go per capita than anywhere else. But now its schools systems are running an intense physical education program aimed at instilling a lifetime approach to fitness among students.

  Owensboro adopted the Fit for Life program that aims to teach students how to create their own fitness plans. A partnership between the city's hospitals and schools provided nearly $750,000 to equip extensive fitness centers at 11 schools. Teachers were trained on "New PE" techniques that stress keeping an entire class active for 30-60 minutes on treadmills, stationary bikes, towing machines and weightlifting stations.

  At Owensboro's Newton Parrish Elementary School, a quarter-mile asphalt walking track has been built on what used to be a swampy, grass field. The school's parent-teacher organization raised the $18,000 needed to build the track. At 7:30 a.m. about 80 of the school's 325 students voluntarily walk, skip and run laps for a half-hour before school. Collectively, the students have amassed 3,500 miles, and one dutiful first-grader, Marcus Russell, 7, has logged a pack-leading 140 miles.

- Rick Schupbach, an innovative PE teacher at Grundy Center (Iowa) Elementary School has his thoughts on how the kids are affected by the new "PE". "It's absolutely amazing to see how much self-directed activity these students are involved in. They're getting their heart rates up, and they don't have to run a mile to do it. Every kid can succeed.

As with all New PE programs, personal improvement is the goal, and students are not rated against others for strength, stamina, or speed. The program embraces aerobic activities such as jogging and swimming. It disdains old-school competitions such as dodge ball that tend to quickly relegate slow-moving students to the sideline.

"What I've seen in my 21 years as a PE teacher is that kids have almost gotten to the point where movement is perceived as work to them, and now we have a society where we're much more fearful of allowing a child to go out and play."

For schools that say they can't get funds for fitness centers, Schupbach points out that he started his program in 1992 with a $5,000 grant and has largely supported it since through traditional school fund raising events. Also, the federal government issues about $69 million in Physical Education Program (PEP) grants a year.[118]

- In 1999, Tennessee coordinated a school health program and piloted it in dozens of schools in ten districts. The program works to increase physical activity, give students someone to talk to when they're upset, check children for health problems, boost community awareness of school health, create a safe school environment and educate students about healthy living.

Those in the participating schools aren't waiting for a report to sing its praises. They say increased physical activity, full-time nurses, better nutrition and other initiatives are paying off with more alert students, fewer discipline problems, higher attendance and better test scores.

Better nutrition and more exercise are key parts of the program. Health committees can negotiate with vendors to provide healthier snacks, partner with mental agencies to provide counseling, have the school building checked for mold, conduct workshops to boost students' self-esteem or participate in activities to reduce substance abuse.[119]

- Morgan Spurlock revealed some fascinating facts not only about fast food, but also about the effect that poor nutrition has had on our school systems. Sodexho has been the lowest bidder for a number of school food service contracts, resulting in their servicing over 400 k-12 school districts in the United States. Sodexho operates prison food systems worldwide also. In fulfilling their contract, Sodexho provides our school-age children with menus of candy, chips, cheese-laden pizza, sugar-heavy soft drinks, little debbie snack cakes, french fries, onion rings, macaroni & cheese, fried foods, and cookies. All of the foods that growing boys and girls do not need.

Another school that was visited in the movie provided students USDA reimbursable meals in which approximately 85% of the meals were of the reheated, pre-cooked variety. Most of these meals either came out of a box or a can. Some of the meals topped over 1,100 calories, whereas the recommended calorie intake for the average person is approximately 2,500.

Dr. Neal Barnard, President of the Physician's Committee for Responsible Medicine, says that fast-food restaurants use all of the addicting components they can when producing their food. Components such as caffeine, sugar, and cheese, which is filled with casomorphins. Casomorphins are the opiates found in cheese proteins, and they are similar to morphine. He goes on to say that the brain of an adolescent is no match for that combination.

- Still another school, Appleton Central Alternative High School was visited in the movie. This school houses students with truancy and behavioral problems. This school has achieved a success story of its own by turning things around through diet, not discipline. Natural Ovens Bakery of Manitoc, Wisconsin, takes a healthy approach to providing meals for schools systems. They believe in low-fat, low sugar, non-chemically processed foods. They also favor food full of whole grains, lots of organic foods, and a lot of fresh fruits and vegetables. They use no beef at all! There is no frying, but there is a lot of baking. Fresh preparation as opposed to opening up food out of cans or thawing things out of a box proves to be beneficial also. There are no candy machines or soda pop machines in the school. Instead they provide bottled water.

The costs for this healthy and nutritious food program are about the same as the school lunch programs that provide the unhealthy food choices. The question was asked, "Why isn't everyone doing what Appleton Central is doing? In reply, Mr. Paul Stitt, Ms., the founder of Natural Ovens Bakery, replied: " There's an awful lot of resistance from junk food companies that make huge profits off the schools at the present time. They don't want to get kicked out of the school system. They want to be there to addict the children for life".

I WAS OF the opinion that American schools needed to change the food and drink menus long before I saw the Appleton Central Alternative High School example. Sugar and fat-laden foods most certainly need to be replaced with healthier choices such as fruits and juices, especially since statistics show that Africa-American children are the most sick and unhealthy children in America, bar none.

An example of how profit, no matter how small, takes precedence over health, takes place daily at a middle school in which my son attended right here in Nashville, Tennessee. This school has a practice that allows children to interrupt class every second hour of every day to sell candy and pop. The interruption is enough in itself, but allowing the kids to hype-up on sugar just makes matters worse. And this is a school that on a banner states that it strives for excellence. It seems as though it might be time for a reassessment of that statement.

The Corporate Angle

CORPORATE AMERICA SPENDS unholy amounts of money on marketing to get people addicted to their food products. In 2004, McDonald's spent $1.4 billion dollars on marketing, Pepsi spent $1.0 billion, and Hershey's spent $200 million. In contrast, total spending for the five-a-day fruit and vegetable campaign spent a paltry $2.0 million dollars touting nutrition, which is 100 times less than the direct media budget of jut one candy company.

The marketing campaigns of these companies include t-shirts, coupons, toys in stores such as Wal*Mart and Kmart, giveaways, birthday party programs, play areas, storytelling, and of course, radio and television advertising. Ultimately, American citizens are left to foot the bill and deal with the consequences, such as very bad health, obesity, low self-esteem, and staggering financial costs.[120]

Corporate America and the federal government have vast amounts of information, studies and even experiments ranging from sleep to social behavior to mortality to flatulency. In essences, they know all that is needed to be effective in what they do and what they sell. In addition to that, they have tons of money and favorable laws on the books that allow them to sell and place various harmful food products all the way to the classrooms of American schools. They know that the scientific phenomenon known as the human body, which is strong, enduring, recharging and versatile. Although ultimately to be left in a rag-tag and sickly condition, the human body will continue to function until dead. However, along the way before death, the Pharmaceutical Industry will be sure to get into the act by advertising and supplying its drugs to help keep the body functioning, thus getting their cut. This all makes the human body the perfect dumping grounds for chemical and preservative-laden food products that Americans are gobbling up. And guess what? Those that are hurt the most once again, are the children.

The food our children eat at fast-food joints and at schools are loaded with fats, sugars, preservatives, antibiotics, hormones and chemicals. One of the reforms needed is that food be labeled not only with the fat, fiber and sugar content, but also with disclosure of the amounts of preservatives, hormones, antibiotics, fertilizers, chemicals and filler material. This information would be important and useful. It would also be somewhat scary to see just how much unnatural substances people, and especially the children, are putting in their bodies.

The desired alternative is to stay away from fast food and go back to the practice of home-cooked meals. This option is healthier because you would have better control of sugar, fat and all the other harmful ingredients that are consumed by families. It is safer because of the spreading of disease such as HIV/AIDS, which is growing out of control, and thus the chances of an infected person cooking food at a fast food restaurant of choice increases. Regardless of what medical authorities say or do not say about communicable diseases such as HIV/AIDS, one has to wonder of the chances of diseases such as HIV/AIDS spreading through food. Lastly, the home-cooked meal option is heartier because it brings back the presence of the family eating together at home, which is one of the ties that bind loving families.

The Importance of Physical Exercise

As a child growing up, I can remember the first meaningful award I won, The President's Physical Fitness Award. Winning that award meant a great deal to me. It marked the beginning of what would be a lifetime commitment to physical fitness. There are now six different awards that have evolved from just the one that was in place in the 70's: The Presidential Active Lifestyle Award, Presidential Champions, The Presidential Physical Fitness Award, The National Physical Fitness Award, The Participant Physical Fitness Award, and The Health Fitness Award. However, there is not much talk of them anymore, and that does not pose well.

Physical exercise has become quite an ignored activity. As kids over-indulge in video gaming and channel surfing, they also suffer the consequences of bad health and being overweight due to a lack of physical exercise. The love for the joystick has replaced the love for any type of game or activity involving physical activity. The days of eating a good home-cooked breakfast to get the day off to a good start has been replaced with a quick fast food breakfast sandwich from a fast food restaurant or worse yet, a microwave meal. Aaarrgghh! This food is often heavy in taste and light on nutrition. Badly missed are the days of healthy, home cooked meals being the foundation of a family.

Limiting television time, eliminating video game systems in the home, enrolling the children in sports, encouraging exercise, and preparing healthy home-cooked meals is large in the search for educational and family redemption in BA. Kicking Corporate America and its useless products out of inner city schools and homes is key in reaching the goal of having smarter and healthier children.

Pursuit of Educational Excellence

How does the vision of a new BA become a completed reality? As mentioned earlier, by pursuing educational excellence. The Reformation of Public Schools can get BA back in the game and give it a fighting chance. Cleaning up the streets of the communities while spurring investment via Community Action and its Urban Law fortifies BA by giving hope and instilling pride in every citizen in every Black community that partakes in this turnaround. Shunning the electronic squadron of useless gadgets and winning our children's minds back makes the playing field even again for the children. Controlling television and internet viewing increases the odds for the victory BA so badly needs.

The renaissance can be completed by helping every inner city student a solid education of a quality that puts them on par with students from every other school system of America. Education in all of its covetous forms has to be the foundation of BA if it is to gain respect, good fortune, and any hope for a promising future. Black American students, as well as adults and parents that seek educational growth must want, seek, and find the knowledge of the book. With that said, BA changes its destiny through educational excellence and encouraging new educational attitudes which will lead to never before educational accomplishment. From kindergarteners to high school seniors to adults simply going back to school for the high school diploma or additional college degree, everyone is invited to be a part of this new collective education explosion facilitated by the new Black American that chooses to become dedicated to education.

Education is the ticket. There is almost no end to the amount of improvement needed to fix the dilemma of BA. It will be a difficult, unique, and very, very long process, but it will be a magnificent one as well. New schools and new attitudes are the only elixir that will make BA well. BA, it's time to get well.

The Educational Dearth

PROSPERITY IS TO the gate, as education is to the key. BA is having problems connecting the dots to successful and healthy living, and this is due to a lack of commitment to educational excellence. Exceedingly too many Black youth are failing, underachieving, or dropping out of school altogether, and the price paid is dear. In its rebirth, BA will have to stress education from the cradle to the grave. Education determines the ability to pay the bills, and the quality of meals. Education will also determine whether or not BA will win or lose.

BA ranks last in virtually every educational statistical category there is. With that said, a lot of love goes out to the Latino brothers and sisters also, as they rank a close second to BA in a number of categories, and it is my sincere hope that they, too, will have better success in the years to come. In fact, it appears that as families of the new Latino American contingent move on to just their second generation, they actually do begin to enjoy successes, including that of education. That can be a good thing for all involved, as competition can breed character, and character can breed success. As for BA, that effect, and any other that lends itself to giving BA a boost in improving its educational health, would be a good thing.

IMAGINE A CRAZY dream where a great majority of Black children's brain-power has atrophied away, and now they wander the streets aimlessly, lost in cognition, having given up on school altogether. In the dream, the schools have been sealed off to the public with yellow crime tape. Teachers, staff, students, and parents are all suspects waiting to be interviewed, as the cops try to determine who was minding the minds, and where in the world are those precious minds now. The evidence and forensics conclude that the adults involved, namely the teachers, principals, and parents are all responsible for letting the children down. It was concluded that the kids were not intellectually challenged, and that as the expectations decreased, so did the interest of the children. It was determined that the children are not intellectually dead, but rather do not know which way to turn, as they did not know how to demand the most from themselves. Once this was figured out, life became better than it was ever imagined. The minds of the children were found. They were being held captive in the limited imaginations of the adults.

In reality, this is close to what is actually happening right now. The adults have let the school children down. At some point, the children are expected to become scholars as though they have been bred to be. The schools have lost control and direction. The world continues to pull away from BA day by day. As circumstances stand right now, there is absolutely no respectable or desirable future in sight, unless an insatiable thirst for education is discovered.

The dismal results of Black students from elementary to high school, has resulted in a lifetime of makeup work to do, no pun intended. Black children of all grades of all ages in all cities are experiencing the same negative educational phenomenon of either lagging behind all other students in core subjects or outright failing school. The National Center for Education Statistics has the following average scores for 8th and 12th graders in mathematics (M), science (S), and writing performance (WP):[126]

Grade 8/12	M	S	WP
Black	252/8th only	122/123	135/130
Hispanic	259/8th only	128/128	137/136
White	288/8th only	162/154	161/154
Asian/Pacific Islander	291/8th only	156/153	161/151

- On the 2000 National Assessment of Educational Progress reading assessment national test that gauges states academic progress, 40 percent of white 4th graders scored at or above proficient, compared to only 12 percent of their African-American peers.

- In math, African-American achievement also lagged: 35 percent of white fourth graders scored at or above proficient, and just five percent of African-Americans scored as high achievers.

- The racial achievement gap is real, and is not shrinking.

- Educating every child is the greatest moral challenge of our time.[127]

- Only 51% of all black students and 52% of all Hispanic students graduate, and only 20% of all black students and 16% of all Hispanic students leave high school college-ready.

- The graduation rate for white students was 72%; for Asian students, 79%; and for American Indian students, 54%. The college readiness rate for white students was 37%; for Asian students, 38%; for American Indian students, 14%.

- The portion of all college freshmen that is black (11%) or Hispanic (7%) is very similar to their shares of the college-ready population (9% for both). This suggests that the main reason these groups are underrepresented in college admissions is that these students are not acquiring college-ready skills in the K-12 system, rather than inadequate financial aid or affirmative action policies.[128]

African-American Degree Attainment Breakdown

ACCORDING TO THE U.S. Census Bureau, there are about 2,676,000 Blacks in this country that hold a bachelor's degree only; 829,000 African-Americans whom have a four-year degree plus hold a master's degree; and an additional 135,000 Blacks hold a professional degree in fields such as law, business, or medicine. Another 100,000 African-Americans have obtained a doctorate. Overall, 3,736,000 African-Americans possess a four-year college degree or higher.

Despite the good news, the figures show that Blacks still have a long way to go before they reach higher educational parity with White Americans. Overall, 27.6 percent of the White population over the age of 25 holds a college degree compared to 17.3 percent of adult Blacks. There are 44,129,000 Whites that have a four-year college degree. Thus, there are 12 times as many Whites with a college degree as Blacks that hold a college degree, although it must be noted that Whites outnumber blacks in the U.S. by a ration of about 8 to 1.

BLACK WOMEN HAVE built a huge lead over Black men in college degree attainments. There are 1,530,000 Black women with a four-year degree compared to only 1,146,000 Black men. Therefore, it turns out that Black women hold about 57 percent of all the bachelor's degrees earned by Blacks in our country.

Some 539,000 Black women hold a master's degree compared to 290,000 Black men. Thus, Black women hold nearly two-thirds of all African-American master degrees, an even larger share of their total in bachelor's degree attainments.

In regards to professional degree, Black women hold 72,000 degrees compared while Black men hold 64,000. But Black men still hold the lead in Doctorate's with 64,000 while Black women hold 36,000.[129]

PROFESSIONAL DEGREES SHOULD play an even bigger role in the lives of African-Americans, according to Joe Goldthreate. Mr. Goldthreate is the Founder and Executive Director of the Hadley Park Junior Development Tennis Program in Nashville, Tennessee, which is one of the top Black tennis programs in the nation. Mr. Goldthreate has had extensive experience teaching, nurturing, and counseling young Black children. As I spoke with him one day on the choices that kids today make in regards to college majors, the subject of professional degrees such as those found in medicine, education, law economics, or a Ph.D. in any field came up. In response, Mr. Goldthreate bellowed, "Professional degrees are definitely a smart way to go! Simply put, by getting a professional degree, a young person does not have to succumb to the job market and those that dictate when, where, how, and if he or she will have a job. With a professional degree, young people can start their own businesses, and that is the way to go." I strongly recommend a professional degree for anyone going to college."

Additionally, Mr. Goldthreate wants to point out that college is not the only avenue en route to professional certification, as he is a nationally certified professional tennis instructor, and it is this professional certification that has allowed him to build a very successful tennis organization in Nashville. It is not too difficult to concur with Mr. Goldthreate. As more Black people obtain professional degrees and certifications, there will be more consulting practices, law practices, doctor offices, franchise businesses, psychologists, CEOs, college professors, managers, and various other professional, corporate, and entrepreneurial options, and BA needs more of everything that higher education has to offer.

IN 2002 BLACKS earned 6.3 percent of all doctorates awarded to U.S. citizens. This is the highest yearly percentage in history. The overall progress over the past 15 years is very strong. As recently as 1990 African-Americans earned only 3.6 percent of all doctorates awarded to U.S. citizens. Since 1987 the number of Blacks earning doctorates has more than doubled. One area of concern, though, is the fact that African-Americans made up nearly 13 percent of the U.S. population in the year 2002. Therefore, Black doctoral awards were earned at only one half the level that racial parity would call for.[130]

DIVERSITY FACTOIDS FROM *Diversity Inc. Magazine' October/November 2003* issue:

- The percentage of bachelor's degree earned by African-Americans in year 2000 was 8.7 percent, while African-Americans made up 12.3 percent of the U.S. population.

- The percentage of bachelor's degree earned by Latinos in year 2000 was 6.1 percent, while Latinos made up 12.5 percent of the U.S. population.

- The percentage of bachelor's degrees earned by Asian-Americans in year 2000 was 6.3 percent, while Asian-Americans made up 3.6 percent of the U.S. population.[131]

African-Americans and Black Immigrants

BLACK PEOPLE WHO immigrate to the United States from the Caribbean and sub-Saharan Africa tend to earn more money and have a slightly higher level of education than native-born Black Americans, according to a report by researchers at the State University of New York at Albany.

The report, "Black Diversity in Metropolitan America," said Afro-Caribbeans stay in school for an average of 12.8 years, compared with 12.5 for Black Americans. African immigrants, most of whom live in the Washington area, stay in school an average of 14.5 years, a level that is "higher than [the level for] whites and Asians," according to the report. "The main routes to America for Africans is through institutions of education," said John Logan, director of the Lewis Mumford Center for Comparative Urban and Regional Research and author of the report.

Nearly 70 percent of the Afro-Caribbeans living in the United States were born overseas, earned a median household income of $40,000 and attended school an average of 12.8 years, according to figures from the 2000 Census.

The number of Africans in the United States passed the half-million mark during the 1990s, with a population that was 85 percent foreign-born. Their median household income was $40,300. Africans from Ghana, Nigeria, Somalia and Ethiopia largely settle in Washington, New York and Atlanta.

African Americans had a median household income of $33,500 and attended school an average of 12.5 years. Their unemployment rate was 9.9 percent, while unemployment among Afro-Caribbeans and Africans was 7.3 percent and 5.1 percent, respectively.

ASIANS LIVING IN the United States earned a median household income of $64,000 and remained in school an average of 13.9 years. Among Hispanics, those numbers were $37,600 and 10.7 years in school, the report said. Among White people, they were $52,000 and 13.5 years.[132]

The message is that education is a formidable foundation in which to build income and success. The dedication to education of the immigrants from Africa and the Caribbean is to be commended, and whether or not there is a selective policy on entry into America of people from these nations does not, in any way, take away from their accomplishments here in America.

Indigenous Americans already know of the roads to success, and that includes BA, and as such, really has no legitimate excuse as to why it is not taking advantage of the American educational opportunities here at home. Every individual member of Black society has to answer that question. BA must ask itself, why is it that foreigners can come to America and take advantage of the many wonderful opportunities it has to offer and then prosper, while BA finds basically locked out of substantive living. It brings to mind the old saying: "One man's junk is another man's treasure." How true.

Oh, How The World has Changed

On November 27, 2005, while viewing the coverage of The National Book Festival on C-Span 2's Book-TV, I got a chance to listen to Mr. Thomas Friedman, author of "The World is Flat. A Brief History of the Twenty-First Century". His book, which received rave reviews, brings awareness of the clear and serious changes to life in the United States, as we know it. His book discusses the internet, Microsoft Windows, telecommunication technology and the advancement of fiber optics technology and how they have combined to bring about possibly the greatest changes the world has ever known. As a result, American jobs are up for grabs. The citizens of China, India, Japan and the world over are players in a game that many Americans are not prepared for. Black American youth are especially vulnerable in terms of competitive disadvantages due to educational non-achievement, a lack of awareness of current events, as well as international competition for jobs and businesses.[133]

The editorial review section of Amazon.com in reference to Mr. Friedman's book offers some keen insights. One review mentions that the service sector (telemarketing, accounting, computer programming, scientific research, and engineering, etc.) will be further outsourced to the English-spoken abroad; manufacturing, meanwhile, will continue to be off-shored to China. As anyone who reads his column knows, Friedman agrees with the transnational business executives who are his main sources that these developments are both desirable and unstoppable.

Another review offers a more sobering insight into Friedman's elaboration on Bill Gates' statement, "When I compare our high schools to what I see when I'm traveling abroad, I am terrified for our work force of tomorrow. In math and science, our fourth graders are among the top students in the world. By eighth grade, they're in the middle of the pack. By 12th grade, U.S. students are scoring near the bottom of all industrialized nations. The percentage of a population with a college degree is important, but so are sheer numbers. In 2001, India graduated almost a million more students from college than the United States did. China graduates twice as many students with bachelor's degrees as the U.S., and they have six times as many graduates majoring in engineering. Experts have concluded that Oriental IQs generally average 10 points higher than those of Americans. China and India graduate a combined 500,000 scientists and engineers a year, vs. 60,000 in the U.S. In the international competition to have the biggest and best supply of knowledge workers, America is falling behind." "In China today, Bill Gates is Britney Spears. In America today, Britney Spears is Britney Spears -- and that is our problem." [134]

IF MAINSTREAM AMERICA is falling further and further behind, then BA has a foot in the educational grave. And how are the vast majority of Black students dealing with this international flight of American jobs? By practically doing nothing, remaining totally unaware of the tremendous challenge entering their shores from across the seas. They do not realize that American jobs and wealth opportunities are shrinking everyday, that the times of the future holds devastating bad news for those that choose to be uneducated. They fail to realize that America is not the same America anymore.

Mr. Friedman put it best in his closing statements at the National Book Festival when he said that the best skill to have is to 'learn how to learn'. He advises that in order to do that, people have to 'love to learn', and this can be accomplished by listening and talking to educators, teachers, and professors.

A Superstar amongst Superstars

THERE IS A particular former professional athlete that is well known across America. He has earned the titles of Father, Husband, Professional Basketball Player, Musician, Naval Academy Graduate, and Philanthropist. Well, now the title Master Planner can be added to the list, as he has provided a blueprint for the success of Black America.

In my eyes he has bcome the greatest professional athlete/ hero since Muhammad Ali. His efforts and contributions are matched by a simple few in today's world of professional athletes and entertainers. He has created a body of life-long work that will forever reap dividends in the lives of those that he will touch. He has also provided a shining example of what needs to be done by those in the position to make a difference.

As the bedrock of the NBA San Antonio Spurs for more than a decade, David Robinson has amassed a list of accomplishments that would be more than enough for any lifetime: one of the 50 Greatest Players in the National Basketball Association; the NBA's Most Valuable Player in 1995; Defensive Player of the Year in 1992; three-time Olympic Games competitor ('88, '92 and '96); member of the NBA All-tar Team 10 times. He led the San Antonio Spurs to a World Championship in 1999. But these on-court accomplishments just begin to tell his story.

His greatest legacy may well be his contributions to his community, driven by his strong Christian faith and strong sense of duty. David and his wife, Valerie, created the faith-based David Robinson Foundation in 1992, through which they invest in "Mr. Robinson's neighborhood," the name of the special seats he reserves for underprivileged families during Spurs home games. The Foundation's mission is to support programs that address the physical and spiritual needs of the family.

The Carver Academy

THE DAVID ROBINSON Foundation's most significant accomplishment to date is jump-starting The Carver Academy in downtown San Antonio. The school offers elementary school-age children a challenging academic program featuring small classes, leadership opportunities, and a nurturing, family-like environment based on the foundation of Judeo-Christian scripture. David and Valerie donated $11 million to the Academy, named for botanist George Washington Carver.

The Robinson's vision for the Carver is "to build a foundation for future generations. We want to make these children the heroes of tomorrow, by teaching them principles of integrity, discipline and faith," states David. Even after retirement from professional sports, David plans to continue in an active role with The Carver Academy. "My career as a sport has been exciting, but its main purpose is to provide a platform for me to impact people's lives in a positive way. My plans for the immediate future are to build my own family and work on raising endowment funds for The Carver Academy.

Since announcing plans for the Academy, David has received support from foundations, corporations, philanthropists, and individuals who have been motivated by the Robinson's efforts to help inner-city children find a successful path in life. Has the support surprised them? "Not really. I always felt strongly about the vision. I know there are many people who are focused on education and raising leaders. I'm happy that so many people are excited about what's happening at the Carver." Robinson says. "From the beginning, The Carver Academy students have performed extremely well. They take the Stanford Achievement Test, a common test for schools across the nation. And they've scored consistently in the top 25 percent of all schools tested."

The world-class school is the first of its type in an area that has been historically underserved. "The quality of education at The Carver Academy is phenomenal. We expose the kids to a tremendous balance of culture," David explains. "We have wonderful partnerships with the Institute of Texan Cultures, the Japan America Society, the Jewish Community Center, and the Carver Cultural Center. Our children are not only going to learn from books, they're going to live it."

FOCUSING ON FIVE basic principles, The Carver Academy seeks to instill discipline, initiative, integrity, service, and faith. "We want the kids to understand that when they live their lives, each one of these qualities must be present. They won't leave here without taking these principles with them.[135]

"This school is not for poor kids. Sometimes I feel like there are schools that internalize that idea: "We're here for poor kids.' And what happens? Once you decide that, the school becomes second-class, the standards become lower. Not here! Our standards are high, and all of these kids have tremendous pride in their school."

Robinson recounts the story of a seventh-grader in San Antonio he mentored; the two would communicate by e-mail. I'd say to him, "You can't even write me a letter that isn't misspelled. How are you going to get job, a good life, if you can't spell?" He didn't think it was important, because he was going to be a ballplayer or a rapper. That's the attitude. We need to change the culture of minorities families when it comes to education."

BRENDA MURPHY, INTERIM director at Carver and a 30-year veteran of San Antonio public schools, agrees that cultural change starts with changing the expectations kids and parents have for schools in the inner city. So Carver deliberately builds its facilities to exact specifications and maintains its buildings beautifully. She calls the atmosphere "restful. There are no fights, no discipline problems. For many of these kids, it's the least chaotic atmosphere they have ever been in." Carver's well-maintained grounds also serve as a kind of community center for the east side, and the presence of the school has sparked something of a renaissance in the surrounding neighborhood, says Murphy, who's watched several new businesses go up around the school in the past two years.

Carver is Robinson's attempt to change the educational attitudes and expectations of low-income and minority students, one child at a time. Carver kids take a rigorous mix of reading, writing, math, science, history, and foreign language classes. The school stresses faith in God, good citizenship, and above all, high achievement. "We tell parents, we're going to push your kid as far as they can possibly go," says Robinson. "We want to produce kid who have passion, who are on fire with the idea that they can accomplish anything."

"This school isn't for everyone, we know that," says Robinson. "But even if it helped us get more kids into the school, we're not going to compromise what we think is right. We're not going to let any kid who can do better settle for less, no matter where they come from." That's straight from the Admiral, and it sounds like an order.[136]

The potential is there in all young Black students to achieve high academic marks just like the students at Carver. They just need to be in the right environments, coupled with high expectations and personal challenges. The children, grandchildren, and generations to come of the Carver kids will all benefit from the successes that will surely radiate outward from the halls of the Carver Academy. Schools such as the Carver offer the best opportunity to break cycles of poverty and academic shortcomings. The power of education must no longer be overlooked in Black communities. To borrow from an old marketing campaign of Starkist Tuna, " We don't need tuna that tastes good............We need smart tuna."

All kids can succeed at anything they set their minds to if they get sufficient help and guidance. David Robinson is providing the type that inner city children need. For all of the talk by professional athletes of their desires to win world championships, David Robinson has won the most meaningful and important championship of his career, and he did it away from the basketball court. When the children of The Carver graduate with high performance thinking skills, clear and challenging goals and solid educational pedigrees, they will all feel like champions of the world. To have world-class physical skills like professional ballplayers is great, but to be blessed with world-class academic skills is even more impressive. The students at The Carver will accomplish great things, and because of David and Brenda Robinson, their successes are sure to reverberate for generations to come. Now what are needed are sibling schools that can share their successes. And therein lies the key to the survival of BA. Schools: Bigger. Better. Bountiful.

Other Educational Options

THE CARVER ACADEMY may be unusual in urban education, but is not completely alone. Carver is one of a handful of private schools across the nation that are having tremendous success in education poor and minority students who might otherwise get lost in urban public school districts. Schools such as Cristo Rey and Cornerstone schools in Detroit are all having a great degree of success.

AN EXCITING OPTION that is producing terrific results is the year-round school concept. At Valley View Elementary School in Las Cruces, New Mexico, the kindergarten school year is an 11-month, full-day year. The program is called The Kindergarten-Plus program. It is a three-year experiment seen not only as a cost-effective way to help prepare disadvantaged children for school, but also as a way to reduce a stubborn achievement gap between poor and middle-class children. Unlike other year-round programs, which simply rearrange the typical 180 days of school, this one actually adds 40 days onto each kindergartner's school year.

Kids who have been through Kindergarten-Plus are almost a full year ahead of typical new first-graders. Virtually all are beginning to read when they enter first grade, which is a dazzling success. The kids are writing stories, have achieved excellent work skills and critical reasoning skills. In short, the program is producing kids who are very advanced. These types of gains used to be basically unheard of.

A lot of success of the program is attributed to the fact that the kindergartners spend an entire month alone with their teachers before older kids arrive. The school atmosphere is very quiet and calm, which allows the children to get into their routines without any distractions. Valley View Elementary School has found their niche, and it is a very successful one.[137]

THERE IS STILL another vision created by the great Oprah Winfrey: *The Oprah Winfrey Leadership Academy for Girls* in South Africa. The mission for the school is to teach girls to be the best human beings that they can be; it will train them to become decision makers and leaders; and it aims to be a model school for the rest of the world. It will allow girls to explore the changing world through advanced education techniques and advanced technology including a telecommunications system, which will allow Oprah to teach from Chicago. South African teachers and administrators will be selected from the best and the brightest of South Africa's educators.[138]

Ms.Winfrey, she of kindness, philanthropy and possessor of the Midas touch, once again is providing hope and opening doors. Africa itself is in great peril, and it is easy to overlook its many problems when keeping an eye on BA. However, anytime the Motherland can do better, it generates a warm feeling in all who care about Africa, and should touch a special place in the hearts of BA. Like David Robinson, Oprah Winfrey has also decided that the futures of young people will be best served through the creation of an institution of learning. Education: Always a wise choice.

Professional Athletes & Private Foundations

ONE WAY THAT professional athletes of today show love and support of youth is through their very own private foundation, which id a Temporary Intervention Measure. Many professional athletes create these foundations to serve as a link between themselves and their communities. These athletes bring joy and fellowship to the youth they touch in an attempt to fill the gaps in areas such as role modeling, charity, and positive activity, even if only on a temporary basis. Acts of goodwill such as these prove meaningful to young people in need of a positive light, and the abundant joy that the kids experience is easily imagined. Here are three private foundations along with their respective superstar athletes and missions:

1) Homes for the Holidays. NFL running back Warrick Dunn of the Atlanta Falcons is quite a player on and off the football field. He is the 2004 Walter Payton NFL Man of the Year. Warrick launched "Homes for the Holidays" program in 1997, when he made down payments on four homes in Tampa. To date, Home for the Holidays has assisted 52 single mothers and profoundly touched the lives of 135 children and dependants in Atlanta, Tampa, and Baton Rouge.[139]

2) In 1997, Steve Smith, who believes you can never give too much, and The Steve Smith Scholarship Foundation, donated $2.5 million dollars to Michigan State University. This donation helped construct the Clara Bell Smith Student-Athlete Academic Center, in honor of his late mother, Clara Bell Smith, who died of cancer during Steve's rookie NBA season. This remains the largest single donation ever made by a professional athlete to an alma mater. The building was formally dedicated on September 12, 1998, and it remains a state of the art facility in this country. At Steve's insistence, a portion of this generous donation also funds The Steve Smith/Pershing High/MSU

Scholarship for Academic Achievement. In 2001, Steve donated an additional $600,000.00 to fully endow the scholarship. This scholarship provides, on an annual basis, high-achieving students from Detroit Pershing High School the opportunity to attend Michigan State University.[140]

3) The Jalen Rose Foundation. The Jalen Rose Foundation opened its doors in 1999. It has given more than $500,000 to single-parent families, soup kitchens, and students who need scholarships. The JRF has given thousands of game tickets to children and has also procured thousands of coats through winter coat drives for the needy.[141]

Professional athletes and entertainers are icons in American society. They are adored by kids, admired by young adults, sought out by autograph seekers, penned by journalists and blessed with fortune. In the entertainment industry, the social and economic power that Black superstars possess is mighty, and it is general common knowledge that in this industry, Blacks are well represented.

THERE IS ONE athlete whom, in the prime of his life and career, gave all he had to represent Black people. He stepped on stage in front of the entire world and showed the utmost respect not only for Black Americans, but colored people in the continent of Asia. His mission had an immense sense of purpose, was guided by love for his race and country, and was shaped by unlimited courage. This man literally put his life on the line, and in the end paid a dear price by losing his freedom, not to mention millions upon millions of dollars. He is a champion in the heart of hearts of many Americans, and he was definitely a hero to me as a kid. He is the incomparable Muhammad Ali.

Missing Muhammad Ali

ON MARCH 6, 1964, Cassius Clay took on the name Muhammad Ali. Not many knew at the time that he would go on to take one of the greatest stances in history, and subsequently become possibly the bravest and most unselfish Black American heroes of all time. His stance against the Vietnam War will be remembered for all time:

"I ain't got no quarrel with no Viet Cong......No Viet Cong ever called me nigger. I will die before I sell out my people for the White man's money."

"No, I am not going 10,000 miles to help murder, kill, and burn other people to simply help continue the domination of white slave masters over dark people the world over. This is the day and age when such evil injustice must come to an end."

" If I thought the war would bring freedom and equality to twenty-two million of my people, they wouldn't have to draft me. I'd join tomorrow. But I either have to honor the laws of the land or the laws of Allah. I have nothing to lose by standing up and following my beliefs. We've been in jail for four hundred years."

"Why should the ask me to put on a uniform and go 10,000 miles from home and drop bombs and bullets on brown people in Vietnam while so-called negroes in Louisville are treated like dogs.[142]

It wasn't until the summer of 1955, as David Remnick writes in *King of the World,* that Ali saw the face of racism in all its horror. Emmitt Till, a 14-year-old boy from Chicago, was spending the summer with relatives in a Mississippi River town called Money. The Supreme Court had ruled in *Brown v. Board of Education* the year before, and Mississippi seethed over the integration decision. After Till made a flirtatious remark to a grocery cashier, the woman's husband and the husband's half brother broke into Till's uncle's house, shot the boy in the head, then threw his body in the Tallahatchie River. Cassius was a year younger than Till, and the murder affected him deeply.

Ali says his real motivation in standing against the government was to protest the way it treated Black Americans. "If it was about helping Blacks," he said of the Vietnam War, "I would have gone in a minute." [143]

ON APRIL 28, 1967, Ali refused induction into the Army at the height of the war in Vietnam. He was criminally indicted and on June 20, 1967, convicted of refusing induction into the U.S. Armed Forces and sentenced to five years in prison. He was stripped of his title, sentenced to prison, and fined $10,000. Although freed on appeal, he was inactive for over three years while his case dragged on. He eventually obtained a license from the state of New York, and in 1971 the Supreme Court ruled in his favor. He was free by every measure once again, but not until he left a permanent mark on America's conscience.

Muhammad Ali is indeed an American hero. He is respected by millions, crosses over to all races, and in the eyes of many has indeed attained hero status. He achieved an unparalleled level of respect and admiration due the strength of his convictions and the reasons of his actions. History taught him that most wars are wrought on people of color. As a result, Muhammad Ali sacrificed millions of dollars and almost four quality years of his life and career to stand up for his convictions, and this was in a time when Black people had to endure some of the most vicious and cruel treatment that White America could dish out. He was a fighter that refused to fight in a war that was not his. He told America and the world that Black people were important and that even if it meant his life, he would not raise one finger to kill a member of another colored race of people that had done absolutely nothing to him or his people. He meant it, he lived it and he will forever be remembered for it.

What would a youthful Muhammad Ali do today, given the present situation Black people are in? What example would he set as he observed his people on the brink of extinction? If he were in his prime today, would he still be the highest paid athlete of this generation, surpassing the great Michael Jordan or the incomparable Tiger Woods? The answer could quite possibly be yes. Would he make continuous visits to inner-city schools, create scholarship funds, and conduct marches, rallies and speeches? Probably yes. But he probably wouldn't stop there. Would he spend a significant portion of his fortune to further the Black cause of prosperity, respect and life? Probably yes. Yes. Would he stand by idly, as the Killer Systems and Afflictions pummel BA into extinction? Probably no. Muhammad Ali would do today what he did yesterday, and that is show the world that he believes in, and loves his race, no matter how downtrodden they might be. He loved his race because he loved himself. He was a rare person who truly used his star power and charisma to make America a better land for all people, and for that, he is surely missed. Today, Muhammad Ali would make a difference unlike no other. That is what his legacy whispers to me.

The Standard of Leadership Today

BUT FEAR NOT, as there is one who has picked up the torch and continues to run with it. David Robinson is today's Muhammad Ali. He goes about his business quietly, and without much media attention, but has lit a fire nonetheless. He will not call anybody out, but then again he doesn't need to, as his actions speak much louder than words. He has quietly, professionally and perhaps unknowingly, shown us the way to rebuild a contingent of people who categorically and undeniably need rebuilding. And although The Carver Academy is not a household name within BA, it is heretofore hailed as one of the great examples of what BA needs.

David Robinson and his wife, Valerie, donated $11 million dollar to the Carver Academy. By any measure, that is no small drop in the bucket. Together, they also contribute countless hours to the commitment of excellence and purpose of The Carver Academy. In short, they have dedicated their lives to their purpose. This is the type of leadership that BA needs. A special thanks goes out to Mr. and Mrs. David Robinson, a special couple with a special way of caring.

To Whom Much is Given, Much is Expected Of

IT IS QUITE possible that you may be asking, "Where is this all going?" The answer resonates, "To the Promised Land, to make Dr. King's dream a reality!" BA needs superior educational achievement from top to bottom. BA has to take the high road of education because it is the lack of superior educational achievement that has gotten BA into this fine mess in the first place. For all of the annual homage paid to Dr. King, for all of the replaying of his legendary speeches, and for all of the regression and inaction by BA since the death of Dr. King, absolutely nothing substantial has been done to elevate BA from the pits of hell on earth. It is as if not only has the rest of the world become satisfied with Dr. King's speeches, but BA has also. Dr. King talked about where we needed to go! And now I am talking about it also. Do not lose sight of that, and never let it stray too far from your thoughts. There is a place that BA needs to go, and it is called the Promised Land. Let us not disrespect Dr. King's efforts one more day with ceremonial reprieve. Let us honor him, as well as all the other s that valiantly fought for BA's rights, with intelligent action. There is work to do. Let us complete the dream.

Black Professional Entertainers – Our Obe Won Kenobe

THE PEOPLE THAT have the capability of leading BA out of mediocrity are today's Black professional entertainers. The task of asking Black superstars to donate their time, money and star power is not something that I am shy of. It is only natural that for once and in the most dangerous of times, the ones to help BA are Black people themselves. It is logically the first and only place to start. BA should not be ashamed to lean on its own for help. The United Way gets its way because of donations from millions of people and corporations around the world. The Red Cross stays in the black and out of the red as a result of philanthropic gifts and volunteerism from thousands of people and businesses. Right now, BA needs help. Black superstars can provide that help. This particular cause just happens to have a targeted group of people to lead the way in saving lives: its own people.

Not the government, nor Corporate America, nor the M.O.C. can be expected to save BA. This time, it must be that Black people help themselves at a time when everything is on the line, and this is the way it should be. If BA can come together to perform so great a duty, it will never again need to rely on the government or anyone else for that matter. It simply comes down to pride and self-love.

With the support of Black superstar athletes and entertainers, the condition of BA improves commensurate to the rate in which BA buy into the vision. Simply put, Black superstars are the ones. It must be remember that BA's entertainers cannot do it by themselves, but only lead the way. There are millions of Black Americans that are able to contribute in some way to the cause of saving BA, and make no mistake about it, it will take every last member make this miracle happen.

And so the question remains, why do I state that today's Black multi-million dollar superstar athletes and entertainers need to lead the charge of emancipation from extinction? The answer is because BA needs new schools, and it needs new schools now. There is no time for any more panels, roundtable discussions, think tanks, meetings, reports, or symposiums. We know what is happening. The whole world knows what is happening. It is time to do something. An immediate enactment of a plan for survival can begin, and Black superstars can get it started as expeditiously as is possible.

Making Sense of The Call to Service

THE IDENTIFICATION OF Black American superstar entertainers as BA's saviors may come as a surprise to many. It is like the prophecy that was not prophesized. The coming of the Lord and Savior Jesus Christ was foretold way back in the Old Testament. However, the elite group of people that can save BA was not envisioned. There was nothing from Nostradamus. The Swami was on vacation. The memo was never sent. Up to this point, there has not been a clear vision that has been formulated to put a stop to the decimation of BA, but there is now. So it is understood and expected that some may not see how Black superstars can achieve such a dream. I say to you, you should believe. I say to you, get ready to be a part of it. I say to you, stop what you are doing and look around. The time is now to take a stand.

Soon after America came out of the Civil Rights Era, professional sports became totally integrated. Gradually, salaries, endorsements and recognition power went stratospheric. What role did the Civil Rights conquests play in the successes of today's Black entertainers? Much credit is often given to athletes and entertainers of years past, but how much credit does the freedom fighters deserve? It just may be possible that the reason Black people have been blessed with the ability to be amongst the world's greatest athletes and entertainers is because of where BA finds itself today. Does BA have its own set of disciples waiting to set their people free? Has BA suffered its own 40 years in the wilderness, only to have one last opportunity to get it right, to make amends, to live?

Looking back, it was only forty or so years ago when Black people were victims of American apartheid. It took the power of the Civil Rights movement to negotiate a standard of living that resulted in a much more level playing field in life. Nationally, schools opened their doors, jobs became more plentiful, the American dream opened up to Blacks, and most importantly, professional sports and the industry became fully integrated. The work was done, the best came out of it, and a man had a dream. That dream has only been honored one month a year, when the intent was to be for a lifetime.

QUESTION. WHAT DO you do with more money than you will ever be able to spend in a lifetime? You build a New School System for inner city America!

New School Systems

NEW SCHOOL SYSTEMS! An ultimate Action Plan Implementation technique! An awesome and effective way to create strong, visionary and effective school systems! A new educational system calls for new schools. The more schools BA can build, the better BA will function. BA needs more schools like the great Carver Academy, and as the Stars Wars character Yoda would say, "Build them we must!" A school system is one that consists of an elementary, middle, and high school. A graduating class of two hundred to three hundred students would be ideal. Each school system will start with an elementary school, followed by a middle school, and finalized with a high school. The New School Systems are to be placed in at least the top 100 cities across America, all built to accommodate grades k-12. The goal is to create an annual graduating class of ten to twenty percent of the entire graduating class of Black students in the entire United States. According to the Digest of Education Statistics approximately 330,000 Black high school students graduated in the year 2001, which makes the goal to create a national school system that would graduate somewhere in the neighborhood of 33,000 student-leaders. This calls for a goal of approximately 200 school systems.

Keep in mind that even with the realization of these new school systems, the rebuilding process is now complete unless BA pursues the 'Reformation of Public Schools' and its 'Transition Classes and Schools'. Both new and old school systems have to working at top proficiency to realize the dream. Every resource must be employed. Better and healthier menu choices are vital. Down with sugar, soda pop, and fattening snacks, and up with fruits, vegetables, nuts and water. Academic competitions and dress codes can be of considerable significance. More traditional tools such as parental volunteerism and involvement will also help to make the dream come true. The present assortment of enrichment programs and private foundations will continue to do their part also. Once again, remember that BA must find a way to allow its students to reach their academic potential, to allow those who want to learn be allowed to learn, and to make it all happen.

AND SO, HERE is the ultimate goal of the Pursuit of Educational Excellence: **To transform Black American students into the top-rated students in both the public school system and the private school system sectors!** There is no other way, as the greater the reward, the greater the price. Dr. King never said it would be easy. He just wanted BA to get there. The Promised Land has to be a place that we reach in our minds. Yes, there are others already where BA needs to go, but the goal of BA will be to join the club, and hopefully push the envelope that only our ancestors from Africa could appreciate. That will be the Promised Land.

Lofty goals some might say. "Impossible!" others may blurt. I say this is what BA needs, and that there is no other choice. The number one educational status can be accomplished school system by school system and student by student. Principals, teachers, parents, volunteers, and Black Superstars are needed to sign on. People have fought harder for lesser causes, and there is no greater cause that deserves the total effort and dedication of all other than the pursuit of educational excellence by BA.

A goal of extremely high altitude it is, yet one that will bring out every inch of charity, work ethic, and character of all who partake. I cannot think of a more worthy undertaking. It can be accomplished brick by brick, and nail by nail, in building new schools. And along the way, a very large contingent of folks will forever be grateful. A New School System not to be confused as being the new status symbol of the wealthy, but ran extremely important and necessary investment into the future and survival of BA.

Strength in Numbers

THERE ARE A substantial number of Black and Latino professional athletes in the NFL, MLB and the NBA. In the year 2005, the Black athletes numbered 1,228 in the NFL, 311 in the NBA, and 111 in MLB. In regards to Latinos, there were 9 in the NFL, 5 in the NBA, and 326 in MLB. There were 3 Black Head Coaches and 0 Latino Head Coaches in the NFL, 4 Latino and 3 Black Managers in the MLB, and 11 Black and 0 Latino Head Coaches in the NBA.[144]

The salaries that are paid out in all three men's professional sports leagues are indeed exorbitant. In the NFL, the top twenty-five salaries range from number one at $35,000,000 per year to number twenty-five at $9,300,000 per year. In the MLB, the top twenty-five salaries range from a high of number one at $26,000,000 to number twenty-five at $12,500,000 per year. In the NBA, the top twenty-five salaries range from a high of number one at $27,696,000 to number twenty-five at $12,900,000 per year. Multi-million dollar salaries reach as far as the top one hundred players in the NBA, and when combined with the other sports leagues, the number grows. When endorsements are figured in, some of the athletes find their annual revenues doubled and tripled. There are also superstars in Golf, Tennis, and Track & Field.[145]

There are a number of CEO, President, Vice-President, Head Coach, and Assistant Coach positions held by minorities, in addition to one Owner and several Minority Owners. Head coaches earn multi-million dollar salaries as well as many of the athletes, and like the athletes, have lucrative endorsement contracts tacked on. The synergy of it all is that professional sports create incredibly wealthy athletes, coaches, executives, and owners, with tremendous recognition indexes and incredible fundraising abilities.

IT DOESN'T STOP there. There are many Superstar actors, actresses, businessman, businesswomen, television personalities, physicians, attorneys, and philanthropists that possess the financial wherewithal to make great things happen. Even the sports teams themselves can play a major role in the rebirth of BA. In all, there are thousands of entities, both inside and outside BA that are capable of assisting in the rebirth of BA. BA has been America's weakest link, henceforth bringing to mind the old saying, "A chain is only as strong as its weakest link". Thus, helping BA to grow strong grows All of America strong.

This is no attempt to keep track of the salaries of rich athletes and entertainers. That is not the case at all. Besides, the approximately salaries of the public entertainers is generally public knowledge, and can easily be ascertained by anyone seeking this information. My goal is to connect the dots between the massive needs of BA and its potential saviors. BA needs to be saves, and the only way that will be accomplished is for all of BA's superstars and supporters to pitch in and help. The truth is, for many of today's entertainment superstars, the sort of undertaking of building a New School System would be fairly easy. The key is to get those that are able that it is the right thing to do.

Location, Location, Location

THERE ARE MULTIPLE professional sports teams in practically all of the major cities in America. American mid-size cities, and even some of the smaller cities are home to at least one superstar. Major cities such as Atlanta, Boston, Chicago, Cleveland, Dallas, Detroit, Houston, Los Angeles, Miami, Minneapolis-St. Paul, New York, Oakland, Phoenix, Pittsburgh, Philadelphia, Seattle, and Washington all have at least three sports teams from the NBA, NFL, and MLB, with an NHL franchise thrown in for good measure. These cities should have at least three New School Systems built.

Cities such as Cincinnati, Indianapolis, Nashville, New Jersey, San Diego, and Tampa Bay have two sports teams. The goal for these cities would be to build at least two New School Systems.

These same cities also tend to have numerous Superstars from the business, movie and recording industries. This seems to be the case because the cities that have professional sports franchises always seem to have peripheral professional growth. Upon the arrival of a professional sports franchise, there is always an influx of corporate, professional, entrepreneurial, census population and celebrity growth that follows. While sports franchises steal the daily headlines, the width and depth of the total professional landscape of these new metropolitan juggernauts is often overlooked. What we are talking about here are resources. There cannot be a movement without them.

The Benefits of Investing in a School System

THERE ARE MANY benefits for those that choose to become a New School System founder. There is the beauty of seeing future scholars grow and blossom directly under their leadership; direct involvement with the biggest social movement since the Civil Rights era; personal involvement in the uplifting of local communities and BA; tax write-offs for multiple years; Board of Directors Presidency; a post-retirement career; the showcasing of leadership, charitable, and fundraising skills; and finally, the opportunity to make healthy, productive families for generations to come.

In regards to the financing of New School Systems, the financial commitments would be funded not all at once, but rather over a number of years, such as five or ten, and in a way that is advantageous to the founder. Fundraising activities include private contributions from philanthropic individuals, small businessmen and women, and corporations. Fundraisers spearheaded by the founders themselves, telethons, local charitable productions, payroll contributions, productions brainstormed by students, parents and school staffs are options as well. The possibilities are endless, and all are very important pieces of the fundraising process.

There also are some very important benefits to the children that are involved in these new school systems. These benefits are synergetic in nature, as they positively affect the families, communities, and especially the futures of the kids. Here are some of the benefits:

- Healing – From the first day a commitment to build a New School System is made, the healing of BA begins. As the press conference unrolls, the entire nation becomes aware of this new commitment. The respective communities immediately gain much-needed respect. Expectations climb as the community follows the infallible blueprint to success, the Pursuit of Educational Excellence, and in doing so, failure will not be an option.

- Symbolism – The New School Systems will be foundations of strength in the lives of the children for the rest of their lives. BA will now have a number of 'smart-headquarters' capable of supplying inner city communities with ample future leaders that not only will be capable of doing great things, but actually do them as well. The New School Systems will be the new symbols of the rebirth of BA.

- <u>Spirituality</u> – The pride of the children will be reborn. Their self-esteem is now high up in the clouds as they have a chance to be whatever they want to be, without interruption. They get the chance to set high expectations and goals, reach them, and then set more.

- <u>Respect</u> – The children will feel a newfound respect as they claim ownership of a new movement that is both for, and about them. And with studious brows on their faces, the children can earn that respect everyday.

- <u>The Future</u> – From the first day they set foot in their new schools, the children of the New School Systems will know what direction they are headed in. They will both understand and commit to hard work every single day. They demand the best from themselves, and then put out the needed effort to meet those demands. They know where they are going, and can now become the very best students and people they can be.

BUILDING NEW SCHOOL Systems would be like planting new fruit trees. As new students are planted within the systems, fresh, vibrant minds are harvested, and a slew of academic scholars, teachers, principals, geniuses, business executives and new leaders will bloom into welcomed additions to inner city communities.

The positive effects that New School Systems will have on Black families have no boundaries. The increased emphasis on better education will significantly help Black communities as it relates to homicides, drug trafficking, role models and families. These effects will grow stronger with time, as long as BA continues to do whatever is needed to not fall back into the circumstances that were once the root causes of all its problems. As BA turns the corner, there should be no looking back.

These are serious but exciting times, and all of BA must do whatever is necessary in order to make a difference. There is quite a lot of work to be done, as there are hundreds of thousands of minds to shape, and even more lives to save. BA is responsible for providing its own solutions. Once the ball is rolling, others are sure to join in and be a part of the new BA. As BA dwindles, so does the customer base of just about Black entertainment superstar, business, and corporation that calls Black Americans "customer". Along the way, it is important to fight against government dis-investment in inner city schools. The right and expectancy of equitable investment dollars into inner city schools is not a handout or a freebie, it is a right. It is important that inner city schools get their proper amount of tax dollar investment. The government can take back its healthcare, its parks, and its food stamps. But let them be held accountable for inner city schools, and know that BA expects and demands the school investment dollars its schools are entitled to, and not a penny less.

Who 'Dose Cities That Need New School Systems?

ON THE FRONT page of the USA TODAY edition dated June 21, 2006, is an article entitled "Big-city schools struggle", subtitled 'Low graduation rates may also be a national problem'.

According to research released on June 20, 2006, fourteen urban school districts have on-time graduation rates lower than 50%. Included amongst those fourteen cities are Detroit, Baltimore, New York, Milwaukee, Cleveland, Los Angeles, Miami, Dallas, Denver and Houston. It goes on to say that while the nation's overall graduation rate is about 70%, the study suggests that graduation rates are much lower than previously reported in many states. (See the heading 'Accurate Information' on page 111. Let us hope this scenario does not repeat itself in relations to HIV/AIDS).

The study finds three school districts graduate fewer than 40% of its students: Detroit (21.7%), Baltimore (38.5%), and New York City (38.9%). Although this is harrowing information to many of us, there are those entities, such as the Killer Systems and Industries, which will benefit from this situation.[146]

As BA's SCHOOLS continue to be dumbed-down, the children will continue to pay the price. Unemployment, prison, and death await those that do not come out of school with direction, purpose, and intelligence. As the schools continue to be adverse to effective discipline and order, the situation will only get worse. As the schools allow kids to be harassed, assaulted, ridiculed, and enticed with drugs, sex, and violence, the base of good students will continue to erode, and the list of lost students will grow. As inner city schools continue to lose more and more tax dollars, continue to be reactive instead of preventive, and lose those tax dollars to the commercial coffers of the M.O.C., the road ahead will only get bumpier

In light of all this, there are creative solutions. By utilizing Action Plan Implementation measures, by effectively re-building and augmenting on the three fundamental elements of society, which are, new jobs, new legislation, and strong, visionary and effective school systems, BA has a much better chance at prosperity. In fact, it could then be said that the odds would be in BA's favor to succeed. BA needs action, not reaction. Community Action, The Reformation of Public Schools and New School Systems are the platforms in which survival and success can be built on.

PART VI

THE PROMISED

LAND

LEADERSHIP

EVERY FORM OF HUMAN ENTITY DEPENDS on some form of leadership to provide direction, ensure safety, and promote prosperity.

A CORPORATION HAS a CEO. A church has its pastor. A school has a principal.

Who will lead **BA**?

Help is on the way.

A World of Sorrow

ON AUGUST 29, 205, Hurricane Katrina arrived and unleashed its
awesome power on the states of Alabama, Mississippi, and Louisiana.
Later that day the rampaging Katrina departed, but only after leaving
a legacy of being the most destructive natural disaster in the history of
America.

In the following weeks and months, news coverage provided story
after story of personal tragedy and loss, governmental failure and cover-
up, and of a nation torn. One of the stories covered was that of star guard
Stephon Marbury of the New York Knickerbockers. As Mr. Marbury
recalled the events of the hurricane tragedy and the losses incurred by
the people of New Orleans, he emotionally and unabashedly broke
down into a man overcome emotionally by the power of the chain of
events that had taken place almost right before our eyes. The images of
the disaster had taken a toll, as the realization of the enormous loss of
life and property seemed surreal.

For many, Mr. Marbury capsulated the tragedy better than all
the news coverage combined. All across America, those who witnessed
his outpouring became connected through his personal expression.
Hurricane Katrina's destruction made sure all had taken notice that
life is precious indeed, and reminded us all that tomorrow is not
promised.

I, TOO, WAS deeply moved by the event of Katrina, and in more ways
than one. I have close family in New Orleans, numbering a dozen
or more that were affected by this disaster. My roots go back to the
year 1976, as that was the year I attended the Summer Engineering
Institute at Southern University in Baton Rouge, a school in which I
would attend my first year of college beginning the fall of 1977. With
my grandfather, grandmother and dozens of other relatives being from
Louisiana, it is somewhat of a second home to me. One of the first news
shots of the disaster that I witnessed on television was the neighborhood
where my Aunt Pearl lived, at the intersection of Leonidas and Earhart.
As was the misfortune of many other New Orleans families, we, too,
lost an important family member.

As shocking and painful as the Katrina saga is, I cried long before Katrina touched land. The fact of the matter is that before the dreadful day of August 29, 2005 arrived, I was already in a grievous state because I understood that BA was already being pummeled by forces that in effect wreaked more damage on BA than Hurricane Katrina ever could. For me, it did not take that acutely tragic day in August to stir up my emotions and feel the pain. I already understood that BA had already been awash in a human flood of pain, suffering, apathy and death. I knew that the Mortality Metrics and the Afflictions have been running rampant throughout Black families and communities unabatedly for decades, leaving death and human destruction in its wake, just like Hurricane Katrina.

HURRICANE KATRINA SHOWED the world what Mother Nature could do, American government showed the world what it will not do, and the entire ordeal showed BA what it needs to do: Take control of its destiny. The entire world took note of the acute and sudden effects of a hurricane and its power, and for a relatively brief period of time, the victims mourned. Rest assured though as sure as day turns to night, the flood waters will recede, and the eradication of BA will go back to its trickle state, and once again this phenomenon will not only go largely unnoticed, but not acted upon as well.

BA is swimming in sorrow and destruction. The anesthetized mindset of BA is embarrassingly evident. It's like being in a house of mirrors, as BA sees what is happening, but does not see what is happening. BA feels the pain, but cannot touch the pain. BA talks about its problems, but does very little to solve its problems. BA cannot stop the bleeding, and likewise, the healing process cannot begin. BA is besieged by a seemingly never-ending list of problems that in no short order is killing it into extinction. Swiftly and deftly, BA must find a way to fully utilize all of its resources so that collectively it will not only no longer be sitting ducks for natural disasters, but human ones as well.

Bigger, Faster, Stronger and Smarter Capitalists

I HAVE PEGGED Black Superstars as the conduit for the redemption of BA. This is based on the need to ascend as a race intellectually on a plan to build approximately 200 New School Systems, which are guesstimated to have building and start-up costs in the 20 to 25 million-dollar range. From there, the necessary funds are needed to cover administrative and other costs to run the school systems. This can be done also, as BA wields amazing earning and recognition power in the entertainment industry, and has all of the necessary resources, and then some, to transform from its present condition into one of great accomplishment, promise, and excellence in all things. It is all about the people and the vision. Selfishness must take a back seat, and charity, commitment, energy and vision must drive the bus.

Ironically, as well as Black entertainment superstars seem to be doing, there is an old reality show that bears a theme that directly relates to the current state of Blacks in the entertainment industry. Black superstars have not really flexed their collective muscle and star power, and in realty, there is room for a tremendous amount of growth in terms of business enterprise and artistic projects. Although they cannot be blames for taking the money and running, they do have the capability to run faster and further.

There was once a television show entitled, "The Six Million Dollar Man", where Lee Majors played a character, Steve Austin, who was badly hurt in a plane crash. Subsequently, this character was rebuilt with bionics that made him bigger, faster and stronger. Black American sports and entertainment professionals have that same capability. A realization of their true worth and power would result in an exponential growth of their present net worth, which could ultimately offer even more financial power to build a united moral infrastructure that would rebuild BA. Black American entertainment superstars can be rebuilt. They can be made into bigger, faster and stronger capitalists. However, they will not be rebuilt with bionics. They will be rebuilt with courage, passion and a purpose that hopefully "Hindered" will provide.

Collegiate Athletics and Opportunities

He starred at Tuscaloosa High School in Tuscaloosa, Alabama. Additionally, he:

- He lettered for three seasons from 1972-74 at The University of Alabama.

- He was on just the second team—1972-- that allowed black players to suit up in The University of Alabama's all white uniforms.
- He was the starting center on The 1973 University of Alabama National Championship team.
- He was all SEC and Kodak All-American at The University of Alabama his senior year in 1974.
- He was a defensive coach on The University of Alabama's back-to-back National Championship teams of 1978-79.
- He has an award named after him due to his dedication and commitment, called the "Sylvester Croom Commitment to Excellence Award."
- He earned his Bachelor's Degree in History from The University of Alabama at the age of twenty years.
- He earned his Master's Degree in Educational Administration in 1977 from The University of Alabama as well. His father was an All-American football player at Alabama A&M University and served as the team Chaplain at The University of Alabama.

In 2003, The University of Alabama had a head coaching vacancy. Ladies and gentlemen, I present to you, the new coach of The University of Alabama.......Mike Shula? [147]

Yes, that's right. Mike Shula. It would be difficult to come up with a more storybook tale of a standout athlete, outstanding person and genuine homeboy who had the perfect opportunity to lead his alma mater in the pursuit of intercollegiate athletic success, only to have the story ending subcontracted out to Stephen King. Everything about Mr. Croom's resume says University of Alabama, and yet he was passed by like a mailbox on a afternoon neighborhood stroll. Instead, Mr. Croom would go on to become the first Black head football coach in the Southeastern Conference at Mississippi State University, and not the University of Alabama. Hats off to Mississippi State, good luck to Coach Croom.

SINCE THAT MOST insulting day, BA could have flexed its muscles by the speed of thought and changed the entire complexion of Coach Croom's career. All eyes should have gone from looking at the University of

Alabama, and in one slow motion blink and turn of the head, swiveled toward Mississippi State University. But it did not happen, and instead, every Mississippi hopeful and Alabama redneck probably said, "What the hell?" They're still sighing on at the University if Alabama! They still don't get it, do they? It apparently looks that way.

At a time when the intelligent decision by every Black recruit (especially their parents) of the University of Alabama should have found the fortitude and common sense to abandon the University of Alabama and instead attend Mississippi State University, they instead moseyed right along and went to "that school in Tuscaloosa" anyway, seemingly without a clue to the insidious decision of the University of Alabama.

What about Coach Croom? Sure, he's a grown man and a professional. But what happened had to hurt him. From what I have seen of him, he might never say what I'm printing, but the inability of Blacks to recognize and correct the contempt of a Black coach by the University of Alabama probably hurts worse. The fact that Black players and their parents still choose to attend the University of Alabama is the worst aspect of this entire debacle. Do they have a clue to the fact that the University of Alabama will treat them the same way it treated Coach Croom? What about dignity, support, opportunity, and networking? The inability of BA to make the wise and practical choice instead of the inconsiderate and judicial one is its biggest weakness. As for the mindset of Black students and parents that chose to look right through Coach Croom and attend the University of Alabama anyway, they will have their day in the courtroom of conscience. Will BA ever learn?

Collegiate Coaches

AT THIS TIME there are 117 colleges participating in Division 1-A Football. Fifty percent of the athletes are Black; Twenty-five percent of the assistant coaches are Black; Only three head coaches are Black, and they are: Tyrone Willingham at The University of Washington; Karl Dorrell at U.C.L.A., and Sylvester Croom at Mississippi State University.

Says Terry Bowden: "In the last dozen years, my family has made $20 million dollars as Division 1-A Head Football Coaches." His father, Bobby, is the head coach at Florida State University; His brother, Terry, is the head coach at Clemson University; and Terry is the former head coach at The University of Auburn, and is presently a football analyst for ABC Sports.[148]

In the 2004-05 season, only 24 of the 325 Division 1 Women's Basketball Programs had black female head coaches. In women's college basketball, 41.6 percent of the players are Black, but less than 8 percent of the coaches are black women. Vivian Stringer at Rutgers University and Terri Williams-Flournoy at Georgetown University name a few.

By comparison, 58.2 percent of men's college basketball players are Black, with nearly 25 percent of coaches being black. The 11-member ACC has no black female head coaches.[149]

So why is it important to support and attend universities that hire minority coaches? Self-respect is the number one reason. Throughout American history, Black people have been grossly disrespected in terms of opportunity, from 'coloreds can't eat here' to 'Blacks can't coach here', the message has been the same: 'you are not good enough'. How dare BA give its blessing in being disrespected! After the way The University of Alabama treated Coach Croom, it is hard to imagine that a parent would still allow their child to attend the University of Alabama, which has said to Blacks, "You can play football for us, and you can bring in tens of millions of dollars in revenue every year to the university, but you are not good enough to coach here."

BA could have built a bigger, faster and stronger capitalist by supporting Mississippi State University, Coach Croom and every other university with a Black coach by simply attending the universities that have Black coaches. American universities that hire Black coaches should be overflowing with All-American and All-State athletes, simply because they gave Blacks the opportunities to have the same benefits and rewards that Coach Bowden spoke of. These Black coaches should almost be recruited by the players, and not vice versa. If Tommy Amaker can coach at Michigan, any Black ballplayer has a chance to coach at The University of Michigan. If Coach Croom can coach at Mississippi State University, any Black ballplayer can coach at Mississippi State University. Instead, some Blacks still display the lack of vision and intelligence that has always been attributed to Blacks. And therein lies a major fault of BA, one that touches family, community and sports: the lack of unity, purpose, pride and self-respect.

FINANCIAL ENE IS reason number two. As can be seen with the Bowden family, head coaching jobs are not only lucrative, but can be springboards into various other career opportunities, with or without nepotism. Head coaches, athletic directors, television sports analysts, scouts, agents, play-by-play announcers and endorsements are all part of the equation. We're talking tens of millions of dollars here. Hello! The more successful Coach Croom is, the more successful he will be on and off the field. The more successful he is on and off the field, the more he can help others. The business of sports is just that, a business, and with that, the opportunities to make tons of money and help others to be successful are as wide as the Grand Canyon and as tall as mountains. BA needs to understand the big picture, and create more opportunities.

The world needs to see that BA can make logical and sensible choices. More importantly, BA needs to see that it can make logical and sensible choices. BA as an entire group needs to be respected for its intellect, and not just athletic or acting ability. Decision making without deliberation and discretion renders BA somewhat silly-looking time after time. Support the ground breaking, history making Black coaches and not the biased universities. BA does not have to repeatedly go for the carrot. In-state rivalries, smooth talking and high-strung personality coaches, recruiting visits, in-state colleges, the illusions of multiple television appearances, immature affinities for school colors, helmet styles or uniform designs are pathetic reasons to sign on to collegiate athletic programs when compared to the much more meaningful principles of respect and opportunity.

Until Black Americans can make the proper and intelligent decisions concerning not just sports, but every aspect of society, it will never fully flex its muscles to the extent that it can. There will always be whispers of a lack of intellect, purpose, or vision by BA by those that cannot speak in a microphone due to the Gag Order principle, but will indeed talk about it at the bar over a drink. In the meantime, BA will continue to be the joke of society. To the parents of young Black All-State and All-American athletes, put yourself in the shoes of the

Black coaches working hard to get the opportunity to coach your own children. Who will your child play for? Coacg Croom, or Coach Billy Bob? Keep in mind that one day your child may hope to be a coach also. Here's to hoping that coaching opportunities will still be there for your children, as they are here right now for Coach Croom and the other handfuls of Black collegiate football coaches.

Professional Agents

SPORTS AND ENTERTAINMENT at the professional level offers some scenarios that are very similar to the University of Alabama and Coach Croom situation, only in a 'other side of the coin' flavor. Take brothers Carl and Kevin C. Poston III, of Professional Sports Planning (PSP), superstar professional agents whom negotiate deals for more than 40 players, mostly National Football League stars. Their clients include Kellen Winslow Jr. of the Cleveland Browns, Charles Woodson of the Oakland Raiders and Charles Rogers of the Detroit Lions.

Carl was practicing law in Houston in 1989 when a friend referred a Houston Oilers football player who had a tax problem. At about the same time, Kevin, also a lawyer, was working on financing for a new basketball arena outside Detroit. They decided to try their hand as agents, printed up a brochure, and began a tour of NFL tryouts, college stadiums and the living rooms of prospects such as Terrell Buckley, their first star client.

In regards to the race question, all of the Postons' clients are African American, leading some to speculate that PSP prefers to represent only Blacks. Such talk mostly amuses the Postons: "We'd love to represent white stars," says Carl, 49. "We don't get the time of day from White players and their families."[150]

Is it racist for White players and families to not give Black agents their business? Possibly? Or it could simply be that White ballplayers deal with agents whom they feel comfortable with, those being of there own race. There are possibly many reasons as to why this is so. I, for one, cannot recall a situation where a Black agent signed a superstar White ballplayer. On the collegiate, I cannot recall a season where a Black head sports coach signed any first team high school All-Americans to their respective college sports programs. The reasons could range from comfort, to racial unity, to trust, to stereotypical attitudes, to friendship, to a host of other reasons. However, the bottom line is that Whites do not sign with Black coaches and agents. Period.

THE BIGGER PROBLEM is trying to find an intelligent answer to the question of why Blacks do not support Black agents or coaches to the extent that they should? To debate this question and argue with the component that does not support Black agents and coaches is destructive in itself. That is where the water really gets murky. Within BA, the loyalty, the genuine and total support, and the unspoken intelligent behaviors are absent. Maybe it is too simple to understand. A life based on principle would never allow a Black ballplayer to stray away from a school that provides Blacks an opportunity to coach, an agent that can be truly like a brother or father figure with the added bonus of growing the Black professional representation business. Again, it's about opportunity and self-respect. At some point BA must learn to live on sound and good principles.

What when wrong with the attempts to cross over by the Poston brothers? They are amongst the best in the world in their field. I happen to know Kevin personally. He is a wonderful human being who over the years has remained grounded as a person while achieving astronomical success in his profession. Yet, he and Carl cannot get the time of day from prospective White clients. The situation deserves much scrutiny. It is feasible that professional athletes of any race would choose to gravitate towards competent professional representation of their own race. For reasons that defy common sense, Blacks tend to not do the same.

BA could flex its muscle by supporting the Postons, just as collegiate athletes should be supporting the Amakers, the Crooms, and the Willinghams of the collegiate sports world. The Postons should have cups that runneth over with clients. In a simple world, if sixty percent of players are Black, then sixty percent of agents should be Black. The Postons should have enough clients to justify the creation of a major professional sports representation firm, with a full lineup of attorneys, paralegals and complete staff. This in turn could result in spin-offs of additional professional sports representation firms. This is how BA *could* flex its muscle. However, it is also how BA *does not* flex its muscle, and that is one of the reasons that BA finds itself in the position it is in.

IF ONLY BLACK collegiate and professional athletes could see beyond the statistics, television appearances and bank accounts, and realize the immense and mighty potential that offers itself for magnificent creation, and not imitation as it relates to maximization of blessings. In the end, it's not about being racist or biased, but rather being aware of and supporting the respect and opportunities that are given to us. BA needs all the opportunities it can find. The process starts with educating young athletes from grade school about the real world, past, present and future. The ability to make intelligent decisions throughout their young lives is the critical lesson. It is filled with both the appreciation of opportunity and the dedication to hard work. It ends with self-respect, a stick-together type of existence, and business empires that go way beyond the multi-million dollar salaries and contracts of today's Black superstar athletes and entertainers. It may be difficult for some to fathom that the awesome ten, twenty, and thirty million dollar salaries of today's Black superstars could be suffixed with an additional zero if only those same superstars were to decide to maximize their own total potential, and not let others take home the vast majority of their earnings by maximizing their potential for them. It's possible. In binary language, just add a zero to the total collective revenue of all of BA's superstar athletes and entertainers. You do speak binary, don't you?

Professional Sports Business Opportunities

WORLDWIDE ATHLETIC-GOODS GIANT Nike, Inc. started out as Blue Ribbon Sports in the early 1960s. With humble beginnings, Knight distributed athletic shoes imported from Japan from his father's basement and the back of his car. In 1972, the company changed its name to Nike, and its legendary "swoosh" is recognized around the world, as Nike products are available in nearly 200 countries. Since its origin, Nike has become a $15 billion dollar global business, selling shoes, sports apparel and equipment.[151]

The most popular professional athletes sign lucrative endorsement deals with companies such as Nike for the use of their name and image on its products. Nike signed Kobe Bryant of the Los Angeles Lakers to a five-year contract worth at least $40 million dollars. Kobe also signed sweet deals with McDonalds, /Coca-Cola, Nutrella, sports memorabilia company Upper Deck and basketball maker Spalding. Nike also signed superstar Lebron James to a seven-year, $90 million deal. The list of superstars with deals such as these is impressive, and there are other professional that sign deals that are not as large as these examples, but nonetheless do have endorsement deals that bring in significant amounts of money. Good deal, right? It all depends on how you look at it.[152]

In 1996, the NBA pulled in about $3 billion from licensed merchandise – with 30 percent of that ($900 million) coming from Chicago Bulls or Michael Jordan merchandise. Michael Jordan is in a world all by himself. At one time, Jordan-brand sales made up eight percent ($736 million) of Nike's $9.2 billion in revenue. Recently, that percentage has been reduced to four percent ($368 million) as the brand has sought to diversify and not be to dependant on the Jordan name brand. Still, the brand would be the no.2 basketball shoe and apparel company on its own. Bob Williams, President of Burns Sports in Chicago, says that a great endorser typically increases a company's sales by 1-3 percent. Of course, Jordan is quite the exception.[153]

The National Basketball Association, The National Football League and Major League Baseball all had sales topping $3 billion dollars apiece in the year 2005. The sales of all three professional sports leagues, Nike, Reebok, Puma and other major sports retailers that use the names and images of professional athletes are somewhere in the neighborhood of $30 billion, and with the exception of Michael Jordan, none of the athletes probably come close to earning their rightful share. However, business is business. With Black athletes accounting for the lion's share of athletic goods revenue, there are many compelling reasons for Black superstars to start their own sports apparel, shoe and novelty manufacturing company.

Keep Your Name

THERE ARE BILLIONS of reasons as to why professional athletes should not sign away their names. Does it make financial sense for an athlete to sign a deal paying $40 million dollars when he can make tens times that amount if he were just willing to put in the work required to start his own brand? Let me name just a few individuals who would not dare to even think about signing off on hundreds of millions of dollars: Bill Gates, Phil Knight, Warren Buffet, and It all comes back to the matter of Self-Respect, Financial ene and Pride. When you think about it, it all seems too easy to just have to sign a name on a piece of paper, sit back and wait for television and radio shooting dates, view the finished product, smile, and fly home on a plane and wait for the checks to come in. However, what these contracts really comprise are the world's biggest carrots. The reality is that Black superstar athletes have the grandest of grand opportunities to create the kinds of empires that small nations would be proud of. Although a five-year, $40 million endorsement deals is striking, how does it compare to a five-year, $400 million dollar business enterprise, which is the type of money an athlete like Kobe Bryant could make if he were to take the time to endure the growing pains of starting his own enterprise.

A simplified business model is one where a superstar creates a sports apparel company. There is an open door policy that allows additional superstar athletes to sign on whenever they want. When they do sign on, at that moment they create their own independent division of the company, in their own image, and thus, their own brand. The building, equipment, marketing, employees, logistics systems, corporate logo, administrative costs, human resources and product design team would already be in place and used by the superstars that sign on with the company. No one superstar makes any money off of the other superstars, and all costs are shared. The name of the game is to create, facilitate, and keep all of the money, jobs and other economic gains the company makes.

The difference is that this company is in business to uplift Black communities, and not exploit them. The beauty of it all is that the Superstars do not sign away control, and would receive 90 percent of revenue and pay out 10 percent commissions versus the other way around. All of the Superstars would utilize the same company name and logo in order to grow the brand in a uniform fashion. The only difference would be the name of the superstar athlete on the apparel, just like it works today. This could happen for *every* superstar athlete, if he or she would only keep their names, and not sign off on hundreds of millions of dollars. It would not be as difficult as it may seem. Why would it work? **Because the brands Nike, Reebok, Puma and any other apparel name, are practically worthless next to the names "James", "Wade", "Jordan", or "Magic".** The names of Superstar athletes such as the aforementioned are 'priceless' in the endorsement world.

Imagine if Michael Jordan took his no. 2 rated sports shoe and apparel ranking and had started his own business in his hometown city of Wilmington, North Carolina. His business operation would be the pride of the city and the state. With gross revenues hovering around half a billion dollars, "Air Jordan Enterprises" would probably employ hundreds of employees. This would keep money in the community, strengthen families, and allow great investment in inner city schools.

ANOTHER KEY COMPONENT to all of this is when athletes settle for endorsement deals, they also sign off on life's lessons in business. Signing on the dotted line means to also sign off on the gaining of business knowledge and experience such as tax financing, deal structuring, contracting and subcontracting, codes, accounting, public relations, marketing, consulting, and networking, to name a few. On the civic side, there is the rebuilding of inner-city infrastructures, increasing home ownership for families, improving local schools through investment and increased tax base, jobs, job shadowing opportunities for youth, and the support of minority-owned professional services such as attorneys, certified public accountants, finance managers, and cleaning services. When they sign off, it may seem to cool to let others do all of this work for them, but it makes much more business sense for them to hire their own to have their own attorneys and accountants not only do the work for them, but teach them as well. It comes with the building of the empire.

There is nothing wrong with rolling up the old sleeves and creating one's own enterprise. Phil Knight started Nike with $3,240 in 1964 as Blue Ribbon Sports, and with no name recognition. The superstars of today receive more than $3,240 just by signing an autograph. If Black athletes would only stop biting the bait like little fish and instead, attack the entrepreneurial opportunities in front of them like sharks, the athletic apparel industry landscape would be entirely different, and BA sure does need the assist. Mr. Knight has given hundreds of millions of dollars to The University of Oregon. Imagine how far that type of money would go if invested in New School Systems for inner city youth, who dearly need it. Bill Gates is one of the biggest philanthropists in the entire world, and it's all because he did not, would not, and will not ever sign off on his name.

Every last one of today's superstars could easily make hundreds of millions of dollars over the course of their careers, while also creating jobs and assisting Black families. This is the wise choice, versus settling for endorsement deals. Crucial to this model is that the jobs created could be located in Black communities, and this could mean jobs with benefits for inner city residents, which are quite difficult to come by these days, and also are usually seen leaving inner cities, and not coming into them. Many Black communities could have an entirely different look and feel if these ready to be made empires existed in the inner cities. Every athletic apparel chain in the country would clamor to have this new line apparel gear, only now the superstars are the endorsers, and not the endorsees. This is how BA has the ability to flex its muscles. It's all just an electrical impulse away.

Is It Really That Bad?

AFTER ALL OF the statistics, conditions, and prognostication, a logical question to follow could be, "Is it really that bad?" It is difficult to imagine that an entire race of people could be on the brink of social and mortal extinction. After all, 30+ million people do not vanish overnight. And therein lies the confounding degree of difficulty that can be applied to the plight of BA: it is extremely troublesome to get BA to recognize the slow-kill process that is approaching the 'wind down phase'. The extinction of BA will finalize over the next 50 or so years if the right changes are not made immediately.

How does one create a sense of urgency amongst BA and the general public? So many young people are caught up in the bull crap that television offers. The reality shows that show the lifestyles of Hip Hop millionaires, millionaire athletes, and the Hip Hop culture are very popular amongst Black youth. They are too caught up imitating a group of people that they will never become. There is so much sexual imagery within Black America culture that sexual conquests and activity will seemingly never cease. Black youth are assuredly caught up in a 'feel good' mental state, and they are dying for it. Black adults are caught up trying to make ends meet at one end of the spectrum, and failing in the sense of family on the other. Rich Black folk are holding on to their resources with all their might, feeling they are doing just fine by today's wealth standards. But it is a foolish king who lets his people die off. In time, there will be no constituency, and then, it will be the king's time to die. In the meantime, everyone else is watching television all of the damn time, doing nothing and committing to even less. There are so many ways in which BA is failing, and yet, the vast majority of Black people are doing nothing of substance to put an end to the demise of BA.

IF BA IS doing so badly, how is BA surviving? The answer is, BA is not surviving. BA is struggling, BA is holding on. BA is in fact dying off in numbers greater than births, and at a frightening pace. This is not a test of the local emergency response system. Understand that this is for real! The health, mortality, social, family, poverty, exploitation, drug, HIV/AIDS and education issues are real, and BA's condition in America is definitely one of peril. Too many of BA is standing on the sidelines not even trying to get in the game, and because of that, the fat lady is ready to sing.

There is a way for you to personally capture the state of your piece of BA. In your own city, conduct your own investigation into the quality of life. Search your local newspapers, take a tour of your city with a keen eye of observation, search the Black Yellow Pages if you have one, talk to people, sit in on your city council meetings, ask questions of your middle school and high school principals and get information by any and all means in order to determine the current state of affairs in your hometown:

- Look in the business section of your local newspaper and see how many Blacks are hired or promoted in the legal, medical, media, public relations or other professional areas. Check for managers, consultants, pharmacists, etc.

- Who are the managers of the stores you patronize?

- What is the unemployment rate in your city for Blacks?

- What is the HIV/AIDS rate at your local middle schools? High schools? In your city?

- Do the high schools in your city have extra-curricular activities besides football, basketball, and track?

- Are minorities finding decent jobs in your city?

- Is the homicide rate high among Blacks?

- Is the Black on Black crime rate high?

- Is drug dealing prevalent, persistent, and growing?

- What is the media coverage like of minorities?

- Is there an abundance of obese people?

- Who are the business owners in your community? Do other races of people own the businesses in your community? Do the Black businesses, if any, thrive?

- Are your senior citizens locked in their homes, afraid to come out, or are they enjoying their golden years?

- Are minorities losing jobs at an increasing rate?

- What are the effects of the Killer Systems and Industries in your town?

- Do you even know anyone that is ultra-successful?

- Are the high schools graduating fewer and fewer students?

- Are Blacks hurting in regards to medical insurance?

- Is there a dependency to rely on the church to solve every issue that makes headlines?

- Are Blacks involved with any or many volunteer agencies in trying to attempt to make positive changes?

The answers to these questions will tell the story. If you are not satisfied with some of the answers you get, if you are unhappy with what you discover, then you may want to get involved in such a way that you can make a difference in your community. You will no doubt be moved by what you find. On the other hand, the MO of BA has been to not be moved enough. You can help break that trend. There is enough charitably and spiritual work to be done in Black communities to last of all the rest of our lifetimes. There is a historical stand waiting to be made, and the least we all can do is attempt to make a difference.

Safe Preaching & Black Representation

TODAY, BA NEEDS more than 'Safe Preaching'. Safe Preaching is when week after week, Pastors preach primarily to the same members, the same way, and basically to the same effect. It is Safe Preaching because typically, the vast majority of their congregations are not in any immediate social crisis, and a spiritual and Godly level, it takes more than thirty minutes of ritualistic preaching every Sunday to save a soul. There are those who do not go to church, do not drive nice cars, and need the most help. It is required that Pastors step out of their comfort zones and put in work where it is needed, on the streets where the young roam aimlessly and adult alcoholics, drug addicts and illiterate can be found.

As strange as this may sound to some, BA also need less from Pastors in a certain way. One part of Black American culture that needs to change is the relying on the church to represent BA in every single instance of hardship and turmoil. Historically and invariably, BA has looked to the church for direction and opinion, regardless of the social situation. In the past, the Pastor was handed the microphone to speak, regardless of the crisis. Medical problem – call the pastor. Water main broke - call the pastor. Need our vote – call the pastor. Today's pastors are very popular individuals, and some are quite wealthy, even becoming millionaires, on the strength of tithing. It is true that Pastors have a stronghold in Black society, and because of this fact, they have been retained to a fault to represent BA.

Today, the game has changed. The situations of today call for specialists, professionals, and subject matter experts, and for the leaders of the church need to re-invent themselves. Safe Preaching cannot educate Black youth if they are not present in the churches. Safe preaching will not save people if the churches are taking in lots of money, and not giving enough out. BA does not need any more stage shows with robe-draped actors. BA needs solutions. Because Black churches occupy such a prominent role in Black American society, it is important that they become as effective as possible. And this needs to be done now, before it is too late, 'lest they run out of souls to save.

In general, BA does not need 'leaders' to lead them anywhere. Black people must not view themselves as sheep lacking a sheepherder. Black people need only to lead themselves, one family at a time, and one person at a time. Black people need no longer to look for Black activists, preachers, educators, politicians, business and community leaders to lead them anywhere. The 'help wanted' ad looking for a Black leader can be pulled. Black people need only to lead themselves back to awareness, back to school, and back to their families. Stay on top of current events, have an educational vision for yourself and your family, and understand that BA is in a war. The 'need' for one person to lead millions of people is unrealistic, and surely does not speak to the collective intelligence of BA.

Talk, talk, talk, talk, talk, talk.......talk.

It would be very interesting to count the number of panels, councils, hearing, symposiums, reports, recommendations, papers, studies, and meetings that have been convened in the name of solving the problems of BA. I am sure that an entire slew of newly–laid plans for even more of these activities are in the planning stages right now. Some of these events are chaired and attended by very educated, highly respected and well-known individuals. I'm sure that on the surface many of these 'high-powered' activities appear to be a sure thing to bring about positive change. But that is not the case.

When the adjournment of these activities occur, BA is no better off than it was when the activities convened, and in fact is sure to be incrementally worse. By the time the individual attendants of these get-togethers wake up the next morning, the answers to the problems have still not been found. However there are still the self-appreciative feelings of a job well done. "We met, we talked, we conquered……..lunch!" The wisdom bought by the collective social standing and brainpower of those in attendance was refunded due to a lack of a plan. In the end, it was all about talk.

Why All of the Partying?

THE SENSE OF urgency needed to combat BA's many problems is surely missing in some of the most important segments of Black American society. For example, if one were to listen to Black radio talk shows, one would get the impression that 'life is great, so let's have big fun'. It always makes me quiver when I check in on some of the radio broadcasts and listen to what is being put out to Black society. BA is in a state of war, and every opportunity should be made to get the message out that BA is losing the war, and some things of real substance and power must take place. Black people do need to laugh all the way to the grave, and the crap on the radio about the ridiculous, meaningless aspects of Black dating and loving within relationships is bull crap.

If you were to turn on your television or radio right now, there would probably be very little in the way of awareness messaging, educational documentaries, investigative reporting or public service announcements in regards to the dreadful BA plight. What you will find are an infinite supply of musical videos revealing young Black women shaking their asses on BET, watered-down R&B gospel-party music on BET, disgusting reality shows of sex, narcissism, egotism, and materialism, hysterically fun times on one nationally syndicated Black radio show and stupid 'relationship information' as it relates to the Black dating scene on another Black nationally syndicated radio show. And as everyone is having a grand old good time, it only adds to the illusion that all is well in BA, when just the opposite is true.

Do these entertainment venues have a home within BA? Obviously they do. But does it make sense from an intellectual and social level to have them exalted to the place they occupy? The answer is a resounding no. The fact that HIV/AIDS, teen pregnancy, physical health, foster care, and all of the other Mortality Metrics and Afflictions get incrementally worse everyday needs to take precedence. The Blacks that have a say in the media are too busy partying and having a good time. Having party cruises and creating scholarships are not the answer to solving BA's problems. Maybe the responsibility to save Black lives as efficiently as possible is not at the top of the priority lists for many, but at the same time and in repeat fashion, "to much is given, much is expected".

'Feel good' moments will not get the job done. All is not well in BA, and the continuous commercial partying is sending the wrong message not to Black people, but to society in general. Black people need to be made aware of the seriousness, the depth, and the width of its current social and medical situation in an ongoing fashion. Leading the charge should be the Black media and the Black well to do. America in general depends on the media to tell it what is going on, what to do, and how to do it. If the media reports it, then America listens. When the media broadcasts sensationalist stories such as kidnappings, shootings, murders, natural disasters, roofs that collapse, the latest diet plans, prostitution stings, volcano eruptions, mining disasters, pro athlete amoral shortcomings, drug stings, and other forms of excitement, it gets the nation's attention. The Black media though should have a bit of a different agenda. BA has issues that require the broadcast of one message loud and clear – BA is dying. To accomplish that task, a cessation to the celebration of wealth and status is needed, and all of the partying needs to stop. We don't have the luxury other groups of people have. It is time for the 'feel good' era to end, and the healing process to begin. Party time is over.

The Ascension Team

HELP IS ON the way. It is coming in the form of a new organization formed by this author to be known as The Ascension Team. To ascend means to rise, and The Ascension Team will have as its purpose the task of uplifting not only BA, but the inner city as well. There will be five business models that The Ascension Team will seek to build with the mission of investing profits into inner city public schools systems. The Ascension Team will have one purpose and one purpose only – to facilitate the rise of BA and the inner cities. It will be an all-inclusive organization, By accomplishing this mission, the Ascension Team will help all members of America realize the American dream, which is one of family, education and success. To a person and to a people, a nation is only as strong as its weakest link. BA must not be that weak link anymore. That will be the mission of The Ascension Team.

The Ascension Movement

THE CIVIL RIGHTS Movement was indeed a very important chapter in the history of BA. It was a movement that sought equality, respect, and protection. It was a movement about non-violence, basic protections, the right to vote, the end of racial discrimination, the fight for the poor, and equal employment opportunities. The achievements of the Civil Rights Era are of epic proportions, still serving as a measuring stick for race relations and social conditions on many fronts today. But make no mistake about it, any notion, claim or testimony that Blacks have overcome is fallacious. And since that era, times have gotten much worse. This has resulted in the need for a new movement, one that embodies the complete slate of work to be done by all of BA. This new tour de force is known as the Ascension Movement.

The Ascension Movement has inherent meaning, to rise, and has come about because BA is in a time that actually poses greater threats than those that were present in the Civil Rights Era. This is because BA is depopulating without a clear plan of cessation in sight. The Ascension Movement is about new value systems, newfound self-respect, economic development, intelligent consumerism, educational excellence, and new school systems. It is a movement about the right to live, the choice to live, and the fight to live.

The primary objective of the Ascension Movement is to not only take action to save BA, but also to raise the level of consciousness of all America so that this massive and all-important end can be accomplished. Everyone can play even a minute role, and everyone is asked to play at least a small role, as this mission is sure to appreciate even the smallest of contributions.

Do you want to be a part of the biggest movement for BA since the Civil Rights era? Would you like to assist in possibly the most important cause in the history of America? Well, here it is front and center. The goal is to push, push, and push BA into academic excellence of the likes BA has never seen before. Educational excellence is at the forefront of the new BA existence. That much has been said. What are you prepared to do to make it happen? Whom better than BA to jump-start its own survival process? That is what the Ascension Movement is all about.

The Ascension Plan

THE ASCENSION TEAM will develop its five business models to make money to build New School Systems. Along the way, The Ascension Group will instill values, honor, and pride, as it will diligently work on everything from A-Z in order to make its it's 'National Blueprint for Success' a reality and a win. Only through the utilization of Action Plan Implementation can this be accomplished.

BA does not, and will not, listen to people such as William Bennett, who suggested that in order to bring down crime rates, one idea is to "abort every Black child." There are better options than that. Black people do not have to be washed away by hurricanes. BA can stay dry and hold its collective heads high in the process. Blacks can succeed right here in America.

Some of the tools of the Ascension Plan to be utilized are:

1) The promotion of books through a variety of methods and ideals.

2) The propulsion of Black American students to the top of the educational achievement list. The Pursuit of Educational Excellence via The Reformation of Public Schools and New School Systems will give BA the opportunity to reach this goal. The transformation of BA from worst to first in terms of educational achievement is the ultimate goal in itself. The goals of healthy food and drink choices, cognitive clubs and more parental involvement in inner city schools across the nation are important parts of the agenda as well.

3) HIV/AIDS information disclosure in inner-city middle schools and high schools. Every middle and high school in BA needs to have all of its students tested for HIV/AIDS. Of course, any

positive test results would be kept confidential, made known only
to the family of the student. The reform comes by informing the
student body and its parents of the total HIV/AIDS percentage of
the school itself.

Black students are privy to what is going on in their schools. They
deserve at least the knowledge of the conditions of what is the most
important institution they will attend in their young lives, and that
is school. They deserve the opportunity to make better decisions,
including those of a sexual nature, with as much information as
is possible. They could and would make better sexual decisions if
they knew the direct and real risks associated with those decisions.
HIV/AIDS is rampant right where the kids least acknowledge
it to be. Schools are where the kids spend the most time, have
the most fun, socialize, hang out, and party, together. It is in
school where they learn to both trust, and sometimes deceive, each
other. Most importantly, school is where they make their first,
and often regrettable, sexual decisions. And because of this, it is
imperative that they know the sexual status quo of their school,
and they should not be kept in the dark any longer. The message
of abstinence is a priority also.

4)   A.C.E. Groups (Ascension Community Education) – A.C.E.
     Groups are community education groups that focus on community
     needs. Topic areas such as updates on the Mortality Metrics and
     Afflictions, ways to combat Killer Systems and Industries, local-
     state-federal politics, voting, drugs, gangs guns, personal health,
     finance, education, property values, national community trends,
     schools, and any subject matter that has a direct effect on inner-city
     communities will be explored. The objective is to uplift all inner-
     city families and residents through comprehensive awareness along
     with useful information that will lead to a better standard of living
     for BA.

5)   Intelligent Consumerism. An emphasis on strengthening Black
     households through resistance in purchasing the electronic gadgets
     that dominate the time of the youth of today. Like the HIV/AIDS

situation that is present right in the schools the children attend, these pitfalls are even closer to the children due to being right in their own homes. Electronic gadgets play a damning role in the destruction of BA. This objective is about convincing BA that these time-wasters are indeed destructive, and either need to be tightly controlled, or completely eliminated out of the homes and the children's lives altogether.

Number One

IN SPEAKING OF the goal to transform Black students into one of the top educational groups in America, the acronym 'Number One' will serve as both a rallying cry and a reminder of what BA needs to accomplish. There needs to remain a clear vision in the minds of everyone of the goal, and also to help everyone get accustomed to the idea that BA can make it to the top. The hope is that BA will not run from this aspiration of becoming number one, but instead will believe in it and work hard to make it happen. You have to know in your heart that we have the power to effect positive change, and only then can we make it happen. Number One:

N. Never give up on the quest of BA to ascend to the top.

U. Understand what is at stake and seriously get involved.

M. Make a new commitment to combat drugs, gangs, and guns in your communities. Remember to report all illegal activity in your communities.

B. Books, books, and more books. Bombard our kids with books. Believe in books. Make weekly library trips. Have storytelling sessions. Join or create Book of the Month clubs in the neighborhoods. Bring books back in style.

E. Education Elevation. Support The Pursuit of Educational Excellence for our children by getting involved in The Reformation of Public Schools and the building of New School Systems.

R. Respect. BA must respect the intelligence of the youth in school and make sure they know the HIV/AIDS facts in their schools. They must not be blind to the truth. Let them be well-informed and thus have the power to make intelligent decisions.

****

O. Outlaw technological candy in your homes. Get rid of or limit the use of video game systems, excessive television viewing, and sex-laden music videos and music of radio stations. Enroll the children in sports, school clubs and other cognitive activities, and be sure to transport them to their practices and events.

N. Nothing is more important than saving Black America.

E. Education Elevation of the second kind. Adults of all ages need to take their education to another level. Get that high school diploma, first college degree, or second college degree. Everyone that can should to go back to school.

A RECENT ARTICLE in the Tennessean newspaper by a Mr. Bob Herbert talked about a couple of ill-natured magazines now at newsstands. One is entitled Felon, and the other is named F.E.D.S. These magazines are about convicted criminals and their 'gansta' mentality. These magazines tie-in their messages through music, fashion, film, etc. The stories are about cocaine, snitching, murder, and letters actually written to "bitches".

This is what the youth of BA is up against. This is what The Ascension Group will fight to eliminate. It is because of madness such as 'Felon' and 'F.E.D.S.' magazines that BA has to regroup and decide just what direction it wants to continue to go in. This is why the goal is to be N.U.M.B.E.R. O.N.E.

One Probable Future

As THE CLOCK ticks, the situation of BA worsens. The Latino population is increasing in both numbers and political power, while BA's population power and political base erodes. Privatized prisons are booming, and so is the Black prison population. Blacks continue to find employment evasive not only to jobs going overseas, but more importantly because of educational achievement shortcomings.

The Mortality Metrics and the Afflictions grow stronger everyday. As the HIV/AIDS rate continues to swell, more and more Americans want absolutely nothing to do with BA. Blacks who are not infected may as well be, as know one wants to take a chance and get infected by any Black person. The social crippling extends to the workforce, as those employers that can hire will not because of the social, insurance and healthcare ramifications resulting from the perception that any Black hired just might be infected. This is what the actuarial studies show, so it must be right, they say.

It can go on and on. Insults are whispered and labels are administered in hush tones: Crime-mongers. Ignoramuses. Bitches. Bastards. Dead weight. Prison population incarnate. The pain increase as the panic ensues. Is this scenario impossible? Possibly. At what point does this type of mentality sweep the nation? Is it when there is a 1-in-20 HIV/AIDS rate amongst Blacks? How about 1-in-10, or 1-in-8? This future possibility will mean a lot more than one might imagine to those who have to stand in line at grocery markets, use the same workplace bathrooms, swim in the same swimming pools, or whose children attend the same schools as the children of the 1-in-8's. It is not a nice subject to think about. However, these types of scenarios have to be considered in order to cover both the gamut of social possibilities and reasons why BA has to trek that long road to respectability and mortal longevity.

This is why it is of pre-eminent importance that BA go straight into action mode, hard and heavy, and serve notice to each other and to the world, that there will be no more ineptness, no more inaction, and no more excuses. The future of BA will not be *that* future just described, but rather it will be a future of promise and long life.

The Year 2050

THE FOLLOWING PROJECTIONS are based on the HIV/AIDS and prison population percentages of 7.7% and 2.3%, respectively, as mentioned in Part I. These same percentages are now used to project out, to the year 2050, the number of Blacks that may be infected with HIV/AIDS, and the number of Blacks that may be in prison as well.

These projections represent just two of the Mortality Metrics and Afflictions. Not included are the dozens of other metrics and conditions that take BA down, such as the number one killer of us all, Cardiovascular Diseases of the Heart, in addition to the other conditions of Cancer, Coronary Heart Disease, Stroke, Accidents, Diabetes, High Blood Pressure, and Infant Mortality. And there are also the other Afflictions that do what they do. In all, these projections give one and all something to think about.

	HIV/AIDS	**Prison Population**
2000	121,903	871,867
2001	131,290	891,920
2002	141,399	912,434
2003	152,287	933,420
2004	164,013	954,889
2005	176,739	976,851
2006	190,348	999,319
2007	205,005	1,022,303
2008	220,790	1,045,816

2009	237,791	1,069,870
2010	254,436	1,094,477
2015	368,687	1,226,266
2020	534,240	1,373,924
2025	774,130	1,539,362
2030	1,121,741	1,724,722
2035	1,625,441	1,932,401
2040	2,355,318	2,165,086
2045	3,412,934	2,425,791
2050	4,945,457	2,717,887

The increases in both HIV/AIDS infected and prison population is quite sobering. Of course, there are going to be many who will choose to argue with the numbers. Keep in mind that these numbers just might be fairly accurate. However, debate is not my goal, nor my desire. But alerting and saving BA is my goal. Time may even prove these numbers to be conservative. Remember, BA does not need that corrective headline: "Earlier estimates in regards to HIV/AIDS infections were wrong. New estimates place HIV infections amongst Blacks as much higher than previously stated". The anxiety and stress levels would become meteoric, and an ensuing panic would be almost imminent. It can happen. But of course, we collectively pray that it will not.

Withstanding, there could also be increases in the number of deaths in any of the eight Mortality Metrics that caused more deaths in the year 2000 than HIV/AIDS, and they are: Cardiovascular Disease, Cancer, Coronary Heart Disease, Stroke, Accidents, Diabetes, High

Blood Pressure, and Infant Mortality. And of course, there are the other Mortality Metrics and Afflictions that will still be present as well within and without BA.

How will you react when the announcement comes that population of BA is spiraling downward, to 31 million, to 29 million, to 27 million, while the HIV/AIDS, prison population, and other Mortality Metrics and Afflictions prosper? Whatever your reaction may be, whatever your intent could be, let that reaction and intent be today, and not in the year 2010, 2030, or 2050. Make sure you keep this very simple and direct fact at the forefront of your minds: Black America is dying, and once we are gone, there is no coming back. Get up. Be moved. Let's all do something about it right now. We're all just a decision away from change.

Have Faith

By now, I hope that many, if not all of you, have been moved to action, or at the very least the contemplation of action. Contemplation is okay, as everything starts with a thought. After the thought comes a decision, followed by action, guided by faith.

Here is a little something about faith. You have just read a book calling for a national movement to be manifested by BA that will culminate in an entirely new destiny for not only BA, but America as well. And in case you haven't noticed, the author's last name is not Jackson, or Sharpton, or Obama. The author of "Hindered" goes by the last name Young, first name Mark, who just happens to be a person that practically no one has ever heard of, a guy once known as moose, lemonhead, and Jack Murphy to his childhood friends. How dare this unknown write about a probable total devastation, and then a seemingly impossible reincarnation. Well, "Dare I must." Ladies and gentlemen, I am so far out there on faith that I have disappeared to many, I'm sure. However, that is okay because this is something I simply must do.

It took a lot of faith to write this 'save the world' sort of book. A lot of thought went into writing it, and initially just as much thought went into not writing it. But I had to write "Hindered", and it was because I not only see what is happening, but I also care deeply about what is happening. And so it took a lot of faith, and required a lot of courage, but in the end, we all have to do what we all have to do. The love of Black people is my motivation, and faith in both you and I can take us to our destination.

AND NOW IT is requested of all of you to have faith. I want all of you to have faith in knowing that BA can find its way. I want all of you to have faith in knowing that can get back into the fight right now. Have faith in knowing that BA does not have to perish, and that BA can prosper to any degree it wants to.

Have faith in knowing that enough members of BA to recognize the enormity of its task and that BA will understand, with crystal clarity, the work that must be done. Have faith that as you excuse yourself when stepping by those who choose to do nothing, they too will have a change of heart, and will ultimately meet you in the Promised Land.

Have faith in education. Educate yourselves. Educate your family. Believe in BA's Pursuit of Educational Excellence. Have faith that one day your very own children and grandchildren will benefit from the Ascension Movement and find his or her way to the profession of his or her blessing. Have faith in the blueprint for success to ensure the rebirth of BA in ways only dreamt of. Have faith in knowing that it is BA's time.

I hope that I have not failed in lighting a fire underneath you. The intent is to motivate as many as possible into taking action to save BA. The process works like this: First, one must to be informed. Consider yourself informed. Second, acknowledge and believe that BA's occupation with the dire is true. It is. Third, be touched to your hearts through the conscience of your minds. I hope that you are. Finally, be inspired to do something. I have faith that you will.

The Promised Land

I TRULY BELIEVE that the process of getting to the Promised Land will be one of Public School Transformation, Community Action via its components, and The Pursuit of Educational Excellence through the building of New School Systems. Many may wonder, "Just how can it be that simple?" Well, not to say that the mission of BA is on par with that of salvation, but the direction given by Jesus Christ for any, and all, to make it to the Kingdom of God was simple in nature also. Not necessarily easy, but simple. His counsel for those seeking the kingdom was to:

1) Obey the Ten Commandments

2) Confess with thy lips and believe in thy heart that Jesus Christ died on the cross for your sins.

3) Have Faith

THE ASCENSION MOVEMENT is bigger than all of us. Everyone so moved to action will definitely have to step out of his or her comfort zone and do whatever possible to save BA. It seems surreal to think that all of BA needs saving I know. But BA is destined for extinction at the present rate, and it is happening right under our noses. Dig deep to see for yourself. Become convinced and find the necessary passion to do whatever you can to assist in the ascension of BA. Remember, every little bit counts.

BA SHOULD STRIVE for Number One. Never in history has BA been challenged so completely and so directly. History allows the opportunity to learn from past failures and successes. The present allows us the opportunity to do great things. The future is ours for the shaping. For the love of family, friends and community, we must succeed. In the words of the incomparable Muhammad Ali, it is possible to "Shake up the World!" We just have to believe.

WHO WILL LEAD Black America? **You** will lead Black America.

In Saying Farewell

IN CLOSING, I wish you well. I wish us all well. Here's to meeting you on the front lines. Receive. Believe. Achieve.

FOOD FOR THOUGHT. In meditation:

"Where there is no vision, the people will perish".
George Washington Carver

"All that is necessary for evil to triumph is for good men to do nothing.
Edmund Burke

"The world is a dangerous place to live in; not because of the people who are evil, but because of the people who don't do anything about it.".
Albert Einstein

"A man who stands for nothing will fall for anything".
Malcolm X

"We've got some difficult days ahead. But it doesn't matter with me now. Because I've been to the Mountain Top… And He's allowed me to go up to the mountain. And I've looked over. And I've seen the Promised Land. I may not get there with you. But I want you to know tonight, that we, as a people, will get to the Promised Land".
Dr. Martin Luther King, Jr.

ENDNOTES

PART ONE: Numbers

1 Resident population by race. (July 1, 1998). Retrieved October 30, 2003 from www.census.gov/population/estimates/nation/intfile3-1.txt

2 United States Citizenship & Immigration Services: (n.d.). Immigration by region And selected country of last residence. Retrieved October 30, 2003 from http://www.uscis.gov/graphics/shared/aboutus/statistics/IMM00yrbk/ExcIMM00/ Tab2.xls

3 American Heart Association: (n.d.). Facts About African Americans, Heart Disease and Stroke (pgs. 1-6). Retrieved November 7, 2003 from www.americanheart.org/ presenter.jhtml?identifier+3003839

4 Intercultural Cancer Council: (n.d.). African Americand & Cancer (pp.1-4). Retrieved November 7, 2003 from http://iccnetwork.org/cancerfacts/cfs1.htm

5 National Vital Statistics Report: (September 16, 2002). Deaths and percent of total deaths for the 10 leading causes of death by race: United States 2000. Retrieved August 30, 2005 from www.cdc.gov.nchs/data/nvsr/nvsr50/nvsr50_16.pdf

6 Center for Disease Control: (September 16, 2002). Infant, neonatal, and postnatal deaths, percent of total deaths, and mortality rates for the 15 leading causes of infant death by race and sex: United States 2000. Retrieved June 6, 2006 from www.cdc.gov/nchs/data.dvs/LCWK7_2000.pdf

7 Center for Disease Control: (n.d.). Estimated numbers of deaths of persons with HIV/AIDS, by year of death and selected characteristics, 1998-2002-United States. Retrieved December 20, 2003 from http://www.cdc.gov/hiv/stats/hasr1402/table7.ht

8 Deaths from Asthma (n.d.). Retrieved June 7, 2006 from http://www.wrongdiagnosis. com/a/asthma/deaths_printer.htm

9 Dr. Meg Meeker (2002). *'Epidemic: How Teen Sex is Killing Our Kids'.* Washington, D.C: LifeLine Press

10 Blacks Against Drunk Driving. Building Safe Communities. *Building Safe Communities.* Volume 2, Number 3 – March/April 1999.

11 *African American Youth and Alcohol Advertising.* Retrieved November 7, 2005 from http://camy.org/factsheets/index.php?FactsheetID=11

12 African Americans and HIV/AIDS. The Henry J. Kaiser Family Foundation. *HIV/AIDS Policy Fact Sheet,* September, 2003.

13 *HIV/AIDS and African Americans.* Retrieved August 25, 2005 from www.balmingilead.org/aidsfacts/aidsfacts.asp

14 *Cultural Geography of Sub-Sahara Africa.* Retrieved June 7, 2006 from www.homestead.com/parkview/SubSahara.html

15 *HIV/AIDS Information released for the year 2002.* Retrieved June 7, 2006 from www.hardtruthaboutaids.com/statistics/2002.htm

16 Abai, Mulugeta. (2001). *Africa: A Continent in Turmoil.* Retrieved January 31, 2005 from http://www.ccvt.org/springsummer2001.html

17 *The UN is in crisis over Africa*. Retrieved June 24, 2005 from www.arcuk.org/pages/un_is_in_crisis_over_africa.htm

18 Knickmeyer, Ellen. (2004). *DRC death toll at 3.8 million*. Retrieved January 31, 2005 from http://africa.iafrica.com/c2cnews/398255.htm

19 Montague, Dena. *War Profiteers, in Africa, as well as Iraq*. Retrieved January 31, 2005 from www.commondreams.org/views03/0422-09.htm

20 *Marshalling Africa*. Retrieved June 7, 2006 from www.amren.com/mtnews/archives/2005/06/marshalling_afr.php

21 *The 'Real' Costs of the Iraq War*. Retrieved June 7, 2006 from http://washingtontimes.com/upi-breaking/20040701-024236-4063r.htm

PART TWO: Afflictions

22 Smiley, Tavis. (2004, February 28). *The Black Family*. C-Span.

23 Hearn, Ted. *McCain Introduces a la Carte Bill*. Retrieved June 26, 2006 from www.multichannel.com/index.asp?layout=articlePrint&articleid=CA6341831

24 *African American Television Usage*. Retrieved November 11, 2003 fromwww.nielsenmedia.com/ethnicmeasure/african-american/indexAA.html

25 *Television Viewing Habits*. Retrieved November 11, 2003 from **www.aspe.hhs.gov/hsp/97trends/sd1-5.htm**

26 Black Female Sexual Exploitation. *Youth Action Forum*. Summer 2003. Retrieved October 22, 2004 from www.nya.org.uk/Templates/System/journals.asp?NodeID =89073&ParentNodeID=89058

27 *The National Campaign to Prevent Teen Pregnancy.* General Facts and Stats. Retrieved November 1, 2003 from www.teenpregnancy.org/ resources/ data/ gen1fact.asp

28 *Poverty and Income.* Retrieved June 6, 2005 from www.infoplease. com/ ipa/ A0854972.html

29 Asthma: A Concern for Minority Populations. *National Institute of Allergy and Infectious Diseases.* October 2001. Retrieved December 16, 2004 from www.niaid.nih.gov/factsheets/asthma.htm

30 Race and the Drug War. *Drug Policy Allowance.* 2002. Retrieved November 11, 2002 from www.drugpolicy.org/library/factsheets/ raceandthedr/index.cfm

31 *Incarceration vs. Education.* Retrieved October 24, 2002 from http:// stacks.msnbc. com/ news/803010.asp?cp1=1

32 Souls of Black Men. *Black Mental Health Alliance.* Retrieved June 7, 2006 from www.communityvoices.org/Uploads/Souls_of_Black_ Men_00108_00037.pdf

33 Null, Gary. *Gary Null's Natural Living.* Retrieved August 12, 2005 from www.garynull.com/Documents/PathologizingAfricanAmerican Pt1.htm

34 *Black on Black Violence.* Retrieved October 24, 2002 from www. sistahspace.com/ nommo/bmc9.html

35 Bohn, Dean. Shootings Flare in City. (2003, April 24). *The Saginaw News*, pp.1, 10).

36 Beck, Allen J., Harrison, Paige. *Prisoners in 2002.* U.S. Department of Justice. Bureau of Justice Statistics Bulletin. July, 2003.

37 *Statistics on African Americans and the Death Penalty in America.* Retrieved October 22, 2003 from www.imamjamil.net/articles/statistics.asp

38 *Sourcebook of Criminal Justice Statistics.* Retrieved June 11, 2006 from www.albany.edu/Sourcebook/pdf/t41020004.pdf

39 Hocker, Cliff. *More Brothers in Prison Than in College?* Retrieved June 11, 2006from www.globalblacknews.com/Jail.html

40 Black Males in College or Behind Bars in the United States, 1980 to 1994. Department of Justice. Office of Justice Programs. Bureau of Justice Statistics. *Postsecondary Education OPPORTUNITY.* Number 45 – March 1996

41 Current Impact of Disenfranchisement Laws. *The Sentencing Report.* Retrieved November 9, 2004 from www.hrw.org/reports98/vote/usvot98o-01.htm

42 Why Can't Felons Vote? *The Straight Dope.* Retrieved February 8, 2005 from www.straightdope.com/mailbag/mfelonvote.html

43 Reported Voting and Registration, by Race, Hispanic Origin, Sex, and Age for the United States: November 2000. *U.S. Census Bureau.* Retrieved February 8, 2005 from www.census.gov/population/socdemo/voting/p20-542/tab02.pdf

44 Kirk, Dwight. *Taking a Stand: The Unemployment Story You Haven't Heard.* Retrieved June 11, 2006 from www.cbtu.org/2003website/takingastand/ blackunemployment.html

45 Amazing Facts About Trade, Offshore Outsourcing, Guest Worker Programs, and the Economy. Retrieved June 11, 2006 from www.rescueamericanjobs.org/amazing/ index.php?facts=facts-statistics-temporary-foreign-workers-programs-h1b-h-b-l-1

PART THREE: Images, People, and Hope

46 The Victorian Hands Foundation. Retrieved June 11, 2006 from www.tvhf.org/

47 Do Something! Retrieved June 11, 2006 from www.dosomething. org/

48 Downing, Eve. Alumna Makes a Career Out of Helping Others. *Tech Talk*. Retrieved June 11, 2006 from www.pmd.org/mit-article. html

49 Kid Power. Retrieved June 11, 2006 from www.kidpower.org/

50 A.C. Green Youth Foundation. Retrieved June 11, 2006 from www. clubac.com/ news/default.asp?/DocumentID=444

51 *Live Aid.* Retrieved June 11, 2006 from www.nostalgiacentral.com/ pop/liveaid.htm

52 Citizen Change. Retrieved June 11, 2006 from www.behaviordesign. com/work/ case_/studies/images/ctz/canned_site/about_citizen_ change.html

53 The Innocence Project. Retrieved June 11, 2006 from www. innocenceproject.org/

54 The Bill & Melinda Gates Foundation. Retrieved December 28, 2006 from www.Gatesfoundation.org/default.htm

55 East Lake Community Foundation. Retrieved January 28, 2005 from www.eastlake communityfdn.org/overview/main.html

PART FOUR: Institutional Racism

56 Berlin, Ira. Masters of Their Universe. *The Nation, November 29, 2004, pp. 23-27*

57 Hall, Mimi. Group: USA Not Ready for Terror. (2004, December 15). *USA Today*, p. A10.

58 Welch, William M., Tauzin Switches Sides from Drug Industry Overseer to Lobbyist. (2004, December 16). *USA Today*, p. B3.

59 Foster Care. American Academy of Child & Adolescent Psychiatry. *AACAP Facts For Families #64*. Retrieved January 27, 2005 from www. aacap.org/ publications/factsfam/64.htm

60 Simms, Dr. Mark. *What the Experts Say*. Retrieved June 11, 2006 from www. window. state.tx.us/forgottenchildren/ch05/s0502experts. html

61 *Pill-popping Worries Grow in Foster System*. Retrieved June 11, 2006 from www. iamforkids.org/newsdata/view_ind/1205

62 *Kids on Legal Drugs*. Retrieved February 7, 2005 from www. smileandactnice.com/ news/daily/032300.html

63 *"My Lobotomy": Howard Dully's Journey*. Retrieved June 11, 2006 from http:// www.npr.org/templates/story/story.php?storyId=5014080

64 *Creating Safe Learning Zones*. Retrieved June 11, 2006 from www. childproofing. org/ABC.pdf

65 *Green Seal*. Retrieved June 11, 2006 from www.greenseal.org/

66 Weintraub, Irwin. *Fighting Environmental Racism: A Selected Annotated Bibliography*. Retrieved June 11, 2006 from http://egj.lib. uidaho.edu/ egj01/weint01.html

67 Rall, Ted. *Save Social Security with the Flat Tax, Now Wall Street*. Retrieved October 24, 2006 from http://www.the villager.com/villager_ 87/talkingpoint.html

68 Lawson, Richard. Nashville Growth 15th Largest Over Next 20 Years. *The Nashville Business Journal.* Retrieved May 21, 2006 from http://www.bizjournals.com/ nashville/stories/1998/07/27/story4.html

69 Carey, Clay. *Special Censuses Pay Off for Growing Cities.* (2006, January 12). *TheTennessean,* p. B6.

70 Keating, Raymond J. *The NFL Offers: A Case Study in Corporate Welfare.* Retrieved May 21, 2006 from http://www.libertyhaven.com/ noneoftheabove/sports/ nfl offers.shtml

71 Strachan, Al. *The American Experience.* Retrieved June 11, 2006 from http://slam. canoe.ca/StateofHockey/apr29 15.html

72 Pulle, Matt. (2002, December 12). Is Nashville Getting Pucked? *The Nashville Scene.* Retrieved June 11, 2006 from http://www. nashvillescene.com/Stories/News/2002/12/12/Is_Nashville_Getting_ Pucked_/index.shtml#

73 *Nashville Vote is Music to Dell's Ears: Final $166 Million Incentive Package Approved. Online Insider.* (1999, August). Retrieved November 11, 2005 from http://www.conway.com/ssinsider/incentive/ti9908. htm

74 Bush, Bernard and Walters, Kevin. *Nissan Gets $155,000 per Job in Incentives.* (2005, November 16). *The Tennessean,* p. A1.

75 Long, Diane and Paine, Anne. (2005, November 9). *Garcia Would Cut 7 Schools, 490 Jobs.* Retrieved November 16, 2005 from http://www. tennessean.com/ apps/pbcs.d11/article?Date=20051109&Category

76 Lamb, Henry. (2004, December 4). *The Selling Out of America.* Retrieved May 5, 2006 from www.worldnetdaily.com/news/printer-friendly.asp? ARTICLE ID=41770

77 (2006, July 28). *Report on Homeland Security.* CNN

78 *Nissan Helped Develop State Law to Give Company Millions.* Retrieved November 9, 2006 from http://smartcitymemphis.blogspot. com/2005/12/nissan-helped develop-state-law-to.html

79 *The Top 20 Pharmaceutical Companies.* Retrieved April 2, 2004 from http://www. contractpharma.com/JulyAug031.htm

80 *Yahoo! Finance.* Retrieved April 27, 2004 from http://biz.yahoo. com/research/earncal/2004427.html

81 Smith, Phil. (1993). Private Prisons: Profits of Crime. *Covert Action Quarterly,* (1993, Fall). Retrieved April 2, 2004 from http://mediafilter. org/caq/Prison.html

82 *When Companies Profit from Crime, There is an Incentive to Imprison More Inmates for Longer Sentences.* Retrieved May 21, 2006 from www. common-sense.org/ ?fnoc=/common_sense_says/00_march

83 Hoovers. *Research Companies & Industries.* Retrieved June 11, 2006 from www. hoovers.com/free/

84 Racial Inequality in Special Education. *The Civil Rights Project of Harvard University.* Retrieved May 16, 2006 from http://www. civilrightsproject. harvard.edu/research/specialed/IDEA_paper02.php

85 Baxter, James J., NMA President. *The Traffic Ticket System.* Retrieved January 25, 2005 from http://www.motorists.com/issues/tickets/traffic_ ticket_system.html

86 Dedham, Bill & Latour, Francie. (2003) *Traffic Citations Reveal Disparity in Police Searches.* Retrieved May 16, 2006 from http://www. boston.com/globe/ metro/ packages/tickets/010603.shtml

87 Trapp, Doug. (2001) *Moving Violations: Racial Profiling, by the Numbers.* Retrieved May 16, 2006 from www.citybeat.com/2001-03- 08/cover.shtml

88 Williams, Kristiam. *Racial Profiling: Fact, Fiction, and Function.* Retrieved May 16, 2006 from http://www.agitatorindex.org/articles/racial_profiling.htm

89 Facing Up to an Unflattering Profile. *Law Enforcement News,* December 15/31, 2000. Retrieved September 28, 2006 from http://www.lib.jjay.cuny. edu/ len/2000/12.31/coast.html

90 *Profiles in Distortion.* Retrieved May 21, 2006 from http://www.lipmagazine.org/ timwisc/ profilereport.html

91 O'Neal, Lee Ann. *Traffic Stops Just the Ticket for Metro Budget.* (2006, May 28).*The Tennessean*, p. A1.

92 *Abortion and the Black Community.* Retrieved May 21, 2006 from www.black genocide.org/black.html

93 *African Americans and Autism.* Retrieved May 21, 2006 from www.autismconcepts. com/africanamericans.shtml

94 *What Causes Autism?* Retrieved May 21, 2006 from http://www.autism-society. org/site/PageServer?pagename=causes

95 Thomas, R.N., M.P.H., Joyce N. *Dimensions and Critical Issues of Child Maltreatment in the African American Community: Causation, Consequences, and Prospects.* Retrieved May 21, 2006 from www.dvinstitute.org/ Proceedings/1995/joyce.pdf

96 *Child Maltreatment 2004: Race and Ethnicity of Victims.* Retrieved May 21, 2006 from www.acf.hhs.gov/programs/cb/pubs/cm04/table3_12.htm

97 Stone, Robin D. *No Secrets, No Lies.* Retrieved May 22, 2006 from www.random house.com/broadway/blackink/catalog/display.pperl?isbn= 978076 7913 454 & view=excerpt

98 Fotson, Nikitta A. (2003) Behind the Pain Nobody Wants to Talk About: Sexual Abuse of Black Boys. Retrieved May 21, 2006 from http://www.ncdsv.org/ images/BehindPainNobodyTalksSexualAbuse BlackB.pdf

99 *Black Admissions to Substance Abuse Treatment, 1999.* Retrieved May 22, 2006 from www.drugabusestatistics.samhsa.gov/2k2/BlackTX/ BlackTX.cfm

100 *Need for Mental Health Care.* Retrieved May 22, 2006 from www. mentalhealth. samhsa.gov/cre.fact1.asp

101 A Human Rights Campaign Report. Retrieved May 22, 2006 from www.urban.org/ UploadedPDF/1000491_gl_partner_households.pdf

102 Gipson, Michael L. (2005). *With Almost Half of Black Gay and Bi Men HIV+ in Some Cities, the Community Works to Avoid a Repeat of the 1980s.* Retrieved May 22, 2006 from www.condomdepot.com/ learn/2005/11/with-almost-half-of -black-gay-and-bi.cfm

103 Wood, Regina Lee.. Our Golden Road to Literacy: In the Name of Helping the
Disadvantaged, Are We Consigning Them to Permanent Illiteracy? National Review, 10/18/93. Retrieved June 16, 2006 from www. highbeam.com/ library/ docfreeprint.asp?docid= 1G1:14752502&ctrl Info=Roun.....

104 *Adolescent Literacy Research Network.* Retrieved June 18, 2006 from http:// www. ed.gov/about/offices/list/ovae/pi/hs/adollit.html

105 The Associated Press. *Media Under Fire for Missing Persons Coverage.* Retrieved June 16, 2006 from www.msnbc.msn.com/id/8233195/

106 *Internet Porn Statistics: 2003.* Retrieved June 18, 2006 from www. Healthy mind. com/s-port-stats.html

107 *Prostitution Statistics*. Retrieved June 18, 2006 from www.icasa. org/uploads/ prostitution.pdf

108 *High School Dropout Rates by Sex and Race/Ethnicity, 1960-2001*. Retrieved June 18, 2006 from **www.infoplease.com/ipu/A0779196. html**

109 Back to School 2001: Bad Teeth Epidemic Among Poor Children. Retrieved June 18, 2006 from www.poste-gazette.com/ regionstate/ 20010826teeth schoolonereg3p3.asp

110 *Christina's Smile*. Retrieved June 18, 2006 from www.csmile.com/ mission.html

111 Uchitelle, Louis. *For Blacks, A Dream in Decline*. (2005, October 23). *The New York Times*, Section 4, p. 1.

112 Harris, Anne Marie, Henderson, Geraldine R., and Williams, Jerome D. *Summary of Research and Research Findings*. Retrieved November 14, 2005 from http:// www.acrwebsite.org/print.asp?artID=305

113 *Aids – The African AIDS Epidemic*. Retrieved January 31, 2005 from http://www. virusmyth.net/aids/data/pdafrica.htm

114 Wattenburg, Ben J. (2004). *Fewer*. Chicago, IL. Ivan R. Dee

PART FIVE: The Plan

115 The National Center for Family Literacy. Retrieved January 28, 2005 from www.famlit.org/loader.cfm?url=/commonspot/security/ getfile.cfm&PageID=2996

116 Wald, Johanna, Losen, Daniel. Defining and Redirecting a School-to-Prison Pipeline. The Civil Rights Project at Harvard University. Retrieved June 18, 2006 from www.woodsfund.org/community/ Folder 1036081004377 /File 1084877618748

117 Mason, Dr. Terry. (2004). Parents: You Can Set a Healthy Example. Jet Magazine. September 20, 2004 Issue.

118 Hiestand, Michael. 'New PE' Objective: Get Kids in Shape. (2004, December 16). *The USA Today*, Section A, pg. 1-4.

119 Riley, Claudette. Healthy Kids, Better Schools. (2003, November 23). *The Tennessean*, Section 1, pp. 1-2.

120 Spurlock, Morgan. (2004). *Super Size Me*. USA. Samuel Goldwyn Films. Available from: The Con, 76 Mercer, 4th Floor, NY, NY 10012.

121 Bottorff, Christian. *I'm Shot*. (March, 23, 2006). The Tennessean, p. A1.

122 Roker, Al. (2005, October 1). *"Menace on Main Street"*. Arts & Entertainment Channel.

123 Platt, Gordon. (2005, January 16). *"Railroaded in Texas"*. Court TV Network.

124 *City Crime Rankings by Population Group*. Retrieved June 19, 2006 from http:// www. morganquitno.com/xcit06pop.htm

125 Green, Elwin. (2006, April 18). *Black Business Owners on the Rise*. Retrieved June 19, 2006 from www.post-gazette.com/pg/pp/06108/682889.stm

126 *Learner Outcomes*. Retrieved January 27, 2005 form http://nces.ed.gov/ programs/ coe/2002/section2/tables/t12_2a.asp

127 *Reaching Out…..Raising African American Achievement*. Retrieved October 23, 2003 from www.ed.gov/print/nclb/accountability/achieve/achievement_aa.html

128 Kafer, Krista. (2003, November 1). *1 in 3 Students Graduate College Ready*. Retrieved August 3, 2006 from www.heartland.org/PrinterFriendly.cfm? The Type=artId&theID=13539

129 *More Than 3.7 Million African Americans Now Hold a Four-Year College Degree*. Retrieved January 7, 2005 from www.jibe.com/news_views/44_college-degree. html

130 Percentage of Doctoral Degrees Awarded to Blacks has Reached the Highest Level Ever Recorded. Retrieved January 7, 2005 from www.jibe.com/news_views/42_ PhDs_and_blacks.html

131 *Diversity Factoids*. DiversityInc Magazine. October/November 2003.

132 Fears, Darryl. (2003, March 9). *Disparity Marks Black Ethnic Groups*. Retrieved October 13, 2005 from www.washingtonpost.com/ac2/wp-dyn/A63392-2003 Mar8?language=printer

133 C-SPAN Television Network. (2005, November 27). *Thomas Friedman Book Presentation*. National Book Festival.

134 Zxerce, John. Editorial Review. *"The World is Flat: A Brief History of the Twenty-First Century."* Retrieved October 13, 2006 from www.amazon.com/World-Flat-History-Twenty-first-Century/dp/0374292795/sr=8-…..

135 *David Robinson: Founding a Legacy of Leadership*. Retrieved December 10, 2003 from www.philanthropyintexas.com/03MarchApril/davidrobinson.htm

136 *The Admiral Leads the Way*. Retrieved January 10, 2005 from www.philanthropy roundtable.org/magazines/2004/march-april/theadmiralcover2.htm

137 Toppo, Greg. Constant Kindergartners. (2005, August 25). *USA Today*. Section D, p. 6.

138 *Christmas Kindness: South Africa 2002*. Retrieved August 7, 2006 from www. oprah.com/presents/2003/christmaskindness/leadership/ pres_2003_ck_leadership. jhtml

139 *Atlanta's Warrick Dunn named Walter Payton Man of the Year.* Retrieved May 9, 2006 from www.nfl.com/news/story/8163101

140 *Steve Smith Scholarship Fund.* Retrieved October 14, 2006 from www. sssfund. com/about_steve/

141 Pollick, Marc. *NBA Star Joins the Giving Back Fund to Maximize His Generosity.* Retrieved October 14, 2006 from www.jalenrose.com/ jalenrose/ index.jsp? section=5&action=show_review&id=166

142 Remnick, David. *How Muhammad Ali Changed the Press.* Retrieved 10/14/06 from www.sportsjones.com/ali4d.htm

143 Duffy, Brian. (2001, August 20). *15 Muhammad Ali.* Retrieved October 15, 2006 from www.usnews.com/usnews/culture/ articles/010820/archive_038208_2.htm

144 *Institute for Diversity and Ethics in Sport.* Retrieved August 7, 2006 fromwww. bus. ucf.edu/sport/cgi-bin/site/sitew.cgi?page=/ides/index. htx

145 *Sport Salaries Databases.* Retrieved May 9, 2006 from http://asp. usatoday.com/ sports/football/nfl/salaries/top25.aspx?year=2004

146 Toppo, Greg. *Big City Schools Struggle.* (2006, June 21). USA Today, Section A, p. 1.

PART SIX: The Mountain Top

147 *Croom Named Mississippi State's 31ˢᵗ Head Football Coach.* Retrieved October 14, 2006 from www.mstateathletics.com/index.php?s=&url channel id= 18&url subchannel id =&ur.....

148 Bowden, Terry. (2005, June 30). *Uneven Playing Field.* Retrieved May 9, 2006 from http://sports. yahoo.com/ncaaf/news?slug=tb-mino ritycoaches062905&prov

149 Orton, Kathy. (2005, March 16). *Black Female Coaches Few and Far Between.* Retrieved August 7, 2006 from http://washingtonpost. com/ac2/wp-dyn/A38213 -2005Mar? language=printer 8/7/06

150 Hyman, Marc. *Agents Who Play As Rough As Linebackers.* (2004, September 27). Retrieved October 14, 2006 from http://www. businessweek.com/ print/ magazine/content/04 39/b3901094.htm

151 *Nike, Inc.* Retrieved October 14, 2006 from http://en.wikipedia. org/wiki/Nike Inc.

152 Rovell, Darren. (2005, March 2). *Nike Cautious with $40M Investment.* Retrieved December 23, 2005 from http://sports.espn. go.com/ espn/sportsbusiness/ news/ story?id=2002865

153 Caplan, Jeremy, Dogar, Rana. (1999, January 25). *Ambassador of Hoops.* Retrieved October 14, 2006 from http://www.jeremycaplan. com/Jordan.htm

Printed in the United States
80075LV00004B/163-210

9 781434 300911